# The Muslim Midwest in Modern China

# The Muslim Midwest in Modern China

The Tale of the Hui Communities
in Gansu (Lanzhou, Linxia, and Lintan)
and in Yunnan (Kunming and Dali)

RAPHAEL ISRAELI

RESOURCE *Publications* • Eugene, Oregon

THE MUSLIM MIDWEST IN MODERN CHINA
The Tale of the Hui Communities in Gansu (Lanzhou, Linxia, and Lintan) and in Yunnan (Kunming and Dali)

Copyright © 2017 Raphael Israeli. All rights reserved. Except for brief quotations in critical publications or reviews, no part of this book may be reproduced in any manner without prior written permission from the publisher. Write: Permissions, Wipf and Stock Publishers, 199 W. 8th Ave., Suite 3, Eugene, OR 97401.

Resource Publications
An Imprint of Wipf and Stock Publishers
199 W. 8th Ave., Suite 3
Eugene, OR 97401

www.wipfandstock.com

PAPERBACK ISBN: 978-1-5326-3752-0
HARDCOVER ISBN: 978-1-5326-3753-7
EBOOK ISBN: 978-1-5326-3754-4

Manufactured in the U.S.A.                    12/18/17

# Contents

*Acknowledgments* | vii

**Introduction**
A Comparative Description of the Arenas of Gansu and Yunnan | 1

**Part I**

Chapter One
Gansu—the Pattern of Muslim Settlement | 15

Chapter Two
Obsessive Sectarianism: New Sect, Menhuan | 34

Chapter Three
The Ma Hua Long Heritage | 56

Chapter Four
Xidaotang | 73

**Part II**

Chapter Five
The Yunnan Pattern of Muslim Settlement | 125

Chapter Six
The Du Wenxiu Heritage, The Burden of the Past | 142

Chapter Seven
A Muslim Sultanate in Confucian China | 150

**Conclusions**
Two Arenas, Two Patrimonies and One Uniting Islam | 168

**Bibliography** | 177

**Analytical Index** | 183

# Acknowledgments

This comparative study of two major theaters of the Islamic settlement in China focuses on that vast country's Mid-West, roughly encompassing the parallel territory of the American Mid-West from Chicago and the Great Lakes in the north extending to eastern Texas in the south. In that enormous expanse of land, two extensive field trips were undertaken by this author. One in April 2015 in the southwestern Yunnan Province, focusing on Kunming, the provincial Capital, and Dali the Capital of the Sultanate created by the Muslim rebel Du Wenxiu (1856–1873), until destroyed by the Qing Dynasty; and in March 2016 in the northwestern Gansu Province, focusing on Lanzhou, the provincial Capital, and Linxia, the "Mecca of China" and its satellite Lintan. In both instances, extensive visits were made to Muslim sites, especially mosques, mausoleums and restaurants. Interviews were conducted with the local Muslim leaders, both religious and lay, who were gracious, patient and hospitable enough to provide details on the contemporary organization, beliefs, sects, doctrines and relations with their Chinese environment. Whenever printed material was available, it was added to the data collection process.

But one must be wary nonetheless of the temptation to take any honest and forthcoming statement as the definitive one. For example, when inquiring about statistics, such as the population of Muslims throughout China, or in specific provinces and cities, I was always given the official government census, which by nature tended to minimize the numbers and designate the Muslims by their "national minority" status, and not by the Islamic religion uniting them all, like Hui, Uyghur, Dongan, Salar, Kazakh etc. However, as part of the informal dialogue that followed, different figures were mentioned, usually inflated beyond the real data on Muslim populations. One has to stress, however, that the same pattern of question and response can be found by researchers who investigate the realities of the Christian minorities or the banned, but apparently widespread presence of the Falun

Gong throughout the country. Similarly, when I asked to attend a class in Arabic language, I was allowed to enter, and I watched carefully their mode of instruction of verses from the Qur'an, which are memorized through repetition. However, I could sense the students could not speak one word of the language, nor did my hosts feel comfortable with having me intrude into their Muslim world, especially when they learned that I was an Israeli.

In an authoritarian regime like the Chinese, where people are cautious about talking to foreigners, one has to take their statements with a grain (or rather a ton) of salt. Nonetheless, one cannot help noticing the tremendous opening of minds that is now felt throughout China, compared to a mere decade ago. When I inquired about my failure to connect from my hotel on the internet, I was told by the receptionist:"you can ask [President] Xi Jinping why he ordered the disconnection of Google," a remark hardly anyone would have dared to utter in the recent past. On the other hand, when I announced in one mosque in Linxia, Gansu, that I intended to go the next day to Lintan, the birthplace and headquarters of the founder of Xidaotang, Ma Qixi, I was "advised" not to go there due to the "risks" that any foreigner may incur while visiting the autonomous county of the Zhang minority where Lintan is located, because of the "tense situation reigning there between the majority Zhang and the minority Muslims." It was evident to me someone was worried about an investigation of the mysterious Xidaotang, and elected to abort that trip. Only in September, 2016, Hiddai my research assistant, visited Gansu and managed to get to Lintan via public transportation filling the lacunae I had been compelled to leave behind in March.

My last field trip to Gansu in March 2016 was followed by a lecture I presented as part of a seminar at the University of Foreign Languages in Beijing, in which a diverse group of Muslim students from Egypt, Sudan, Turkey and Malaysia took part, so that we might have a dialogue on Middle Eastern and Islamic affairs - a rare opportunity usually denied to an Israeli on the ground in the lands of Islam. We convened for that lively exchange of ideas in the atmosphere of the watershed topics advanced by Prime Minister Li Keqiang. In a special meeting of the People's Congress, the reforms the Prime Minister has in mind to overhaul the economic system of the nation, were as expected adopted by that august forum of thousands of delegates from all over that vast country. The new five-year plan was to slow down the pace of 10–12% growth to 6.5% in a new supply-side shift that was to increase domestic consumption, since the next stage of development for China cannot maintain the previous rate of growth. Slower growth meant less jobs, a slowdown in the mass immigration from the countryside to the cities, which could also lead to social unrest. While everything was booming in the previous phase of development, people saw hope for the future and cared little about politics. But it is not certain that this will be the case in the next 20 years. Those data, and more, were repeated by the Prime Minister at the China Development Forum held in Hainan in the Spring of 2016, where Asian countries, including Israel, also participated.

China's high international visibility during those two gatherings showed how this amazing country had effected a virtual economic *tour de force* since Deng Xiaoping's «second revolution," which turned a poor backwater nation into a dazzling world power, respected by the world and awed by its immediate neighbors. Unlike liberal democracies whose populations are traditionally skeptical about their leaders, the autocratic rulers of China are held in high regard and credited for the turn around of the stature of their country. In remote Gansu, the Muslims who may be otherwise at odds with the central government due to its Muslim policies, were elated and proud to show pictures of the visit of Prime Minister Li in their midst, and they regarded as a great honor his entry to one of their mosques. The rubber stamp approval by the Congress of the economic reforms did not seem unusual to them, because in their eyes Chinese "democracy" under the one-party system means that all discussions, debates, compromises and lobbies conclude their differences prior to the convening of the Congress, thus assuring the unanimous support of the draft resolution in a consensual fashion, unlike the West in which those controversies emerge in parliamentary debate and are decided by the vote of the government over the opposition. The Islamic tradition of authoritarianism lends itself to this kind of decision-making. The general mood in the country, of breakneck development, high-rise construction, modernization and unprecedented prosperity, not only in the Beijing, Shanghai, Guanzhou , Shenzhen and Hong Kong hubs, but also in the provinces, as evidenced in Gansu and Yunnan, and on the smiling faces and diversified attires worn by the young people everywhere, by necessity conditioned the responses of the interviewees we encountered among the general population as well as throughout the Muslim areas.

I am deeply indebted to my Chinese research assistant, without whom this task could not have been completed: Han Luzhen in China, a graduate student from Macao who left no stone unturned to organize my field trips to Gansu and Yunnan, to collect the materials and to help interpret them; and to my Israeli research assistant, Hiddai Segev, who not only harnessed himself to review the field-generated materials and verify them, but also took a trip to Gansu, particularly Lanzhou, Linxia and Lintan in September, 2016, and contributed to the enrichment and the authentication of the field data . I am also in debt to my previous student, and now colleague and friend, Amira Katz, who had helped many years ago in the translation of Qing documents regarding the Yunnan Rebellion, and to whom I am deeply apologetic for the long delay it took between her prompt work of some decades ago until I was able to make use of it. Judy Hershon, my copyeditor is to be commended for her untiring toil in correcting the text. Above all I am grateful to my home institution, the Truman Institute for the advancement of Peace, at Hebrew University, for its assistance, office space, financial aid and the peace of mind it always offers when providing an ideal working environment. But all the errors that may have befallen this book are solely mine.

Jerusalem, Summer 2016.

# Introduction
## A Comparative Description of the Arenas of Gansu and Yunnan

### The Province of Gansu

Gansu, the vast province in the Northwest of China, which is almost the size of Spain, the second largest country in Europe (close to half a million square kms, the largest being France) is partly arid and desert, unlike Spain which thrives on agriculture, and is sparsely inhabited by some 26 million people, compared to twice as many in Spain. However, unlike Spain, which is one vast landmass, very diversified in topography, climate and population, Gansu is divided into two large blocs, roughly equivalent in area (a northwestern and a southeastern) connected by a narrow corridor, commonly known as the «Gansu panhandle» which stretches one thousand kms from Lanzhou the capital to Jade Gate. Significantly for the population distribution and the climate differences, the northwestern part, which is desert and encompasses almost half of the area of the province, including parts of the Gobi desert, has been only one of the 14 prefectures (*Shi*, or *Zhou* constituted around major cities or constituting "autonomous regions") of the Gansu Province (*Sheng*), which are subdivided into 58 counties (*Xian*), 17 districts and four cities (*Shi*). In these administrative sub-divisions, Lanzhou the provincial Capital, Linxia (and its Lintan satellite) and the Linxia Hui autonomous region at the heart of the Muslim country, are at the level of prefectures (*zhou*).

Flying over the southeastern area of Gansu, on the air route from Lanzhou to Beijing, one cannot help noticing the vast arid mountain ranges, surrounded by the deep green color of the cultivated valleys hugging every mountaintop to the upper levels, terraces that are cultivated to the limit the water supply and the desolate ruggedness of the terrain allow. Nearby, the arable land containing patterns of human settlement on the mountain slopes are scattered in single farm houses or in clusters of buildings that slowly build up to remote villages. Along the 1,300 kms that separate Gansu from Beijing, one is reminded by the snowy peaks in the distance of the still lingering winter in March 2016. Making the same route overland, one is struck by the yellow-brown colors of the naked trees which had lost their green foliage in the severe seasonal cold. Nonetheless, one is impressed from a close-up vantage point by the tremendous work of land conservation that was done along miles of concrete-framed squares that are planted along the sloping hills to arrest the land erosion of this loess-blessed expanse of territory.

The legendary River of Tears, known as the Yellow River, which irrigates northern China and symbolizes its birth in many respects, derives much of its water in Gansu, and flows majestically straight through Lanzhou the Capital. Nine bridges connect the two banks of the river within that vast city of 4 million. The Promenade that runs for miles along its southern shore constitutes one of the main recreational attractions for the population, with an open-air available to all display of gym equipment, and an endless procession of walkers and joggers in view. Cafes sit on the dry land reclaimed from the river where one sees incessant digging and dredging by the flat boats constantly battling against the silting of the river bed by the enormous quantities of loess that erode the vast plains of the north and the Qilian mountains of the south and the west, peaking at close to 6,000 m, - 1,000 m higher than the tallest altitude of the Alps in Europe. The Daxia River in the northeast of Gansu is the other noticeable waterway of the province.

The elongated shape of Gansu lends itself to shared borders with other countries and provinces, such as Shaanxi in the east, Mongolia and Inner Mongolia in the north, Qinhai and Xinjiang in the west and the rich densely populated Sichuan to the south. No description of Gansu is complete without mentioning its on-again off-again connection to Ningxia located at its southeastern border. Desert and sparsely populated Ningxia used to be one of the smallest provinces in China ("only" 66,000 sq kms, the size of the Sinai Peninsula and of Taiwan, and three times the area of Israel). In 1914 Ningxia was merged with Gansu, but separated again fourteen years after a long period of Muslim unrest. However, in 1954 it was again incorporated into Gansu, but in 1958 it was once more reconstituted as an "autonomous" region of the Hui Muslims, as something less than a province, squeezed between Gansu and Inner Mongolia and featuring a section of the Great Wall on its northern border. One can assume that the Maoist regime had elected to keep those two parts separate in order to help blunt the potential threat of that restive Hui country when united. Ningxia, which counts about 6 and a half million inhabitants, with the capital in Yinchuan (2 million souls) is divided administratively into five prefectures, and at the level of counties into 9 districts, 2 cities and 11 rural counties.

The theme uniting the border areas of Gansu is the Hui population, which still constitutes a sizable minority in Shaansi, Inner Mongolia, Qinhai, Sichuan and Tibet, and naturally Ningxia, which has become a Hui "autonomy" in spite of the fact that only one third of its population is still Muslim. That entire area used to be Hui country, however due to the many disturbances and rebellions since the 19th Century and throughout the first half of the 20th Century, which the central government quelled in blood, a systematic thinning of the Muslim potential for rebellion has taken place in three different and separate processes:

a. During the years of upheaval, especially during the uprisings of the 19th Century, millions of Muslims were massacred, or else deported or fled into other parts of China or to foreign lands, near and far;

b. A systematic settling of Han people in those provinces has resulted in turning the Muslims into a more or less noticeable minority. For example, in all of Gansu more than 90% of the 26 million inhabitants are Han, and only a few percentage points are Muslims, amounting to one million or two. In Ningxia, the most highly Muslim populated area in China, only one third of the 6.5 million inhabitants are Muslim, but still over two million, namely the largest concentration of Muslims in a restricted territory.

c. Xinjiang, with its 12 million Uyghur Muslims, has a larger Muslim population, but it is spread in an area 15 fold larger than Ningxia.

d. To substantiate its traditional policy of *divide et impera* (Divide and Rule), the Chinese count their 25 million Muslims by their "national minority" status, not by their religion: Hui, Uyghur, Dongan, Bonan, Salar and Kazakh, who are diluted as part of the multifarious 56 minority groups recognized by the State, and in consequence are diminished in size and influence. Therefore, while the government persists in designating them as "national minorities" as part of the demographic mosaic of the State, where the predominant element is Han, many Muslims confidently speak of their Muslim faith which unites them all.

## Lanzhou

Lanzhou the capital, located in the southeastern part of the province, is a large city of more than four million inhabitants. Like other middle size and large cities of contemporary China, Lanzhou has developed over the past decade a bustling steel and glass high rise landscape with heavy traffic, luxury cars, clean streets and trendy restaurants. Chic stores and cafes accommodate the dense population where many ethnic groups mix in a frenzy of activity typical of large international urban centers. The city which is built along the banks of the Yellow River, gets its elongated shape from the river valley, where it lies situated in the midst of the dusty desert. Given the weather which is often hazy and difficult to breathe, its busy population often resorts to masks to filter the pollution. But in spite of the many 40-story high rise buildings accommodating the growing population, one cannot help noticing the modest nature of the popular residential parts of the city as one drifts from the super-modern and dazzling center.

Having been badly scarred from the Muslim Dongan Rebellion of the 19th Century, the city was revived as a major transportation hub, as it was in antiquity, on the Silk Road trajectory, with highways and a railway connecting from Xian to Xinjiang in the 20th Century, thus "deserving" particular Japanese attention during World War II, with frequent and destructive bombing. Though the population is dense as in many urban areas, about half are concentrated in the central and most congested Chengguan district. The balance of the population is spread, with less density, in the other four districts and three counties that are part of the city. Most remarkable throughout the city is the resplendent architecture of the mosques, mostly domed and colored in green or blue, and sporting one to four minarets each, which dominate the entire scene with either their tall sleek Turkic style minarets, their Arab-Middle Eastern design, or their local Chinese style of multi-layered pagoda-shape towers. The immense Xiguan Mosque, constructed in the city center at the intersection of the major thoroughfares during the Ming Dynasty, was sumptuously renovated in the 1990s. The dozens of mosques in the center of Lanzhou and some in its outskirts remind one that although Islam had known better days in Gansu, still the relative stature and visibility of Islam remains out of proportion by far to the current rate of a few percentage points of Muslims in the otherwise overwhelmingly Han nature of the city today. It is difficult not to notice the massive building of new mosques all over the city, even in its very center. It reflects not only the liberal tendency of *laissez-faire* by the government towards Islam, but also the input of foreign Muslim money outside of China, from such countries as Turkey, Saudi Arabia, Qatar and Kuwait, which wish their exhibited Islamic impact to be felt, often beyond the real needs of a population whose youth is undergoing secularization.

## Linxia and Lintan

Linxia today, a county-level city in Gansu, the capital of the multi-ethnic Linxia Hui Autonomous Prefecture, is also located along a river, the Daxia, a tributary of the Huang-ho, southwest of Lanzhou. Only half its population of a quarter million is Hui, namely the Chinese speaking Muslims of China, though small groups identify themselves as Salars, Dongxiang or Bonan. Linxia has become renowned among its Muslim population and other outsiders as the "Mecca of China," due to its profusion of mosques, the prominence of its Hui population in the streets, with white caps as the standard headgear for the men and scarves for the women, the Muslim noodle restaurants everywhere and the exchange of the Arabic greeting : "*al-salam 'alaikum*" in public, and the response "*'alaikum al-salam*" voiced out loud, without restriction or embarrassment. Within the walls surrounding the courtyards of the mosques, one could read running electronic notices in Arabic and Chinese citing verses from the Qur'an, or on the electric sliding doors of access to the prayer hall of the mosque imploring Allah to "open the gates of His grace to the Believers."

In Linxia where modernity and a fast paced lifestyle are self-confidently, smilingly and nonchalantly encountered by Muslims at every step, the city's centrality and sense of comfort had in the past spawned many of the multitude of new ideas brought in by itinerant Muslims. New currents of reform arose there with many *menhuan* (that unique trend of genealogically-based style of sectarianism among various Chinese Muslim groups), and other sects and sub sects that seem to have emerged in Linxia and spread from there to other parts of China. It may well be that for want of a unified hierarchical structure in Islam, just like in Judaism where there is no central authority, and unlike the Catholic and Shi'ite faiths which are led by a strict and rigid graded hierarchy, the Sunnite Islam of the Hanafi brand in China, has also diversified into so many sects and sub sets, as to defy definition by the Muslim standards known in the Middle East.

Linxia is principally an urban county, though a small part under its jurisdiction is rural, bordering on the Dongxiang Autonomous county. Its historical importance lies in the fact that during the 19th Century massive Hui rebellions under the Qing took place in this location which constituted one of its strongholds. But unlike other parts of the rebellion which had resisted government troops that massacred or deported Muslims, the Linxia Hui preferred to negotiate. They surrendered, avoiding prolonged bloodshed, and thus were spared the tribulations and suffering of their fellow Muslims in other parts of Gansu. Their 80 mosques which were built throughout the surrounding area are still the landmark of the county and the symbol of the Hui capitulation to the government troops during that major upheaval. Also characteristic of Linxia are the several mausoleums, or tombs of saints (*gongbei*, or *koumbei*) of past Muslim spiritual luminaries, who founded or led Muslim mystical groups.

When driving from Linxia to the south through S306 Road, one can observe a mosque at an interval of every mile. Most are modest, but some are relatively grand, considering the fact that they are located in local parochial villages. The majority of these, however, are built in a Middle Eastern architectural style, attesting to the sources of their financing, and stand in sharp contrast to the traditional Chinese-Muslim discreet design, which sought to dissimulate the Chinese mosques (*qing zhen* ci *yuan*) and make them appear as pagoda-shaped Chinese temples, as many older mosques throughout China still present in their outward facades today, though inside the Muslim style is preponderant.

Lintan is a small town in the south of Gansu, which earns the special status of being mentioned in this study, due to its distinction as the birthplace and headquarters of the founder of Xidaotang, Ma Qixi. Like Linxia to the northwest, Lintan is also located along a very small river to its west. Most of Lintan's residents are Hui, although very small groups of them identify themselves as Dongxiang and Bonan. Lintan has only five mosques located inside and around the city. As of 2016, only three of them were active while the other two have been undergoing refurbishment. The extent of modernity of the town can be gauged through the number of electronic stores and restaurants, which lend to its avenues the appearance of a typical modern Chinese city. In the middle of the streets adult Hui people play a game called *Xiangqi* (Chinese chess) while others busy themselves with going in and out of the local mosque area.

Perhaps due to the younger Hui generation in Lintan, the community seems to the outside observer to be much more liberal than one would expect. Some attend universities in larger cities and are exposed to modern Chinese society. Thus, fewer people wear the traditional Muslim white caps. When confronting the young Hui generation with questions on 'Islam', 'Hui', or even asking reasons they wear white caps on their head, their responses betray a shallow understanding of their creed. Since they don't learn about Islam or Hui in the public school system, they say they usually draw whatever knowledge they have of their faith from their parents. Those who do go to mosques can absorb and digest more information about Islam, although it is limited to primary data. The largest mosque in town is the Xidaotang Mosque, located in the southwest of the city and can be seen clearly from the mountains to the northwest. Unfortunately, it had been under reconstruction during the visit of our team, so we were unable to find someone who could explain in more detail the story of the Mosque and its special nature. Inside the perimeter of the Xidaotang Mosque there is a *gongbei* (saint tomb), that can be surmised to be the tomb of Ma Qixi, however no local was eager to discuss that topic.

The second biggest mosque in Lintan County *is the Hallal Mosque*, located in the middle of town. Behind it are the residences of the *Ahungs* and their families. At the entrance to the mosque, a large board advertises the specific times of prayer. Most of the *Ahungs* can be identified by the grey outfit they wear, in addition to the traditional white cap. However, some of the younger generation who pray at this mosque, also wear this same kind of grey *garb*. When asked for the reason, they said it was related to the Xidaotang sect. However, it seems that these *garbs* are slowly losing their significance, as they are becoming a fad for many youngsters wearing them that are not related to the Xidaotang sect.

The third mosque is the Lintan County *Hallal Northern Mosque* which is located northeast of the town. It is comparable in size to the mosque mentioned above. The fact that there are no women inside the mosques' compounds, unlike all other Hui houses of prayer in both Gansu and Yunnan, points to the fact that the Xidaotang Hui in Lintan tend to a far stricter attitude when it comes to separation between the sexes during prayers.

Another interesting attraction is the tomb of a local saint, a *gongbei*, located just outside the town. When looking from the outside, one may mistake it for a small Buddhist temple. However, hidden discreetly inside, one can see a small round shaped room surrounded by pictures of Mecca. At the center, there is a tomb covered by many Qur'anic books whose deceased occupant may not be readily identifiable. Although no one volunteered to identify its affiliation, it is probable that it also belongs to the Xidaotang, not only because vestiges of *gonbeijiao* are still practiced by adepts of the New Sect, which at times had cultivated the worship of saints, but mainly due to the conspiracy of silence that often enveloped that sect and its adepts' reluctance to discuss it. The disguise of Muslim mosques as a Confucian or Buddhist temple was quite widespread, especially in the major cities of China, where dissimulation was thought to lessen the friction between Han and Hui. This tendency to strictly cultivate the Muslim content within the outwardly Chinese vessel, has been a characteristic of Chinese Islam especially after the great Muslim rebellions which have forever broken the trust between majority and minority. It was not until the post Cultural

Revolution era (1966–76), when China opened to the world and adopted a more liberal policy towards its minorities, that its new mosques, which are built with Saudi, Kuwaiti or Turkish contributions, afford the Hui and other Muslims in China the pride of boasting Middle Eastern and Central Asian architectural styles.

Among our many interviewees in Lintan, from students to Ahungs, most emphasized their biggest problem was uniting the various Muslim societies in China to create a harmonious bond. This includes sub-societies among the Hui such as those who are affiliated to the Xidaotang and other splinter groups. As far as studying Islam among the younger generations, it seems that home education and the authority of the parents remain the only way for young Hui to absorb the most preliminary knowledge of the faith, in view of the total neglect, if not purposeful disregard of religious education on the part of the state school system. One interviewed student, when asked about what the Hui think of the Chinese government, said that unlike in the past, the present Chinese government treats them very positively. They sense and appreciate the freedom they enjoy to practice their faith, as long as they do it within the parameters of their autonomous county or prefecture. From China's point of view, this is related to the more liberal policy toward Muslims due to the State's expanding ties with the Muslim world. From the Hui viewpoint, the paradox sets in that the more their freedom to worship, the more they integrate into Chinese society and forego their religious duties. Only recently, the abuses of the Cultural Revolution had revealed that when hard-pressed by the regime, the propensity among the Hui was to adhere to the requirements of their religious practice.

## Yunnan Province

One can hardly find a greater contrast than that between Gansu and Yunnan. Larger than united Germany, with close to 400,000 sq. kms, but with a smaller population of some 47 million that populates mainly the eastern part of the province, verdant Yunnan boasts in the north and the west some peaks 3,000 m high, almost half the altitude of the desolate high peaks of Gansu, but with profuse water sources, a clement weather and almost double the population of its northwestern counterpart. Yunnan borders with Guangxi and Guizhou in the east, Sichuan in the north, and Tibet in the northwest which separates it from Gansu. As the southwestern most confine of China, Yunnan shares its international borders with Myanmar, Laos and Vietnam in the southwest, which often made it the prey of imperialist predators such as Britain which ruled Burma and sent long tentacles into

Tibet, and France which ruled the Indochina Peninsula of Vietnam, Laos and Cambodia (latter day Kampuchea).

Three main rivers of southeast Asia originate from Yunnan's prosperous slopes and deep gorges: the Red River, the Salween and the Mekong , which form very attractive destinations for tourism, side by side with its Stone Forest, the Putacuo National Park and other sites designated as world heritage sites by UNESCO, and the historical sites of Kunming the capital (6.5 million population) and greater Dali ( about half that figure). But the most remarkable aspect of its water wealth is the numerous lakes of the province. The most relevant to our Hui story is the large Erhai Lake, with Dali perched on its shore, which served as the capital of Du Wenxiu's Sultanate. Almost 40% of the population identifies itself as "national minorities" encompassing some 25 different groups, among them the Hui, who once dominated the scene until they were decimated or ran for their lives in the aftermath of the Panthay Rebellion led by Du Wenxiu in the 19th Century.

In consequence of its ethnic diversity, Yunnan is subdivided administratively to fit as many of the ethnic groups as is feasible in order to help calm the restiveness of some of those 25 minorities with "autonomous" regions, namely about half of all the 56 recognized "national minorities" throughout the country. To gain official recognition as a national minority, each of those groups has to reach the threshold of 5,000 members, therefore many other affiliates of other minorities, who do not reach that number may be dwelling in the province but are not accounted for in the official censuses. About ten of those minorities, including the residue of the Hui which survived the 19th Century massacre, live in border areas and river valleys, and form a major part of about 5 million varied groups of minorities, in addition to the half million Muslims living in the large cities of Kunming and Dali. Yunnan consists of 16 prefectures, among them 8 prefecture-level cities and 8 "autonomous" prefectures, subdivided into 129 county level divisions, comprising 13 districts, 14 cities, 73 rural counties and 29 "autonomous" counties accommodating various minority groups.

## Kunming

This modern, bustling amazing city of more than six million is not only comfortable and its air relatively clean, but its center is so westernized one could easily mistake it for any large American or European city, with its well-dressed, smiling population, its abundance of high rise buildings, the dominant green colored water surfaces and the multitude of public spaces, well frequented by young people who have discovered the delights of modernity and prosperity, and the self-confidence which comes with them in the post-Mao era. At an almost 2,000 m altitude, this traditional city that was known historically as Yunnan-fu, which was the site of many conflicts and bloodshed, has metastasized into a vibrant, peaceful and pleasant resort area where one can appreciate the gifts of nature and enjoy interaction with its people. It is itself located on the shore of Lake Dian. Its location being close to the southeastern Asian countries, it also constitutes a communication hub for these countries to and from China. Its rail connection to Hanoi and its distance from Beijing had permitted Kunming an early launch on the long journey to modernization.

With only 150,000 Hui people remaining in the city, among its two dozen minority groups, Muslims seem to have been diluted and digested by the population to such an extent that it no longer has the effect of a "Muslim country" that we saw in Gansu. But all those who are aware of Yuan history when (1279–1368) Yunnan was first annexed to the Middle Kingdom and its first Governor was Mongol-appointed Seyyid Edjell, or of the Muslim Panthay Rebellion (1856–73) under the weakening Qing Dynasty (1644–1912), which tore the city apart, with the massacres that had ensued, consequently thinning out much of the Muslim population, bear the scars that have remained thereafter. One of the most vivid reminders of the city's history is the disproportionate number of mosques which survived destruction, and the relatively low profile of the remaining Hui community, compared, to the self-confidence that still animates the Muslims of the Northwest, notably in Linxia. Today, compared with the 4.5 million Han people in the city, there are about half a million Yi people, the largest minority group, followed by 150,000 Hui, while the rest of the minorities dwindles almost to insignificance. But the regime is nonetheless careful to publish the list of dozens of minorities everywhere, down to the "national minority" groups which account for only a few hundred people, probably to exhibit, once again, Chinese respect even for tiny non-Han groups, and also to show how they are overwhelmingly outnumbered by the Han crushing majority.

The prefecture-level city of Kunming governs six districts, one county-level city, four counties and three autonomous counties, and also borders on the Liangshan "Yi Autonomous" region, which is adjacent to its own half a million strong Yi minority. Hence the government's interest in separating the two parts by inter-provincial borders rather than having to recognize one large and unified Yi minority which may cultivate, God forbid, similar secessionist ambitions like the Tibetans now and the Hui in 19th Century China. Significantly, in the area of Xundian within the city jurisdiction, where the authorities constituted an "autonomous" county, it was declared as jointly Hui and Yi (*Xundian Huizou Yizou Zizhi Xian*), thus defeating the very purpose of "autonomous" regions, such as for Hui, Uyghur, Tibetan, Yi or Zhang people, originally made ostensibly to satisfy their local "national" or at least cultural aspirations. In Gansu, for example, two minority «nationalities," which often compete for turf and resources, like the Hui and Zhang, where we saw that Lintan was the capital of the Zhang «autonomous county," but at the same time the shrine, the spiritual center and the birthplace of Ma Qixi, the founder of the Hui Xidaotang, this ostensible partnership has become cause for tensions between the two groups.

## Dali City

If one searches for a *Shangri-la* in China, a peaceful and slow pace stroll through old Dali may reveal that it is right there. One derives that impression, first of all, from the magnificent carved woodwork decorating the doors of all residences as well as the commercial establishments along the avenues. The ornate doors, which seem to exhibit the entire artistic enthusiasm of the local artists, are made of clear-colored panels of yellowish or light brown raw materials, which lend an attractive uniformity, yet give a false impression of diversity and nuance to the rows of doors that decorate both sides of the street. In the middle of the sloping paved alley that accommodates the passersby under leafy trees giving shelter from the sun, a pleasant trickle of clear water makes its way down the alley by force of gravity, imposing a dreamy atmosphere of unreality, where one finds oneself laid back, unconscious of time and place, watching and listening, listening and watching, to the tumult of flowing water.

Dali, which had been chosen by Du Wenxiu as his capital during the Muslim rebellion that threw the entire province into chaos in the nineteenth century, was elected not only for its landscape and its location on the Erhai Lake, but also because it had served as the medieval capital of the Kingdom of Dali, which was razed to the ground by the Mongols and reconstructed as a significant Hui city. It lay northwest of Kunming and in view of its large Bai and Yi minorities, it is today also the capital of the Dali Bai Autonomous Prefecture, exemplifying another attempt to share one cultural and historical patrimony between two contending ethnic groups. At an altitude of over 2000 m. Dali is populated by some 650,000 people, about one tenth of Kunming the Prefecture level capital. Serving as the capital of Du Wenxiu, the city was cleansed ethnically of the rebellious Hui, and only a few of their descendants still dare to mention, though reluctantly and somewhat self effacingly, its past. While an adult Hui would hesitate today to hail Du as their hero, only small children who are not limited by fears of the authorities or restrictions of political correctness, venture to say that he "was a Muslim who was good to his people," meaning that he served the Hui cause, however catastrophically destroying his Dali sultanate.

In the area of Dali there exist several marble quarries of superior quality, rich gold and silver mines, mentioned by Marco Polo in terms of gold dust that was found in abundance in its lakes and rivers, while in the mountains pieces of gold were found in larger size. According to William Gill[1] there were about 300 villages in the plain of Dali, most of them Muslim, each reduced to 200–300 families in the post rebellion era, while prior to the massacres of the uprising and its aftermath, their population used to average 700–800 families each. In Dali City itself, which had been predominantly Hui, only about 3,000 families survived the massacres of the rebellion, while the "native" non-Muslims constituted only about half that amount in the immediate period following the unrest. Gill observes that the Chinese were considered "strangers" until then. Now, the overwhelming Chinese nature of that city is unmistakable and attests to the thorough ethnic cleansing it underwent in the aftermath of the revolt. Indeed, immediately after the repression of the rebellion, what used to be the suburbs of the city lay in ruins, which were grievously apparent to Gill and other western explorers, for there, as well as in all towns within fifty miles from Dali, desperate fighting had taken place.

Also narrated by the same source, during the rebellion a horrible epidemic like the plague appeared, that first attacked the rats, and after they died or migrated from the town houses into the surrounding fields, the disease seized upon the population at large and carried off an enormous proportion of its victims. After the rebellion, large numbers of Muslims, recognizable by the white turbans they wore, remained no less discontented than before the rebellion. All the elements of discord remained, and "a very small spark might rekindle a flame that would again cast its ghastly glare over all the horrors of civil war"[2].

---

1. Gill, *The River of Gold Sand*, 303–5.
2. Ibid.

# PART I

Chapter One

# Gansu—the Pattern of Muslim Settlement

The white caps, which sometimes are nuanced with shades of grey and light blue, are the hallmark of the Muslims in Gansu, who in spite of their less than ten percent minority (less than the Muslim minority in France today, both numerically and proportionately), lend high visibility to the Muslims in this vast province, especially in the cities. Many Muslim men proudly wear their identifying headgear, which is often matched by the head-scarves of their women, less frequently in the streets but more often in the courtyards of the mosques where Muslim crowds cluster prior to Friday prayers, or for communal activities, such as funeral processions and festival celebrations. In the religious schools appended to the large mosques, all students, whether locals or coming from afar, wear that badge of Muslim (mostly Hui) identity. Often, large electronic signs exhibit for public scrutiny and "education," or as a public manifestation of cultural pride, running verses from the Qur'an in Arabic script, that only very few, apart from the *Akhund* (imam) understand, followed by Chinese translations.

As Gladney has noted in his seminal book[1], there has been a remarkable revival of Islam, even of Islamic fundamentalism, in Chinese Hui Muslim communities, in the post Mao era, to the point of causing concern among local government cadres. He referred to his microscopic anthropological analysis of the Na Homestead in Ningxia, but he specified that the radicalism connected to the Islamic revival had become more pronounced in Hui communities in the Northwest in general. He emphasized that this radicalism has been expressed in terms of the purity of the faith, hence the epithets *qing* (pure) and (we might add- *zhen*= true) attached to the religion. These two attributes

1. Gladney, *Muslim Chinese*, 117–18.

have been defining Hui Islam since its beginnings, and probably stem from the natural desire of a minority religion to confirm and assert itself when in constant danger of diluting and eroding in the midst of the overwhelming and self-confident Han culture, but the emphatic use and public display today are a manifestation of a new-found pride in the distinction they offer after a long history of clashes and rebellions of the Hui, and more recently, the horrible years of repression of the Cultural Revolution (1966–76).

One prominent and prolific aspect of this surge of identity I observed during my visit to one of the numerous mosques in Linxia, where a large hall was earmarked for a permanent exhibit of Islamic art, with the artist-creator present and pursuing his work, while visitors looked around in admiration choosing the works they wished to purchase at quite high prices, indicating the market value of the paintings. In view of the probation in Islam to paint any objects or humans which run the risk of becoming objects of worship, calligraphy has developed as a favorite art form in the Islamic world. What is specific about this brand of Chinese-Muslim art is the fact that while the shape and size of the paintings are clearly Chinese, in the form of traditional Chinese paintings, the contents are purely Islamic, citing verses from the Qur'an, in Arabic, as can be seen below. In this case, the same text about devotion and submission to Allah runs in its entirety on two contiguous paintings.

Another manifestation in this surge of identity is the religious schools attached to every major mosque, where young Muslim boys, usually teenagers, wearing their white caps for unmistakable identification, take Muslim instruction, consisting mainly of Qur'anic verses, that are loudly repeated in a chorus after the instructor. Most of the pupils did not seem to comprehend what they recited out loud, although part of their instruction includes classes in the Arabic language. I asked for permission to examine some of the books of instruction and to be present in the classes, and was granted both requests. It vividly reminded me of my religious instruction in a Jewish traditional school in Morocco, before my parents transferred me to the French *Alliance Universelle* network in my native city of Fes. There too, we memorized prayers without understanding their meaning, and we learned basic Hebrew to be able to read the texts, but had no clue about saying one single useful sentence in that «Holy tongue." The boys, who came from all over the province of Gansu were interns in place and accommodated in dormitories within the mosque compound. They seemed cheerful to have left their birthplaces in some remote village to get a taste of the big city and enjoy the company of other boys their age. Some of them said they enjoyed and needed religious instruction while others were poised to advance in their studies so as to become *akhund*.

Akhund ( or *ahung* in another version), i.e. the religious leaders in the Muslim communities (elsewhere known as *imam*), resting on both the Islamic and Confucian traditions, where religion was intertwined with intellectual life, remained the repository of Islamic knowledge of the respected *literati* (at least in Islamic matters) to the entire community which they guide. Given that there is no hierarchy (just as in Judaism, but unlike Catholic Christianity) in Sunni Islamic structures, of which the Hanafite Chinese Islam is a part, there is not only an inherent decentralized character to the various Muslim communities, but also a great propensity for sectarianism and diversification of ideas and rituals, mostly connected with local traditions and local charismatic leaders. The respect the *Ahung* command in their communities usually stems from their personal learning and reputation, and they are hired and fired in accordance with the performance of their religious duties, as estimated and judged by the lay leaders, and sometimes the rank and file of their congregations. Hence the density and visibility of the multitude of mosques in the major cities of the Northwest, in the order of hundreds in a large city like Lanzhou, and of dozens in smaller urban areas like Linxia; in all cases, out of proportion to the minority status of Muslims in Gansu (and Ningxia).

The leadership of the Ahung[2] is essential since in the often suffocating overwhelming Han environment, Muslims follow their own ways since their social and religious norms are different from the norms of the majority, in their prayers and ceremonies, in their calendar and festivals, in their weddings and burial of the dead, in their socializing and eating habits, and so on. Therefore, no matter how much the Muslims wish to put up an appearance of being Chinese, they remain Hui people in their own eyes and in the eyes of the Chinese. For example, some of the mosques, notably the *Nan Guan Da Si* (The South Gate Great Mosque) in the south-center of Lanzhou, which had been destroyed in 1958, but newly rehabilitated in 1988–9, are a combination of traditional Chinese ornamental architecture, with totally modern and utilitarian buildings, with the mosque itself sporting large automatic sliding doors with the script in Arabic inscribed on them: "*Allahumma iftah li abwab rahmatik*" (Oh God! Open for me the gates of your compassion). Nearby, a five story brick-structure houses the offices of the congregation, the religious school and the dormitory of its pupils. But at the entrance to the compound, a towering five-story pagoda, richly decorated in glittering Chinese style, dominates the scene and actually advertises from afar the presence of that temple-mosque in the heart of the busy district of the city.

It was a particularly busy Friday when I visited that mosque for the second time in as many days, since this time I could both entertain a long discussion with the *Akhund* who was disposed to speak at length about the long history of the mosque, and of Islam in the province in general, and to exchange a few sentences in Arabic, in spite of the pressure of his congregants who were assembling in the courtyard for him to lead the funeral of one of their members. On another occasion, on the birthday of the Prophet Muhammed, the ladies of the community, fully dressed in modest Muslim garb, set up large tables with utensils and a huge communal kitchen in the courtyard and were busy manufacturing in a long sequence of a skilled labor chain, and then serving to the men-congregants who attended the feast, the famous dishes of Lanzhou noodles, which have made the reputation of the many Hui restaurants throughout the city, where Muslims and Chinese converge at noon for their mid-day meal. Then the Friday service was officiated by the Akhund, in Arabic and Chinese. After the service came a lengthy sermon, in Arabic that no one understood, save for the speaker and myself, and then in Chinese translation, while the long rows of the believers sat silently on the floor carpets and listened attentively.

---

2. For the status of the Akhund, see Israeli, "Ahung and Literatus," 212–22.

According to Gladney's findings, while the Chinese authorities are accommodating towards the Hui as an ethnic group and "national" minority though shunning religion as such, he found that the religious and ethnic identity in the Northwest were inseparable and truly constituted a return to the roots. Indeed, a close analysis of salient Hui institutions, rituals and texts in Ningxia revealed that a "policy that seeks to make a clear distinction between religion and ethnicity is based on an inadequate understanding of Hui identity." He also found that the interaction of ethnic identity with liberalized government policies has led to important changes in the expression of that identity and in the reformulation of local nationality policies[3]. I could observe evidence of that during a visit to a mosque in Linxia, where the Ahung and the lay heads of the community proudly displayed in the local bulletin, their picture taken in their mosque with Prime Minister Li Keqiang, who sat down on the mosque mats in what appeared as a very cordial and accepting dialogue between the parties. The repeated claims of their Hui identity notwithstanding, they spoke boastfully about "their" Prime Minister deigning to band with them in a down to earth manner on their own turf, in the heart of the "Mecca of China." No greater boost to their identity and self-esteem could be imagined.

That feeling of self-esteem and self-confidence has also been manifested in yet another subtle fashion: on the one hand, the multitude of houses of worship, each sporting its own architecture, magnificent mosques, colorful domes and the choice of one or four slim and elegant minarets, and each insistently emphasizing its affiliation: one of them praised its *Gedimu* (ancient) identity, that is its traditional conservative roots that relate it to traditional Islam, the unaltered Islam that is inherited from its ancient roots; another- boasted its *Hua Si* origin, and yet another its *Xidaotang* connections, which will be discussed below. Only a few years ago many of these various teachers of Islam, not to say sects, were reluctant to reveal their links and affiliations, and even now, under diverse pretexts, I was "advised" not to render a planned visit to Lintan where the HQ of Xidaotang is located. But on the other hand, cognizant of the fact that sectarian divisions had led in the past to Muslim rebellions against the authorities, aided by internal strife between the various sects, part of which had sided with the authorities against their coreligionists, all of them stress today their unity under one Islam, and dismiss their sectarian differences as "insignificant," though they have a hard time explaining why then are so many sects needed if there are no essential differences between them; even more difficult was to justify past open hostilities between various orders and sub orders of the Hui. At

---

3. Gladney, *Muslim Chinese*, 118.

any rate, the admission of internal disagreements and the ability to contain them, seem to indicate strength and self-confidence.

The compelling conditions in which the Muslims in the Northwest live today, where they were turned into a minority in what they considered "Muslim territory," forces them to try to be one hundred percent Chinese, in order not to appear to swim against the current under the prevailing culture and system, and to seem as accommodating and compliant as possible to the Han majority; but on the other hand to continue to close ranks with other Muslims in order to signal their collective separateness, and even to presume that though being a minority, they are not truly strangers and have roots in the Chinese natural environment since time immemorial. And if a narration of facts is wanting for making that case, myth comes to their rescue. The center piece of Chinese Islamic mythology is no doubt, Tai Zong's dream, which allegedly took place in the year AD 630, just two years short of the death of the Prophet in Arabia:

> In the Third Year of Zhen Guan [Tai Zong] of the Tang Dynasty, on the 18th day of the Third Moon, toward midnight, the Emperor in his sleep dreamt of a man with a turban on his head chasing a monster which had rushed into the Palace.... His presence was awe-inspiring and dreadful to behold, as might be that of a sage descending to the palace. When he entered, he knelt toward the West [the *qibla* in China toward Mecca], reading the book he had in his hand. The monsters, when they saw him, were at once changed into their proper forms, and in a distressful voice pleaded for forgiveness. But the turbaned man read on for a little, till the monsters changed into bloody matter, and at last into dust, and at the sound of a voice the turbaned man disappeared...
>
> The interpreter of dreams stepped out of the ranks of officials and said: " the turbaned man is a Muslim from the West ... In Arabia there is a Muslim King of a lofty mind and great virtue, whose country is wealthy ... I have heard that in the West a great sage was born. On the natal day, the Sun showed many colors, the night was lengthened to eight watches [out of 12 a day, each of two hours] while clouds covered the hilltops, and when the True Book came from heaven, a white vapor rose to the sky.... Therefore, because of the birth of the Sage, favorable omens abounded....These monsters, thus, must be dealt with by Muslims if they are to be destroyed...[4]

---

4. .See Marshall Broomhall, *Islam in China: a Neglected Problem* London, 1910, pp. 65–7

The apocryphal nature of the story is obvious, for Muhammed was hardly known outside Arabia in AD 630. But the legend, short of making the Emperor a Muslim convert, at least made the Prophet save his life, hence creating a permanent debt by the Chinese to the founder of Islam. Beyond this first link between Islam and the Tang Empire, one ought to look at the meticulous details with which this myth is constructed, in spite of the fact that here the Prophet reads from a holy book, while he was illiterate in Islamic tradition and the fact that there was no holy book until many years after his death. This transformation is logical, since for Muslims his analphabetic attribute only stresses the miracle of his prophecy, and his serving as the vehicle for their *literati*, since there could be no illiterate sage in existence. Making him read a book was the only way to present him as a true sage. The components of this story are what Muslims were interested in preserving within their Chinese environment, so as not only to survive there but also to show how essential they had become to Han society. They were:

a. The dating of the story, to the day and the hour, is so precise as to lend credence to it. This is not a story of the type of "once upon a time," or "people say," or "I heard from." It is solidly anchored in the reign of a respected Emperor of the glorious Tang Dynasty, and it is worded to sound like a true and concrete event in both time and space, like the many events of the various dynastic histories of China;

b. In one phrase, both the existence of the Holy Book and the Holy City of Mecca were invoked. The story tells that when the Prophet came to the rescue of the Emperor, he held in his hand the *Jen Jing* (the True Classic), *jen* being true (the attribute making up the appellation of Islam in China—the *Qing Jen Jiao*, namely the Pure and True Teaching), and *Jing* , the Chinese designation of a classic, like the *Wu Jing* (the Five Confucian Classics). This is an impossible combination of two terms deriving from the two cultures of Islam and Confucian China, that perhaps symbolizes, and illustrates, the incoherence of Muslim existence in China.

c. The Prophet of Islam not only rivals, but even surpasses the power of the omnipotent Emperor, the Son of Heaven, who is said to maintain, through his moral example, not only this-worldly rule but also the cosmic order. The Prophet can even scare down monsters and condemn them to disintegration by the power of reading from his Holy Book [presumably the Qur'an, the Word of Allah Himself], something the Emperor could obviously not rival by reading his Classics, since he obviously was in need of the Prophet's interference to rescue him;

d. The very fact that the elements of nature had dramatically responded to the birth of the Prophet and to the revelation of the Book, suggests that Heaven was not exclusively the domain of the Emperor, whose annual ritual at the Heaven and Earth Temple were supposed to subdue both.

e. There were in existence outside China (*Zhong Guo*), wealthy nations ruled by lofty Kings and sages whose power was not inferior to the Emperor's, in spite of the latter's universal rule over the *Tian Xia* (Everything under Heaven).

f. The recognition of the Imperial Interpreter of Dreams of the personality, power and charisma of the Prophet, attests to the veracity of the story, which therefore has to be accepted as genuine, and not merely as legend;

g. This situation of a dream by the Emperor, *a priori*, justifies and legitimizes the entrance of the Muslim faith in China. It is strongly reminiscent of the dream of Han Mindi in AD 64, which is cited as the rationale for the spread of alien Buddhism into China[5].

This foundational story had many sequels and variations, made to fit local, regional or national circumstances. A later story, explaining the spread of Islam into Ningxia, narrated:

> The King of the Tang Dynasty dreamt that the beam of the Palace fell down, and a Hui person from the Western Regions supported the beam. Therefore, the King of Tang sent Xu Maogong to exchange 60 Tang soldiers for 60 Hui soldiers to defend the Tang Dynasty. Later, those 60 Hui soldiers married Han women and settled in central China.[6]

Those who collected this story say, unabashedly, that this tale "praises the good relations between the Han and Hui peoples, and shows that long ago the Hui people already became members of the big Chinese family[7]. Regardless, it is clear that the key theme of the rescue of the Emperor by a Muslim, this time by one who was able to substitute for the main beam of the Imperial Palace, again plays a central role. To illustrate the intertwining histories of the Han and the Hui, the great event of the An Lushan Rebellion (AD 755), where some Arab troops came to the aid of the dwindling

---

5. See Reichauer and Fairbank, *East Asia: the Great Tradition*, 123, 146.

6. This story was published in Zhong Guo Huitzu Da Ci-dian (The Great Dictionary of Chinese Islam), Jiangsu Guji Chuban Shi, 1992, 461.

7. Ibid.

dynasty, has turned this mythical story into an "exchange program" of troops between Muslims and Chinese, even though the term Hui, to designate Chinese Muslims did not exist then, if only because there were no Muslims yet in China when the dream allegedly took place.[8] Yet another version reports that during the Tang an evil wind swept the Capital, as a result of which the Emperor had a dream which prompted him to send an envoy to the King of Mecca. He returned with 500 followers, including Wangasi (Ibn Waqqas, a relative of the Prophet), and the evil wind receded. The Tang Emperor chose wives for them, they stayed in China and the Hui nationality took shape.[9]

It is noteworthy that the most updated versions of the Tang legend were collected in the 1970s and 1980s from Hui narrators in Ningxia, Gansu and Xinjiang. These are richer in detail than previous versions, however in various places in northwest China, different narrators varied on the minutiae, which may lead one to speculate on the circumstances in which these varying versions of the tale were told. Some versions vacillate between the Taizong (627–49) and Xuanzong (712–56) Emperors, which places the legend on a flexible scale of one century. This is probably due to the connection of the story with the An Lushan episode which unfolded under Xuanzong, and the difficulty to explain in some coherent fashion how Taizong, a contemporary of the Prophet could have also presided over the coming of the Hui to China during and as a result of the An Lushan Rebellion. To avoid repetition, let us look to the additional details revealed in these versions:

a. The Prophet appeared in the dream wearing a white turban, and also a green robe, and he had a towel draped around his shoulder and a kettle of water in his hand. Xu Mao, the official who stepped forward to interpret the dream, said that the turban and the robe are worn only for prayer, when one goes to the mosque, and the water kettle is used to wash one's body. This was obviously meant to explain the "strange" ways of the Muslims to their Chinese environment, such as wearing green tunics in imitation of the Prophet's favorite color of the Islamic faith,[10] or performing the *wudu'* (ablutions) prior to entering the mosque for prayer[11].

---

8.. The Muslims who had started to settle in China in those days were associated with the Islamic Empire of the early Abbasids. See Drake, "Muhammedanism in the Tang Dynasty," 23, 34.

9. Vissiere, *Etudes Sino-Mahometanes*, 120–21.

10. When the flag of the Republic of China was devised after the collapse of the Empire in 1911, the green stripe among the five indeed represented the Hui people.

11. Reported by Shujiang and Luckert, *Mythology and Folklore of the Hui*, 237.

b. It is interesting to note that while the beginning of the dream is related to the Emperor Taizong, with the exact day and hour, and the talk about the Prophet who came to his rescue from the monster, the other version about the beam of the Imperial Palace refers to the Tang Emperor in general, without any specific time.[12]

c. While in the early version the dependence on Muslims for the rescue of the Emperor is only inferred, in later versions it is clearly stated that the Emperor needed the Muslims to defend his country (presumably from An Lushan), and therefore he summoned them to his aid. This emphasis goes a long way to show that the persecuted Hui during the Qing had a high stake in proving that not only were they far from rebelling, but that the Tang Emperor considered their presence in China as essential to its defense.

d. As a result of this dream, the Emperor, according to latter-day versions, held the following dialogue with Xu Mao, his trusted official, who is identified in some of those versions as the dream interpreter himself. This "deliberate" and "planned" invitation of the Hui, who were not necessarily eager to accept the invitation into China, could not have constituted a better legitimation to the presence of the Hui in the country:

> Emperor: Let us invite some Hui people to come here
>
> Xu Mao: We, may not be able to persuade some to come by invitation but perhaps by trading
>
> Emperor: What shall we give in exchange?
>
> Xu Mao: Exchange people for people
>
> Emperor: All right, it shall be done.
>
> The story narrates that Xu Mao chose sixty young men (the sixty talked about in connection with the dream) and exchanged them for 60 Hui men, led by Gens, Gais and Wangars. Because they could not become acclimated to the climate, most of the men died along the way. Gens died in Xinjiang, Gais in Jinquan. Gars led the 20 remaining men to Changan, on the Day of the Qurban [the Muslim holiday of the Festival of *al-Ad'ha*], considered the holiest in the Muslim calendar. Upon their arrival, the Tang Emperor [ no mention of which], was himself at hand to welcome them outside the Imperial Palace. He addressed Wangars

---

12. See Shanjie, cited in Shujiang and Luckert, *Mythology and Folklore of the Hui*, 239–40.

(Waqqas) as "Brother"!, and decreed that his guest should be free to go in and out of the Palace, and no one had the right to stop him. Wangars could sit at the same table with the Emperor, as an equal and no one could oppose this decree. Moreover, the Emperor ordered his top general to build a mosque where his guest could pray[13]. This guest who was identified as Sa'ad ibn Waqqas, the uncle of the Prophet, is thus made the equal of the Emperor and a member of his household, a status that no stranger, not even any Chinese had ever enjoyed in the annals of traditional China. What was more, even the mosque, the holy place of prayer for Muslims, was given legitimacy by the Emperor himself. Incidentally, the oldest extant mosque in Canton is related to Ibn Waqqas.

According to this story, after having lived in the imperial Palace for a long time, Wangars became homesick as did the people who were with him. One day, as he looked extremely worried, the Emperor ordered a golden water kettle be made for him, to allow him to wash himself; since then, it is said, the Hui have kept a water kettle made of copper in their houses, dubbing it the "Tang kettle," which is reminiscent of the kettle held by the Muslim saint that appeared in the Emperor's dream. After some time, the Emperor became concerned with the loneliness of his guests, who had come alone to China, for when they die there would be no trace of the Hui left to guard the Empire, so he held a big ceremony and permitted the Hui to choose their mates. Since then, the Hui people have been settled in China resulting in the Hui saying among themselves :" Hui Father, Han mother." This collective memory, even if fabricated, is still a great indication of how Muslims have become part of the Chinese social and cultural landscape. It is not for nothing that a researcher of Islam in the Northwest, Jonathan Lipman, entitled his book: *Familiar Strangers*.[14]

> This version not only indicates that the Chinese Empire would always need Muslim protection, but also explains the mixed marriages of Hui men with Chinese women (the reverse would be forbidden by Muslims, since it is the faith of the men which determines the religious affiliation of the family and its children), which was current among the Hui and throws light on their demographic and physical assimilation into the Han majority. In another version, it is a military counselor to the Emperor who came forward to interpret the dream, and said: "The

---

13. This story in duplicated in Wan Lei, *The Hui Minority in Modern China*, 54–55; and in Ma Haiyun, "The Mythology of the Prophet's Ambassadors in China," 445–52.

14. Lipman, *Familiar Strangers*.

Hui people are very honest. They never deceive. If we treat them kindly they will remain loyal to Your Dynasty and never betray you.... Please send an envoy to the Muslim ruler in the Western regions and request the assistance of some able person to defeat the evil spirit."[15] This version, dating back to the Qing Dynasty, when Muslims were discredited for their repeated rebellions against the ruler, nevertheless had a deficient logic: How could Muslims "remain" loyal to Taizong when there were no Muslims there? However, for the sake of redressing the negative stereotypes against the Hui at that time, which usually spoke of their arrogance, disloyalty and deceit, a little distortion of history did not matter.

Yet another tale from Ningxia related some elements of the story in direct connection with the Xuan Zong Emperor, a contemporary of the An Lushan Rebellion, in order to make sense, giving a different explanation of the Muslim troops sent to China. According to this version, Guo Ziyi, the commander of the Tang forces against the rebels "went to borrow troops from the Hui" because his own army was not sufficient for the task. But the Hui made the provision that for each of their soldiers, they must receive ten Han soldiers. Since Guo was "in dire need," he complied with the demand and dispatched 3,000 troops in return for the 300 he received. One wonders, however, how a general "in dire need" could dispose so easily of so many of his preciously needed troops, unless we are led to believe that the Muslim army was qualitatively so far superior to the Han (in fact in a ratio of ten to one) that the deal was worthwhile. Another question: why would Muslims from the outside (certainly not Hui as explained above), be willing to accept 3,000 "inferior" troops to their side? In any case, the battle lasted a long time until An Lushan was defeated, when the Hui suffered very high casualties, and only Wangars and two others were spared. The emperor asked them to stay in Changan and rewarded them with high positions and handsome salaries[16]

The point here, of course, is to stress the Muslim devotion to the Tang and the sacrifices that they made to that effect, to the brink of total annihilation of their contingent. The Hui war heroes wanted to return home, but the Emperor, understanding that they would not be able to take Han wives without the consent of their families, allowed the Hui to take spouses by coercion. Thus, during the Lantern Festival, the Emperor had the streets of his capital decorated with all sorts of lanterns. During the Festival, people

---

15. See Israeli, *Islam in China*.

16. .Narrated by Wu Jinlong from Ningxia and recounted in Li and Luckert, *Mythology and Folklore of the Hui*, 240–42.

from the city and the surrounding area came to view the lanterns, rendering Changan into a sea of people. Then the Emperor told the three surviving Hui men :"Tonight the streets will be much alive. Surely, there will be many pretty girls in the crowd. You may go and take them by force. Those taken by you will be your wives." According to the story, each one of the Hui people carried away nine girls, perhaps duplicating the example of the Prophet who had as many, though post-prophetic Islam does not permit more than four at a time. Eventually, when the Emperor passed away, the three Hui and their families, sensing neglect toward them, moved to Ningxia where they multiplied and were called Hui ever since. Another short version takes us to nearby Gansu, without specifying which Emperor was involved, but Wangars and his two companions were simply the Prophet's envoys to spread Islam in China. The Emperor was so full of admiration for Wangars' knowledge, empathy and wisdom, he allowed him to propagate Islam. Even though he was homesick, the Emperor begged him to stay, every time urging him to prolong his stay by one more month, until the weather permitted his departure[17]

This is unmistakably a deliberate attempt to show that Muslim settlement in Ningxia and Gansu was not a Hui invasion or intrusion from the outside, but made upon the request of the Tang Emperor, and the Muslims obliged, only due to their loyalty to him, having paid a heavy price in human fatalities. When their devotion in war did earn them the right and not only the permission to settle in these areas, it was not a favor that the Han Chinese did for them. Even their weddings with the local Han Chinese, which may have been looked down upon by the Chinese majority, were not a fruit of their whim but a stratagem of the Emperor to reward them and keep them in his realm. Since they settled in the northwest and then multiplied, this explains their pattern of settlement in China, and continues to the present to boost their self-identity and add pride and a sense of entitlement to both being there and claiming that it is "Muslim country." Linxia is considered the "Mecca of China" by virtue of the direct original link between the Prophet and his envoys who came from Mecca and Medina, and the first Muslim settlers in the Middle Kingdom. There were apparently other Muslims, of Arab and Persian origin, during the early Tang, who preceded the Ningxia-Gansu settlers, by taking domicile in Canton and other coastal cities as temporary traders, but the permanent settlers of the Northwest were certainly the most entitled to boast their Chinese-Han connections and roots.

17. Narrated by Ma Jinhai of Linxia, Gansu and reported in Li and Kuckert, *Mythology and Folklore of the Hui*, 242–43.

A variation of the story, also from Gansu, is said to explain the reason why some Hui in China still chase the horse of the bridegroom, a custom that is still common in the Caucasus, and was transported to Palestine-Israel by the Ottoman Turks who re-settled Circassians in the Middle East, where that custom still persists. According to the story, Wangars who was invited by the Emperor into his gardens and to marry any girl he liked, approached one who agreed to follow him (thus obliterating the blemish of a coerced wedding, for the image and reputation of the Hui). The gate-keeper of the imperial gardens, who was not aware of the Emperor's permission, ran after what he thought was a kidnapping by an intruder. The Emperor then held a celebration of Wangars' wedding, which was performed according to "Allah's will" in the Muslim narrator's version of the story.[18] This tale then, not only purported to dig up the roots of the Hui custom, and situate it in the Tang Empire, but stressed that the imperial edict regarding the wedding of Wangars could not be carried out without the Will of Allah. An adjunct story of this sort also attempts to explain the origin of the word Hui (which means return in Chinese), from the perennial requests of the Hui to return to their homes. So, these strangely named people, whose naming was often ridiculed by the Chinese and bastardized into such terms as *Hui-tzi, Hui-Hui, Hui-he* and the like, were finally allowed to rest respectfully in the repository of Chinese-Muslim myth[19]

During my visit in Gansu, reference was often made to the *gongbei*, probably a bastardization of the Arabic *Kubbe* (dome), for the tombs of saints in the Northwest which were usually crowned with a dome. Certain mosques were even said to be affiliated with the *gonbeijiao*, (the Teaching of Gongbei), as if it were one of the many sects of Islam. As Elisabeth Alles has pointed out[20], the constant mention of those monuments are but a permanent reaffirmation of the link of the Hui to their original roots as members of the universal *umma*. From her experience in other parts of China, she tells the "miracles" that those saints had performed in their lifetime and even after their death, like the tale of the "Mysterious Master" who was buried in Henan, and the terrain where he was laid to rest changed gradually, as it rose to become a hill, and the adjoining small trickle grew into a river. These Muslims of Henan are in fact said to have derived from the Arab troops who fought in the An Lushan Rebellion (AD 755) and then migrated, following the symbolic example of the Prophet's migration from Mecca to

---

18. Narrated by Ma Quanfu of Linxia, and reported by Li and Luckert, *Mythology and Folklore of the Hui*, 244–45.

19. For a wider survey of this terminology, see Wan Lei, *The Hui Minority in Modern China* pp. 3–9.

20. Alles, *Musulmans en Chine*, 57–58.

Medina (AD 622), to other parts of China. Thus, the Northwest Muslims not only find legitimacy for their own settlement in China in the Tang myths, but they also presume to have been the source and ancestors of all Chinese Muslims, and believe that their pattern of settlement in the Northwest was duplicated over the centuries as Muslims spread across the area.

Although most of the Gansu and Ningxia Muslims are typically urban, a portion of them has been rural and followed a Muslim lifestyle around a mosque in more or less remote villages. Gladney has minutely documented life in the Na Homestead south of Yinchuan city. It is a formerly walled community of mud houses clustered around one central mosque. At the height of the Maoist period, when collectivization of the countryside was mandatory, 9 work teams, almost one hundred percent Hui in composition, comprised the village, a rare phenomenon in a county where Muslims were a minority among the Han. Another two mixed Han-Hui work teams, which belonged to the village administratively, lived in a separate cluster of houses which were mostly inhabited by Han people. Over 60 percent of the Hui in that village were surnamed Na, following their village name. The Han members of the village admitted the lack of social contacts with their Hui neighbors, who refrained from rendering visits to Han homes, probably due to their dietary restrictions. The Han raised pigs in their yards and ate pork, a high enough obstacle to social interaction between the parties[21]

Gladney also attests to the fact that many Muslims in the Northwest are conscious of their dietary limitations, which help them keep their religious purity, and therefore refrain from visits to the Han houses where they can only accept fruits and plant seeds. Conversely, when Han neighbors visit the Hui, they offer them tea from a separate set of cups, to avoid "contamination," and prepare dishes of beef and lamb that the Han cannot reciprocate. The imbalance in itself contributed to less and less social contacts between the two populations, given the tremendous importance of food in Chinese socialization processes. There is an assertion that the Hui refusal to receive gifts from their Han fellow villagers places them in a position of moral "superiority," in spite of their generally inferior and marginal position socially and economically, and even ethnically, vis a vis the Han people. Contrary to the urban parts of Eastern China, where mosques are not very frequented, in the northwest the Muslim houses of prayer are very much crowded on festive occasions, like the Birthday of the Prophet or the Qurban Festival, and certainly duringFriday prayers, when women also often participate, reinforced by the student residents of the religious schools,

---

21. Gladney, *Muslim Chinese*, 118–19.

who are homegrown "captive audiences" in the religious centers where they live during their study periods.

Gladney also found that similar to other Muslims of the Northwest, the Hui of Na are affiliated with one of the many sects and sub sects specific to Chinese Islam. In the case of Na, it is the *khufya* (silent) branch of the Sufi Naqshbandi order, so called because of their low-voice *dhikr*, the invocation of Allah during the Sufi rituals. As we shall see below, the Sufi orders and sub-orders are usually subdivided into well-defined *menhuan*, those specifically Chinese sub-orders based on genealogies of saints; but the Na are not affiliated with any of those *menhuan*, unlike other mosques in the Northwest, but more like isolated mosques in the Eastern coast of China, and some of the Gansu province, especially in Linxia, which claim affiliation to the *Gedimu* (the Ancients), that is the standard orthodox Hanafi Islam—as it had penetrated into China during the Tang Dynasty. The summon to prayer is called at dawn in the village, and despite the freezing cold of winter in Ningxia, the prayer hall was full of worshippers. Many of the latter prayed five times a day, as required by their faith. During the holy festival of Ramadan, there was at least one member of every Muslim household in attendance at the mosque, and all adults fasted. In Na, Gladney also attended the Prophet's Birthday Festival, where he watched offerings brought by adults and children to the mosque in cash, flour and rice[22].

While Gladney's minute study of the Na Homestead gives us a close up detailed view of rural Muslims living in the Northwest today, Lipman's work[23] takes us far back into the history, and the dynamic processes of how it was shaped and transformed over the centuries. His area of interest includes not only Gansu and Ningxia, but also some regions of Qinghai, which are part of the same cultural landscape. The zones of actual dense Muslim population are in Ningxia and Southwestern Gansu with the adjacent areas of northeastern Qinghai. Nonetheless, despite the long term thoroughness of Gansu integration into the Chinese entity, its people still refer to their province as "frontier" (*bianjiang*), in contrast with China Proper, or the "interior," because Gansu, like the other frontier areas of Qinghai, Tibet, Mongolia and Xinjiang are indeed the limits of Chinese civilization, and being on the edge of China also permits the Muslims and other minorities to think of themselves as border-Chinese, or people who constantly vacillate between China and the outside world, if not politically and administratively for now, then at least culturally and in terms of long term dreams, far into the future. They are only one part of the many nationalities and

---

22. Gladney, *Muslim Chinese*, 122–25.
23. Lipman, *Hyphenated Chinese*, 3–23.

## Gansu—the Pattern of Muslim Settlement

ethno-religious and linguistic groups inhabiting Gansu and its frontiers, the Muslims themselves being divided between Turkic-speaking, Mongolic-speaking, Tibetan-speaking and Salar-speaking. The latter are a variety of the Turkic spoken in neighboring Uzbekistan and Turkemenistan, although standard Chinese has become the *lingua franca* of this medley of peoples, and a strong identifier of the Muslims as Chinese, in spite of their mental and emotional sense of separateness. Nonetheless, due to the abundance of separate minority identities in Gansu, and the *ad-hoc* interaction between them, Lipman has found that in certain areas, one can find the same clan divided between Muslim and non-Muslim followers.[24]

These different shades and nuances among the Muslims of Gansu have created a multifarious landscape of what and who is a Muslim: urban dwellers and rural farmers, avowed and proud Muslims who exhibit their faith outwardly and more low profile half-assimilated Muslims who shy away from showing off their identity, mosque goers who are also part of a sect and belong spiritually and administratively to a congregation headed by an *Ahong*, versus loose and diffuse Muslims who roam about unidentified, living in the comfort of anonymity, assimilating themselves in the population. Examples abound in Lipman's detailed, insightful and thoughtful typology[25]:

a. The market town of Zhanjiachuan on the Shaanxi border, is an almost purely Muslim town, where even the few non Muslims who live there have to be sensitive to the Muslim dietary limitations, in order to avoid wrecking the source of their livelihood. In town, the authority of the local sheikh of the *Jahriyya* sub-order (see the next chapter on sectarianism) reigned supreme in the 19th and 20th Centuries.

b. The Capital Lanzhou, by contrast, comprises only a few Muslim neighborhoods, totaling a minor 10 percent of Muslims in the general population. Thus, in spite of Muslim visibility, with their numerous mosques and the white cap-wearing Muslim men (and less frequently scarf-wearing women) one sees in the streets, Muslims are thoroughly diluted and marginalized in this huge and bustling modern city. Thus, commercial success and economic prosperity has not been matched by political power or influence.

c. Linxia, a three hour ride from Lanzhou, the spiritual heart of Gansu and China, has become the center of the Linxia Hui Autonomous Prefecture. The city is shared equally between Muslims and non-Muslims, but in some domains, like the profusion of splendid Muslim mosques,

24. Ibid., 15–19.
25. Ibid., 20–23.

and the omnipresent Muslim famous noodle restaurants that are perennially frequented by the entire city population, Muslim presence seems prevalent.

d. Tianshui, in the upper Wei Valley, although much smaller than the capital of Lanzhou, has kept the same proportion of Muslims (about ten percent). Its hinterland is entirely non-Muslim. Thus, although the Hui population has been loyal to the *Jahriyya*, it has kept a conciliatory attitude towards its Chinese environment, lest it create the antagonism that in the past had produced frictions and confrontations with the local population.

e. In the town of Fujiang/ Gangu, only a tiny Muslim community survives, far from any major Muslim center and totally integrated within this typically Chinese urban center.

In one aspect of Chinese Islam, nonetheless, the remote and conservative Northwest remains far apart from the revolutionary trend that is gaining currency among the Hui in China Proper, and that is the unique phenomenon of women's mosques (*qingzhen nusi*) and female clerics (*nu ahong*) that serve them. To train them for their posts there are also young, all-veiled, Chinese Muslim women clerical cadets (*hailifan*, from the Arabic *khalifa*, the word for Caliph, meaning, in both cases, a vicar, or replacement for the real thing). This topic was splendidly and thoroughly treated by Maria Jashock and Shui Jingjun in their path breaking book on this fascinating and unique angle of Chinese Islam[26]. What is truly revolutionary in this revelation is that Chinese Muslim women suddenly emerge as "taking over space situated outside their feminine sphere, which is intended for their education, and which became in the course of time a site of religious and social activity over which women have varying degrees of control and influence, in varying degrees of dependence on, or independence from, men's mosques"[27]. This book stresses it is concerned with the Hui who followed the Sunni-Hanafite tradition, and was divided in the areas covered by the book in eastern China, into the *Gedimu pai* (the ancient conservative traditionalist faction), who were challenged by the *Yihewani pai* (in Arabic *Ikhwan*—the Brothers, who were and are different from today's Muslim Brotherhood, in that the latter are conservative and radical, while their Muslim Chinese counterparts, sometimes known as one of the groups of the New Teaching, had preceded their modern, 20th century "reformers " in China.

---

26. Jashock and Jingjun, *The History of Women's Mosques in Chinese Islam*.
27. Ibid., 4.

The revivalist Islam which came to China only in the 1980s and which at the core of the Islamic world is represented by Salafi groups, such as the Muslim Brothers themselves, challenges both of the two rival factions which preceded it on the East coast of China. According to this survey, the original *Ikhwan* of China make up one fourth of all Chinese Muslims, and among them the Women's Mosques movement finds both supporters and detractors. Conversely, the new revivalist Muslim movement, which draws its ideology from the Egyptian Brotherhood and other Salafi (the ancients, the predecessors, which may be mistaken as *Gedimu*) teachings, has had an impact on both Northwest and Southwest China, and has been challenging the old traditions, on the ground that they have both been corrupted by Confucian notions[28]. Jashock and Shui underline that while the new fundamentalist *Ikhwan* were supportive of women's education, they remained opposed to women's separate mosques[29]. This is ample explanation why women's mosques did not penetrate the Muslim West, and as I have noticed in my visits to Lanzhou and Linxia mosques, pious women were in evidence, wearing scarves and other head gear, but partaking of the general rituals in their communities, and roaming the courtyards and corridors of their congregational houses of prayer in par with their fellow Muslim men.

---

28. See Israeli, "Islam in the Chinese Environment," 295–312.
29. Jashock and Jingjun, *The History of Women's Mosques in Chinese Islam*, 14.

Chapter Two

# Obsessive Sectarianism
## New Sect, Menhuan[1]

Either due to the diffused pattern of Muslim settlement throughout Gansu and Ningxia, where Muslim clusters of towns and villages have often converted in modern China into "autonomous regions," or because of the lack of a central spiritual authority and structural hierarchy in Chinese Islam in general, one of the major plights (and curiosity-arousing) characteristics of Islam in the Northwest, has been its obsessive splintering into sects, *menhuan* and sub-sects, "new sects" and "new new sects" that baffle the outside observer. What is more, this extreme propensity for specificity and parochialism is constantly matched by a supreme effort of all concerned to adamantly preserve at the very least the *façade* of Muslim unity, to sing the praise of the universal *Umma,* and to deploy a supreme effort to contain and include all Islamic groups within the pale of Islam. As much as the Chinese government has been striving to break up Chinese Muslims into different "nationalities," like the Hui, the Dongans, Salars etc, in order to minimize their total numbers, most Muslim groups have rather tended to emphasize their Muslim character, hence similarity and unity with other Muslim sub-groups, even though their ethnic identifier is often added to their general belonging to Islam ( *I su lan jiao*) and to their specific affiliation with the many sects and sub sects in existence.

In Chinese these different groupings, sects and sub-sects, orders and sub-orders, are known as *jiaopai (*factional teachings*),* a term that does not reflect the full range of the meanings subsumed under the huge variety of these groups and sub groups in Chinese Islam. Only recently attempts have

---

1. This chapter is mainly based on Israeli and Gardner-Rush, "Sectarian Islam and Sino-Muslim Identity in China," 439–52.

been made, mostly by Chinese scholars, and less frequently by Westerners, to map out that great variety of factions in the Chinese-Muslim landscape. However, due to the usual lack of a fundamental Islamic training among both groups, a thorough understanding of the nuances in the Islamic ideologies of these factions has remained obscure. Even during my field trips and my attempts to interview *ahungs* who were supposedly better-educated than others in the field of Islam, the talks were almost never conclusive and the bottom line always evasive, as if there were something hidden that refused to reveal itself. In the face of the perennial insistence that there was one Islam, and that all the sects were united under its umbrella, there was always resistance to questions trying to dig up the motives of these various factions for insisting on sectarianism and factionalism, if Islam was indeed the supreme unifying factor for all of them.

In different religions and religious traditions, the word "sect" has different meanings. In Islamic scholarship it is usually understood to indicate a movement which has moved so remotely from broadly accepted Islamic norms, that it is seen as heterodoxy. Unlike established Islam which encompasses its four schools of law (*madhahib*- the Hanafis which predominate in China and the Middle East, the puritanical Hanbalites, or Wahhabites which rule Saudi Arabia, the Malikites who prevail in North Africa, and the Shafi'ites who have spread to southeast Asia), and even recognizes the dissident Shi'ites as a legitimate teaching within Islam, radical Muslims, like the Brothers persecute them as of old and even regard them as "worse than Jews." Sect can also be an uncomfortable word to use in Islamic contexts, particularly in reference to Sufism, because of its underlying connotation of exclusivity and heterodoxy. In Confucian China too, there was always a negative connotation to *dang* (faction), which even so has been legitimized today as a political party, but it had meant in the past a deviation from the orthodox norm, and therefore was shunned by Chinese intellectuals and authorities.

*Jiaopai*, a sect or teaching, has become then the most neutral fashion of expressing ideological differences in China, and the freest of all terms from connotations of dissent, division, deviation from the accepted norms, and subversion, etc. In Islam, despite the current enmity between the Sunnite majority and the Shi'ite revolutionary minority (about 12–15 percent of the total, two hundred million out of a billion a half), which came into the open since Shi'ite Iran declared its intention to relinquish the quietist theology of the times of the Shah and export its revolutionary Islam to the entire expanse of Islamdom, there is still sufficient commonality in theology and worship to permit ecumenical prayer in a way difficult to conceive in other multi-denominational religions such as Christianity. This is the conceptual and terminological space in which Muslims in general, and in China in particular, struggle to identify themselves. Among Chinese Muslims, who live within their generally tolerant religious ambience, and specifically in Gansu-Ningxia where the multitudes of national minorities, ethnic groups, religious beliefs and sectarian atomization are prevalent, it seems "natural" on the one hand, that local Islam should behave likewise, but on the other hand it would seem anomalous that at times Chinese-Muslim factionalism should take such a rigid factional character, perhaps as a measure of self-defense and self-perpetuation in the face of the many competing identities for the souls of the same audiences. For although Wahhabi-inspired groups in China are usually discreet bodies, other Muslim congregations never tire of advertising their particular sect affiliation.

There has been great difficulty in determining the exact structural organization, and more so the changes in substance and practice in these sects of Islam in China, due to the nebulous history surrounding their birth and the turbulent circumstances which they have gone through since they emerged in their localities. Similarly, it has been difficult to pin down the precise evolution of the policy of the People's Republic vis-a-vis religion and religious minorities since the mid-1960s, during the Cultural Revolution and the immediate post- Mao era. For this reason, until recently, the dynamic dimension of sectarian Islam among the Hui, has been vague, and only now, due to various descriptive works on the beliefs and practices of this variety of sects and groups, done mostly by Muslim and Han Chinese scholars, do we begin to perceive a clearer picture of this complex array of teachings and groups. Broomhall and d'Ollone had been perhaps the first to recognize the existence of these splinter groups. Broomhall had written about the white and black hats worn by the various sects[2], while d'Ollone described in his travelogue the "tomb worshipping cult" of Gansu and northern Sichuan[3]. Later, several missionary scholars attempted to analyze in greater depth the Sufi orders (or paths as in the Chinese *dao*) in northwest China. Perkins and Broomhall identified the importance of tombs and saints within these paths and realized that there were several, often feuding, paths of Islam within China.

In recent decades, Western authors have turned their attention to sectarian movements within Chinese Islam. This author's: *Muslims in China: a Study in Cultural Confrontation (1978)*, was among the first to attempt an analysis of the origins and practices of the sects within Chinese Islam, drawing on a number of Chinese and Western sources, when China was

---

2. Broomhall, *Islam in China*, 68.
3. d'Ollone, *Recherches sur les Musulmans Chinois*, 105.

still closed to field work by foreign researchers. Gladney's: *Muslim Chinese: Ethnic Nationalism in the People's Republic (1991)* touches on some of the historical issues in the development of Chinese Muslim sects. It further examines questions of sect and identity in contemporary Hui society. Lipman, too has done a considerable amount of work in this field, particularly his excellent book *Hyphenated Chinese: Sino-Muslim Identity in Modern China* (1996).[4] During recent decades of greater openness within the People's Republic, students, tourists and scholars have again had the opportunity to live and travel among the Hui communities of China, including those in the heartland of Gansu and Ningxia. For the first time since the 1940s, Westerners with some knowledge of China, the Chinese language and normative Islam have observed, investigated and interacted with the Chinese Muslim communities. While there remain difficulties in carrying out long term thorough field work, firsthand knowledge gained to date has been invaluable in our understanding of Chinese Muslims.

What is more, the increased opportunities to travel and stay in China over long periods of time, and the desire of the Chinese authorities to develop friendships with Muslim countries, has also led to greater contact between Chinese and foreign Muslims. This, in turn, has promoted an enhanced awareness of the Chinese Muslim communities throughout the core world of Islam, and has resulted as well in various efforts to assist them from the outside. In 1995, for example, a well-attended Conference was hosted by the Fujian Academy of Science in Quanzhou on the theme of the introduction of Islam to China via the maritime Silk Road. At the Conference, delegations from different parts of the Islamic world met for the first time with their Chinese coreligionists, who also sent their delegates from all parts of China, seeking acts of generosity from the "rich uncles" of Saudi Arabia, Kuwait and other wealthy Gulf area countries. Muslim organizations throughout the world, for the first time since the great medieval Muslim travelers to China had recorded their observations, and Muslims at the core have begun to take an interest in the periphery, including China, and this was the main focus of the Conference.[5]

Finally, since the post Mao era and the end of the Cultural Revolution, a growing body of scholarship, written for the most part by Chinese, and sometimes Chinese-Muslim academics, has become available, although some of its authors, who are versed in China's history and culture retain a stereotyped, incomplete and often distorted view of Islam, as a faith and as a culture. As the educational system in China has been reconstructed in the

---

4. Lipman, *Hyphenated Chinese*.
5. Israeli, "Medieval Muslim Travelers to China," 94–104.

post-Mao era, so too has the quality of the materials produced by Chinese scholars improved. Some have launched detailed works on sectarian movements within the Muslim community. Ma Tong, for example, pioneered the re-establishment of the field after the disastrous decade of the Cultural Revolution (1966–76), with his twin works : *Zongguo Yisilan Jiaopai yu menhuan zhidu shilue* ( A History of the Islamic Sects and Menhuan in China) (1981), and *Zhongguo Yisilan Jiaopai menhuan Suyuan* (The Origin of Chinese Islamic Sects and Menhuan, 1986). More recent publications have built on Ma's work. A plethora of writings on and by Chinese Muslims have been available from secular and Islamic bookstores in Lanzhou, Linxia, Yinchuan and elsewhere. Every mosque I visited in 2016 had several books and brochures available for distribution to visitors, often partly translated into English and Arabic, briefly stating the local history of the Mosque, but rarely with a more enriching regional and provincial context. Some of those brochures encompass verses of the Qur'an, in Chinese and Arabic, probably for use by the Chinese-Muslim congregants. These are not always quality academic studies, but we find among them useful contributions by authors like Feng Jinyuan in his *Zhongguo de Yisilan Jiao* (Chinese Islam, 1994), and Gao Zhanfu's *Xibei Musilin Shehui Wenti Yanjiu* (Research into the Question of Muslim Society in the Northwest, 1991). Less significant contributions appear regularly in Chinese-Muslim journals, notably in *Huizu Yanjiu* (Studies on the Hui People), and *Xibei Minzu Yanjiu* (Studies into the Hui people of the Northwest).

The idea that there were three distinct "waves" of Islam penetrating the Chinese experience has become in some academic circles accepted as a paradigm which, like all paradigms, will occasionally need some revision. In brief, this theory posits that a first wave of Muslims migrated to China as traders, artisans and mercenaries during the late Tang (intertwined, as explained above, with history and myth), through the Yuan dynasties, up to the fourteenth Century, settling first along the southeastern coast and then further inland. What is known as the second wave, which was in fact not an outside wave at all, consisted of an internal revival movement, triggered by Sufi saints, which swept China from the late Ming times (sixteenth and seventeenth centuries) until the mid-nineteenth Century. The third wave lasted from the end of the nineteenth Century up until the Communist Revolution when Arabs, Turks and Chinese pilgrims returning from Mecca brought to China modern and radical Islamic ideas of the Wahhabi tribe. Several authors have also posited a fourth wave in the post-Cultural Revolution and the post-Mao era, as renewed contacts between the Muslim core in the Middle East and the Chinese-Muslim periphery generated more interest in Islam in China in particular, and in Muslim minorities elsewhere in general.

The uniquely sectarian nature of Chinese Islam which will be discussed here is generally viewed as having gradually developed during the second and third waves of Islam in China. While it has become conventional wisdom that the wave theory has been useful in providing a framework for sectarian development and identity-building in Chinese Islam, it is proposed here that the analysis take into account a further layer of complexity. Specifically, it has been proposed by Israeli and Rush[6] that sectarian development, or degeneration from normative Islam's point of view, among Chinese Muslims, is constantly seeking to reassert individual, communal, ethnic and religious identity through the adoption of development in the larger world of Islam or more rarely, through building a distinct identity based on a closer synthesis of Islamic and Chinese beliefs. Gladney's three waves, themselves drawn from Joseph Fletcher's scholarship, are similar to Baudel's theory of underlying currents of history which shift direction gradually throughout the centuries. This theory posits that these currents brought with them a myriad of gentle ripples, introducing first Sufism and then modernist and radical Islam to China's shores, primarily through the actions of individual Chinese and foreign Muslims, reflecting the desire of the community to bring about renewal. In other words, while the wave theory is perhaps useful in developing a framework for understanding the broad strokes of the unfolding of Islam in China, it also tends to obscure the fact that Sino-Muslim development is an organic and dynamic continuum which has been closely related to events outside the Islamic heartland, yet at the same time, also underwent evolutionary processes within Chinese Islam as a result of its interaction with Chinese society and culture.

In effect, during my 2016 visit to Gansu's mosques, both urban and rural, it was this sense of the continuum which helped to close the conceptual gap between the insistence on Islamic unity that I heard everywhere, and the equally adamant emphasis on the parochial distinction between various Muslim sects and Muslim congregations, each with its own specific affiliation (Gedimu, Ikhwan, Xidaotang, Huasi, New Sect, and what have you). It is said that only emphatically close groups can rival each other so bitterly, but my impression was that the unity provided by the continuum, was governed in fact by the fear lest disunity and discord would revive the abysmal drawbacks of the past, breaking down the awesome influence of the great mass of Muslims, into the insignificance of small splinter groups. All these factors are contributing their impact on keeping the totality of Muslims, conceptually and emotionally, within one framework of the universal *Umma* of Islam. Indeed, while the gradual yet continual process of renewal

---

6. Israeli and Gardner-Rush, "Sectarian Islam and Sino-Muslim Identity in China."

insured that Sino-Muslims retained a faith that is recognizably Islamic, it is still also admittedly Chinese, namely adapted to Chinese culture. The universality of the Chinese spoken language throughout China, even in areas where it is seconded by some local dialect, is one of the best manifestations of this unique phenomenon.

Therefore, what flows out of these assumptions is that the Islamic adaptations to Chinese culture do not, as some authors argue, make Chinese Islam a corrupt or "less pure" form of the faith, anymore than Malayan, Indian or African Islam does, and all those are arguably contained within the umbrella of world Islam. It has been this capacity of inclusion within the Islamic continuum which has precluded considering any of them as heterodox versions of the faith. The spread of Islam worldwide, over the continents of Asia and Africa, and nowadays in Europe and the Americas, has been facilitated precisely due to the diversity which allows all versions to dwell under the wings of the *Umma*. Even the upsurge of Muslim radical groups, which commit outrages around the globe, has permitted the quietist majority to label them as a "distortion of Islam," at a time when the radical groups battle among themselves (al-Qaʿida against ISIS, Sunnis against Shiʿis) and all blaming the others of "apostasy" and "treason" to the cause of Islam. Paradoxically, it is the diversity in Islamic forms, rituals and loyalties which has spawned the widespread acceptance of each otherʻs rivals, "traitors" and "apostates" as fellow Muslims. Yes, Muslims are not supposed to fight each other, for internecine war is the much shunned *fitna* in Muslim history. Therefore, all belligerent parties in these internal wars claim to fight *Jihad* against outsiders or apostates, which is the only sort of war sanctioned in Islam.

It is further believed that information available in Arabic texts, as well as in Chinese historical works, suggests Chinese Islam was divided along sectarian lines much earlier than is generally understood. In particular, a strong case can be made that Sufism had penetrated China as early as the fourteenth Century, during the Yuan, if we follow credible reports of the famous Arab and Muslim medieval traveler Ibn Battuta, who described the existence of a Sufi *Zawiya* in China. Zuo Zongtang, the great Chinese scholar and military commander, who battled against the Hui uprisings in the Northwest in the 1850s and and 1870s, also distinguished between the "Good Muslims" (*liang Hui*) and the "Muslim bandits" (*Huifei*). While he pursued the latter and exterminated them, on the grounds that they professed «heterodox» teachings of Islam, he supported the former for their docility, although they were to become the ancestors of the present diversity of sects and factions in the Northwest. More recently, it has transpired that while organized Shi'i Islam has left no trace in China, circumstantial evidence is strong, though not conclusive, that some form of Shi'ism had been established in China during the Yuan and that some expressions of it, as detected and reported by Muslim Brother Huweidi, an authority on Islamic affairs, may still be extant in contemporary China[7].

The complex admixture of sects and factions in the Northwest can be divided into five categories according to their chronology, theology and structure. For the most part, these have been accepted by scholars of Islam. These categories differ slightly from Gladney's description of a scale ranging from assimilationist to rejectionist Islam, but the two classification systems are not necessarily mutually exclusive. Gladney's sectarian classifications were intended to describe ways in which various Sino-Muslim groups have attempted to assert their identity within Chinese society, while this proposed categorization has been a means of depicting Sino-Muslim groups in a way that is more meaningful to scholars of Islam, so as to place Chinese Islam in a universal Islamic context, though at the same time remaining useful to Sinologists as well. The proposed categories for the sake of analyzing Chinese Islam in general and in the Northwest in particular, are five:

1. The first belongs to the oldest form of Chinese Islam, the one we can term "pre-sectarian" or traditionalist, in Chinese the *Gedimu* (literally the ancient, from the Arabic *Qadim*). These Muslims and their mosques have chosen not to align themselves with any of the various sects, teachings or factions which appeared in China later on, especially in the fractious Northwest. While dominant in the coastal regions, the first to be settled by Muslims who arrived via the maritime Silk Road, and the Northeast (what used to be Manchuria), many of them remain unaware of the deep sectarian divides among their coreligionists in inland China, thus lending further credence to the appellation "pre-sectarian" attributed to them here. In contrast with more recent *salafi* groups (meaning the ancestors) who wish to refer back emulating the acts of the ancient Muslims from the time of the Prophet and his disciples, the *Gedimu* only state their antiquity as a chronological fact, connoting their loyalty to the old tradition and their reluctance to be drawn into sectarian dividing arguments. During my visit of 2016 to Gansu, only a few mosques and *Ahongs* avowed their *Gedimu* affiliation.

2. The second category is represented in China by four Sufi orders and two dozen sub-orders, based on kinship genealogies, which the Chinese call *menhuan*. These four paths (*turuq*) are the Qaderiyya and Kubrawiyya orders, and the two sub-orders of the *Khufya* (incorrectly

---

7. Israeli, "Is there Shi'a in Chinese Islam?," 49–66.

often transliterated as the *Khufiyya* in Chinese-Muslim writings) and the *Jahriyya* (also often mistransliterated as *Jahariyya*, both sub branches of the great Central Asian order of the Naqhbandiya. *Because the* two branches had been steeped in internal rivalry and had often fought on opposite sides during the great Muslim rebellions of the 19th Century, they were somewhat identified as the Old versus the New Sect. The main bifurcation separating them is ritual, for the former recites the name of Allah (*dhikr*) in a low voice (*khufya*), while the latter performs the same rite loudly (*jahriyya*). In Gansu today many more Muslims and mosques emphatically stated their affiliation with the rebellious Jahriyya, while Khufya adherents seem to keep a lower profile in their low voice. In fact, since Sufism has been accepted as part of traditional Islam, it is easier to associate the khufya current with conservative and traditionalist Islam, both being low-key, without any ambition to cause trouble or to upset the applecart. Conversely, Jahriyya has been associated with indocility, rebelliousness, trouble-seeking and reform, and can be easily perceived by outside observers as a "New Sect."

3. The third category is characterized by the various *salafi* currents, which are represented in China by the *Ikhwan* (the Muslim Brothers), which state their ambition to revive Chinese Islam, pull it out of its slumber and rid it of its non-Islamic accretions drawn either from Chinese culture or from other outside influences. The original Muslim Brotherhood was founded in Egypt by Hassan al-Banna, and then spread around the Muslim world. The Salafi groups have also developed in Egypt as radical outgrowths of the modernists, and across the Chinese landscape which is well fitted with its orientation towards the past. Emerging from the Wahhabi movement in eighteenth Century Arabia, but claiming spiritual ancestry from the earliest days of Islam, this radical group seeks to return Islam to its original roots and to its pristine form at the time of the ancients (*aslaf*), yet another attractive feature in the Chinese environment. In China, as elsewhere, the *Ikhwan* oppose the conservatives whom they accuse of having corrupted Islam. Therefore, they propose returning to the holy text of the Qur'an and the Hadith for reference and they shun later interpretations and modifications. Today's insistence on the unity of Islam that was in evidence in the Northwest during my visit, has naturally reduced the sharp public debates between this group and conservative Muslims, at least on the rhetorical level, but the disagreements always surface when in-depth discussions are engaged.

4. A fourth category comprises the modernists in China who were directly influenced by modernism in the Islamic world. Their presence is strongest in Eastern China in the communities of the *Gedimu*. Modernist concepts were brought to China in the last years of the nineteenth Century, principally through Muslim activists within the influential New Culture Movement, which swept through the country after the collapse of Imperial China in 1912. They demanded that Islam should be modernized by opening channels of interpretation long closed by the conservative traditionalists. These trends have deeply influenced the official China Islamic Association (*Zhongguo Yisilanjiao Xiehui*), which is paradoxically dominated by adherents of the *Ikhwan*. This raises an important question, not yet satisfactorily answered, as to the extent of the *Ikhwan*'s putative transformation from a radical to a modernist movement, as modernist influences appear to be strong in the *Ikhwan* hierarchy, but not totally widespread among the rank and file of those who claim affiliation with that supposedly radical movement.

5. This last category comprises the Chinese Muslims who have succeeded in Sinicizing traditional Islam, represented in China by the *Xidaotang* or Western Path. It blends certain forms of Chinese Sufism with modern Islamic concepts and indigenous Chinese philosophies. It is unique, though not very widespread, in that it is the only Chinese-Muslim faction that was not founded by outside Muslim influence, and has grown as a thoroughly syncretized Islam, much like some brands of Islam in sub-Saharan Africa or in the Malayan world. As a deliberate attempt to accommodate Islam into the Chinese world, the movement represents a Sinicized movement built within the framework of what is claimed as traditional Sufism of a peculiarly Chinese brand. But despite the curiosity it may arouse in scholarly circles, the sect has remained confined to Gansu, principally in Lanzhou, Linxia and Lintan.

To apply some order to the confusing nomenclature of Chinese Islam, one must address the bewildering issue of "Old Sect" (*laojiao*) and "New Sect" (*xinjiao*) and the far-reaching derivative of the New New Sect (*xinxinjiao*). These were appellations used by Chinese officials who in fact, did not know much about Sino-Muslim sectarianism, and by Western missionaries, who knew more, and even by Chinese Muslims themselves who, during my recent field visit, sounded as though the ancient, established and conservative Islam of the pre-reform era deserved that epithet, which often coincided with the *liang Hui* (the good Muslims). These groups tended not to rebel and on the contrary, were prone to melt into the Chinese environment, adopting its material culture, though at the same time clinging to the spiritual core of the faith when they were isolated during imperial times, and more recently insistent on their universal affiliation with world Islam in the post-Mao era. Sometimes, various groups who wished to avoid suspicions and persecution, adopted the "safe" *Laojiao* appellation, in view of the fact that *Xinjiao* had been associated with the *Huifei (*Hui bandits) during their rebellions in the 19th Century. However, this term was also used at times by other sectarian groups, or by others to describe them, right into modern China. During some of the *Jahriyya*-inspired rebellions under the Qing Dynasty, many members of the *Khufya* faction called themselves *Laojiao* in order to dissociate themselves from the aggressive and trouble-making rebels. Thus, it is certainly wrong to suggest, as Joseph Fletcher did, that *Laojiao* applied exclusively to the *Khufya* adepts.

Further complicating matters, some Wahhabi-inspired groups have, from the early part of the twentieth century onward, tended to lump the Sufi-originating *menhuan* and the *Gedimu* together and to describe them all as *Laojiao*. However, while *Laojiao* has primarily applied to the *Gedimu*, and at times to some or all of the Sufi groups, the opposite ter *Xinjiao* has an even more confusing history. In all likelihood, its use predated the arrival of the *Jahriyya* branch of the Naqshbandiya in China. Several newly-established *menhuan* within each of the main Sufi orders, have at times described themselves as *Xinjiao*, or have likewise been so described by others. Occasionally, the *Ikhwan*-prone factions have also used this term to distinguish themselves from established rival groups within China. It is therefore impossible to say that the term *Xinjiao* refers exclusively, or even primarily, to any particular group or faction, except in the context of a single historical document. The term *XinXinjiao* has applied to only two groups within Chinese Islam, the *Salafiya* and the *Xidaotang*, both of which have used this terminology as a self-descriptor. During my field trip in 2016, I was under the impression that the Hui I talked to were quite amused by the confusion their terminology has created, because it was the best way to keep their sectarianism vague and misunderstood so as to avoid any pointed misgivings towards them.

In other communities like Yunnan, the various teachings were so difficult for outsiders to distinguish between, the confused and misinformed Chinese authorities differentiated them on the basis of their rebellion against, or collaboration with, the government troops. Thus, when Du Wenxiu led his rebellion against the Qing, his followers were "bad Muslims," while the docile quietist others, in Yunnan and elsewhere, remained "good" (in the sense of neutral unknown ideological entities). This led to confusion in late imperial writings of both Chinese scholars and Western missionaries as to how the various Sufi groups were interrelated under the overarching umbrella of Islam. The legacy of this confusion continues to cause difficulties for those reading source materials or trying to sort things out on the ground. The field visits of both Yunnan and Gansu in 2015-16 clearly leave that impression. What is clear is that those terms have outlived their usefulness to scholars. Except for the description of singular instances or documents relating to Sino-Islamic narrations of history, the use of these terms in academic writings has almost become unnecessary, and sometimes even counter-productive, because the added aura of "academic authority" to this confused domain only makes it almost impossible to decipher in any conclusive way, without tripping against interminable obstacles, contradictions and dilemmas during the attempt to analyze, understand and explain this enigma wrapped in a riddle.

In the absence of clear, comprehensive and authoritative surveys, it has been generally assumed in both Western and Chinese scholarship, that the majority of today's Hui are the *Gedimu* traditional Muslims. Both Ma Tong in 1980[8] and Gladney in 1991[9] estimated that about half the Hui population belongs to this school of thought, which is also seen as "standard" or "normative" Hanafi Islam. But neither of these two authoritative writers provide us with sources other than their own impressions and field surveys, which though reliable do not constitute conclusive evidence of these otherwise credible data. Another Chinese scholar, Yang Huaizhong has conducted specific surveys aimed at identifying the sectarian affiliation of mosques in Ningxia and the Northwest[10]. The two surveys differ and there is a need to reconcile the gap between them and several ways are available. First, due to the extreme atomization of sects and factions in the Northwest, the national average of 50% who follow the *Gedimu* must be much smaller in faction-ridden Gansu and Ningxia; second, the numerical strength of the *Gedimu* in China is smaller than claimed, if we take the Northwest as reflecting their average distribution, which is improbable. Circumstantial evidence suggests that the former explanation is the valid one, for though the Northwest (Gansu, Ningxia and Qinhai) constitutes the "heartland " of Chinese Islam, the bulk of Muslims in the Eastern cities of China Proper have remained virtually untouched and have not always been *Gedimu*-prone.

The above data are endorsed in the main by the findings of this author's field trips and appears to confirm, at least with regard to the Northwest, the

8. Way, "Chinois ou Musulmans?," 1948-49.
9. Gladney, *Muslim Chinese*, 385-92.
10. Huaizhong, "Gan Ning Qing Huizou zhong de Sufeipai" 10.

thesis of the Chinese scholar Gao Zhangfu that " from the Qing Dynasty onwards, the history of Chinese Islam can be seen principally as a sectarian issue"[11]. The sectarian nature of Chinese Islam and the sectarian allegiances of Hui Muslims, especially in the Northwest, have then become central to understanding the question of Muslim identity in modern China. Much work has been done by several authors, most notably by the late Joseph Fletcher, in attempting to establish the origins of the earliest Islamic sectarian movements in China. Fletcher's historical detective work[12] forms the basis of current assumptions that generally posit a significant Sufi influence in China from around the middle of the fourteenth Century. While this appears to be the earliest date traceable through extant Sufi *menhuan* sources in China, a number of facts suggest that Sufi Islam, which was the basis of later sectarianism there, was present in China even earlier.

Ibn Battuta, the famous Arab traveler of the fourteenth Century, mentions the presence of a Sufi community in Hangzhou and also describes a meeting with a Muslim mystic, presumably a Sufi, in Guangzhou[13]. This credible travelogue appears to indicate that Sufism was well established within China Proper by the time of Ibn Battuta's visit during the Yuan rule. Ma tong also cites evidence that by 1312 the Imamate of the Quanzhou mosque was hereditary, which strongly suggests either Sufi or Shi'i influence, perhaps the precursor of an early *menhuan*.[14] These early records of Sufism are worthy of further investigation, as they constitute a link between early Sufis of the Southeast and the contemporary *menhuan* of the Northwest. They may force a reexamination of the origins of sectarian Islam and suggest that it is insufficient to depict Chinese Sufism solely as a product of a second wave of Islam in China, as conventional wisdom has hitherto dictated. The existence of quietist Sufism in China Proper, even if it prepared the way for the spread of mysticism into the Northwest and the Southwest, means that Sufism does not necessarily have to evolve into sectarianism and unrest, as was the case in the outlaying area of China in the 19th Century. Unless, of course, we embrace the idea that geography can have a determining influence on ideology and political thinking inasmuch as remoteness from the center, isolation, aloofness and sparseness of population lend themselves to introverted independent thinking, hence to mysticism, agitation and messianic delusions.

11. Zhangfu, *Xibei Musilin Shehui Wenti Yanjiu*.
12. Fletcher, "The Sufi Paths(Turuq) in China."
13. Gibbs, *The Travels of Ibn Battuta*, 847–902.
14. Tong, *Zhongguo Yisilanjiao Jiaopai yu Menhuan zhidu shihlue*.

On the other hand, as the talks during our field visits suggest, one has to assume it takes something more than factionalism of this sort to provoke a fateful rebellion involving great risks of annihilation and little prospect of victory in the overwhelming Chinese environment. Even if the major sectarian-motivated uprisings unfolded in areas where Muslims constituted a local majority or a large and viable minority, in contrast to the large cities in the east where the large Muslim communities constituted a generally insignificant percentage of the population, the rebels were still always vastly outnumbered by the huge Han majorities around them, and always stood to be overpowered by the overwhelming number of Chinese government troops, especially when guided by effective determined officials such as Zuo Zongtang. Thus, it was never sufficient to have a restive, charismatic, hard-driven sectarian-religious leadership, in order for the Muslims to resort to a course of rebellion, but they had to effectively control a heartland populated by like-minded sectarians in order to envisage any chance of success in establishing themselves and implementing their goals. Ma Hualong in the Northwest and Du Wenxiu in the Southwest, having taken control of defensible turfs in Linxia-Lanzhou and Dali, respectively, which were populated by their fellow sectarians, aided by their delusions of *grandeur* and divine inspiration, and taking advantage of the simultaneous rebellions of the Taiping and the Nian which preoccupied the fading Qing Dynasty, attempted but failed, even under those ideal conditions which they could never dream of encountering ever again. Hence the bitter and disappointing residues of those past attempts of Hui secession, in the Muslim consciousness today.

It is also interesting to note that the smallest of the Sufi orders in China, the Kubrawiyya, which has more Shi'ite characteristics than one usually finds among Chinese Muslims today[15], and which is represented in Gansu by a single *menhuan, (the Dawantou* or *Zhanmen)* is generally believed to have been brought to China in the late Ming (1368-1644) by an Arab Sufi known in China as Muhunyindeni Yibuni Aluobi. Ma Tong states that there is no historical record of the Kubrawiyya arrival in China and it is only the stories of this order's adherents that posits its transmission to China during the Ming[16]. Chinese scholars are still debating the date of the Kubrawiyya's penetration into China, but Ma Tong determines that the order may have entered northern China as early as the early Southern Song which had immediately preceded the takeover by the Ming in 1368, which would make this the earliest organized Sufi order in China, though earlier in the Yuan ( who were ousted by the Song in 1338) we had noticed individual Sufis

---

15. See Israeli, *Muslims in China*, 172–73.
16. Ma Tong, *Zhongguo Yisilanjiao Jiaopai yu Menhuan zhidu*, 279.

already existed. The Kubrawiyya had certainly been active in Central Asia since the thirteenth Century,[17] but the possibility of connection between the two events remains tenuous.

While, as indicated above, Sufism may have entered China as early as the 14th Century, and perhaps even in the late twelfth Century, and became established in some of the coastal ports, it was in the Northwest, and to a lesser extent in the Southwest that Sufism was to become a powerful force within the Hui community and to spawn many of the bifurcations that made Islam there so fractious and sectarian. It later became the driving engine behind the Muslim uprisings of the nineteenth century in precisely those areas where regional sectarian dynamics were most pronounced. However, while the *menhuan* in China have assumed some uniquely Chinese characteristics, particularly their exclusivity towards each other, the roots of Chinese Sufism are found in Central Asia, Persia and Arabia. For, since the twelfth century, wandering Sufi ascetics, traders and missionaries took their brand of mystical Islam further and further eastward into what had once been the predominantly Buddhist land of Central Asia, including present day Chinese Xinjiang.[18] The principal Sufi orders in this region were the Naqshbandiyya, the Qadiriyya, Khalwatiyya and the Yassawiyya. In Xinjiang the Naqshbandiyya predominated, though divided into the Jahriyya, meaning those who recite the *dhikr* loudly and the Khufya, those who recite it quietly. Those two sub-orders of the Naqshbandiyya were bitterly divided, and violence often occurred in the Naqshbandi-dominated Central Asia, whence it penetrated the adjacent Northwest[19].

Throughout its history, Chinese Islam has always placed a great emphasis on connections with the Islamic heartlands in the West, hence the vitality of the Northwestern link between China Proper, Central Asia and West Asia. In Islamic communities throughout the world, respect is given to those Muslims who have made the *hajj* to Mecca, especially when the pilgrims originated from remote and isolated places where the obstacles and torments of travel were the most difficult, which meant that the number of Chinese Muslims was among the smallest proportionally of any Muslim community in the world. This in turn has raised the status and numbers of Chinese Muslims and foreign Muslims fortunate enough to travel to Muslim countries. Thus, as these pilgrims and some Arab Sufis brought Sufism to China and Central Asia, they were only part of the Muslim travelers who arrived at these confines for study, commerce, research, or other kinds of

---

17. Bosworth, *New Encyclopaedia of Islam*, 300–301.
18. Bennigsten and Wimbush, *Mystics and Commissars*.
19. Fletcher, "Central Asian Sufism and Ma Mingxin's New Teaching," 88–90.

ventures. Thus the principal Central Asian orders, namely the Qadiriyya and the two branches of the Naqshbandiyya, have given rise to the most influential of the *menhuan* in the Chinese-speaking Muslim communities. Much of the historiography of these orders in China has been traced, but the detailed history of each of the orders still remains to be written.

In analyzing the origin and development of these Sufi orders, some striking similarities are immediately apparent:

a. First, there is the deeply fractured nature of all major orders, leading to the plethora of divisions within Chinese Sufism which still cannot be called sects in the sense generally understood by scholars of Islam.

b. Secondly, the *menhuan*, both in the form of orders and sub-orders, were all established in China by either foreign Muslims or Chinese Muslims who had journeyed abroad and developed either a personal or biological connection, or by spiritual descent with the wider Muslim world; except perhaps for the entirely native *Xidaotang*, which will be discussed separately;

c. Thirdly, the geographical concentration of these groups in the Northwest. Indeed, the vast majority of Sufi tombs of saints and the customary pilgrimage to them are found in what can be termed as the "Qur'an belt," i.e. a reverse L-shaped crescent running in a narrow band from Xining in Qinhai, through Linxia, Lintao and Tiensui in Gansu, and then turning sharply northwards through Guhyuan, Tongxin and ending in Yinchuan in Ningxia. The core of this area is the city of Linxia and its surroundings, referred to by the Hui, as I was to confirm during my 2016 visit, as China's "Little Mecca." ( *Zhongguo de Xiao Maijia*).

It is evident that from the 13th or 14th until the 19th Centuries, this Qu'ran belt was undoubtedly the focal point of China's Muslims, and came to be known as "Muslim country," where Muslims either predominated demographically, or were a very sizable and influential minority. Even today, as they are vastly outnumbered by the Han population, and their proportion has dwindled to a few percentage points, save in sizable and some Hui villages where they still constitute half the population, that influence and that salient presence are still striking and a source of pride for the Hui in China in general. To this day, while official Muslim organizations are headquartered in Beijing for closer supervision, the Northwest remains the cultural center of Chinese Hui and especially of the more dynamic, independent-minded and cultural adherents of all Chinese Muslims. Although Muslims in China's Northwest have been at the remote periphery of both China and the Islamic world, they have maintained their strong identity through constant reference to foreign Islam, whether in Central Asia or the Middle East. Their Islam has also been more recognizably and openly Islamic than that of the Muslims in the heart of the Chinese cultural world. This was periodically expressed in the Muslim uprisings in those areas whenever a weak central government provided the opportunity, or whenever the level of oppression triggered the necessity to do so. In sum, as long as Sufism was the main expression of Islam in the Islamic countries where Chinese Muslims traveled, so also was it key in defining Sino-Muslim identity among the most vibrant of China's Muslim communities.

However, since the end of the nineteenth century, when steamboats arrived on the scene of international shipping, Chinese Muslims began making the *Hajj* by the maritime route once again.[20] Thus, contacts between Chinese Muslims and Central Asia became more limited as a result of the reduced travel along the arduous and time consuming land route to Mecca, followed by the eventual closing of this route at the onset of the Soviet rule in Central Asia's Muslim "Republics." Another result was that China's Muslim communities were exposed to the newly dominant philosophies of the Middle East, partly those originating from Saudi Arabia. As with the Sufis, it was foreign or foreign-influenced Muslims, particularly Chinese Hajjis, who brought radical and modernist Islamic concepts to China. Moreover, because this development has occurred more recently, it has been better documented than that of the arrival of Sufism in China. A number of Chinese Hajjis returned from the Hijaz distressed at the obvious variance of Islamic practice in China and Arabia. From 1892 onward, Ma Wanfu and other Chinese Hajjis promulgated a new Wahhabi-inspired teaching throughout northwestern China[21]. Imbued with the charismatic appeal of belonging to foreign Islam, Ma founded the *Ahl al-Sunna* (the People of the Tradition [of the Prophet]), which was later re-baptized as the *Ikhwan* which spread rapidly throughout China.

One hundred years after its introduction into China, the *Ikhwan* claim a membership of over one million followers, making them larger than any Sufi order in China and the predominant force within the official China Islamic Association, the state-approved and supported Muslim body. This raises the question about the extent of transformation of the *Ikhwan* from a radical to a modernist Islamic movement and probably the most popular, to which many Chinese Muslims were boasting affiliation during my field trip to Gansu in 2016, although it was difficult to pin point exactly what people

---

20. Ma Zishi, delivering a lecture in Cairo in 1934, cited Hu Fangquan's "Zhongguo Huijiao Gaikuang."

21. Ma Kesun, "Zhongguo Yisilanjiao Yikhewanpai de Changyi," 439–58.

meant beyond proudly sloganeering their affiliation. Related to the apparent aspiration of many to identify themselves with this popular movement has been the emergence of the Salafi currents, which are also Wahhabi-inspired. This group traces its theological ancestry to Ibn Taymiyya (1263–1328), the famous Syrian theologian and jurist. Emerging from among the Ikhwan in 1936, they spread especially in the Northwest, just prior to the Communist takeover in the country (1949). As happens within millenarian and politically dissenting groups, there always emerge more extremist streams who are not satisfied with the "moderate" line their parent movement has taken. The Salafis in China accused the Ikhwan, in effect, of failing to go far enough with their reforms and of making concessions to the Chinese host-culture. They failed to comprehend that any ethnic or religious minority that is subtly bombarded on all sides by the dominant host culture, cannot avoid being eroded constantly over the centuries as it adopts the majority material culture, its language, some of its mores and the like, to the point of spawning various trends among the minority, from total assimilation, to total rejection and permanent friction that are embraced by the most fanatic reformers who struggle for their survival.

The Salafis promoted a return to the purity of primitive Islam in Medina by seeking to create an Arabic-speaking community in southern Gansu whose inhabitants would relive the experience of the Muslim community at the time of the Prophet. Like other utopians in other times and places, this dream could not be totally implemented, so in many mosques in China, the best that could be achieved was to train young people in the Arabic language so they might at least read the Holy Scripture as it had originally "descended" to the Prophet of Islam. The official establishment of the Chinese Communist Party has shown concern with the "unpatriotic" nature of some Salafi writings and teachings, and has sought to maintain strict control over its followers. Thus, due to the suspicions hanging over its head, it is difficult to gauge its real strength or the extent to which its radical Wahhabi-inspired teaching has been maintained. However, Salafi mosques remain open in Linxia, and its adherents continue to dress in a distinctly Arab dress for prayer. Salafi Students interviewed in two instances in the 1990s[22] expressed their firm belief, similar to that of other Salafi groups in

---

22. Adam Rush, an Australian PhD Student and my partner in writing the article on which this article rests, had conducted fieldwork in that region in the 1990s and he conducted the interviews. During my visit in Linxia in 2016, some Muslims mentioned the evasive Salafis, but no one rushed to identify as such. But those who mentioned them were quick to confirm that, like all other teachings and factions, they were all under the umbrella of Islam.

the Islamic world today, that that the Sufis in the region were not "true Muslims" due to their conviction.

1. that pure Islam required a population literate and conversant in Arabic;
2. that Hui people must spend time in Saudi Arabia, which is imbued with Wahhabism and where the holy sites of Islam are located; and
3. that a situation where women were in a position of power in politics and commerce was inappropriate in the Hui town of Linxia, though it was acceptable in other parts of China.

These discussions with Salafi followers regarding the theological and social implications of Islam indicate that many of the radical beliefs of the Salafiyya have not only survived the decades of Communist rule, but have even received fresh impetus with the greater freedom of Chinese Muslims to go on pilgrimage to Mecca. In more informal interviews, Salafi theological students were asked whether there were any political implications arising from their understanding of Islam, but all of them stated that they were unwilling to discuss such matters with non-Muslims. The evasive nature of the Salafis in 2016, and their secretive attitude toward discussing these topics today, have been the main manifestations of the presence of these radical Muslims among the lot. But one can conclude that on the periphery of the Chinese cultural world, an overtly Islamic and foreign expression of Sino-Muslim identity was allowed to develop, inspired by the Wahhabis, freely expressed internally among the Hui, but kept discreet vis-à-vis non-Muslims and foreigners, out of self-preserving caution. But in the heartland of China, where Muslims have always constituted a small minority, Sino-Muslim identity had to be expressed only in a manner less likely to arouse suspicions. Thus it was that the increased communication with the outside world since the 20th Century led to a different development in Sino-Muslim communities along the East Coast. Yet, even in the areas where Muslims are more well-versed in Chinese culture and philosophy, and where all of them are under tremendous Chinese pressure for acculturation, Sino-Muslims sought renewal of their communal identity through reference to new teachings and ideas from the core of Islam in the Middle East and not from within China.

In the early twentieth century it was Wang Haoran (in Arabic—Hajji Abd al-Rahman), the Akhund of the dominant Oxen Street Mosque, who was decisive in the introduction of modernist Islamic concepts to China. In 1906 Wang made the pilgrimage to Mecca, but rather than returning immediately, he spent nearly two years studying and traveling in the Middle East, primarily in Egypt and the waning Ottoman Empire. When he returned to

Beijing two years later he used his prestigious position in the renowned Oxen Street Mosque to implement, cultural, educational and religious reforms in the life of Hui in Beijing, thanks to which Muslim translations, publishing and research were expanded during the Republican era (1912-49).[23] Wang and others who visited the Middle East and India during that period sought to end the endemic violence between sectarian groups within the Muslim community, especially in the Northwest, by paring back Islamic practice and belief to its essential elements, namely the five *Arkan* (pillars of the faith: *Shahada*, prayer, fast, alms and *Hajj*). The reform activity that drew its inspiration from Wang and has come to be known as the New Culture, was also guided by an Ottoman educator who had come to China with Wang, and both of them pushed forward modernist concepts of Islam.

In the post Mao era, unlike during the stifling period of the People's Republic, there is something of a return to the Republican period when there was greater freedom for Chinese Muslims to interact with Muslims abroad, a gradual decentralization of political control and the collapse of the dominant state ideology. These factors, along with the less repressive religious ambience in China today and the possibility of overseas Muslims visiting Muslim communities in China[24], are contributing to a new reassertion of Hui identity in China. Even casual visitors to the Muslim centers in Gansu and Ningxia are struck by visible signs of Islamic revival, such as mosque construction and the return to traditional dress, notably the white cap for men, the scarf for women and the distinctly Muslim headgear. The revival of Islam in Hui-dominated areas is not an isolated phenomenon and can be validly interpreted as either part of the worldwide Islamic revival or as one aspect of the overall resurgence of religious practice in China itself, part of which are the Muslim mosques, the Christian churches and such new but widespread phenomena as the *Falungong*. Both factors are certainly at work, and knowledge of both is necessary in unraveling the implications for China's future for a newly self-confident Hui community. The encroachment of some separatist Muslim movements into Xinjiang and from Central Asia in general, are challenging China's sensitivity to religious movements operating outside its control. The ruling Communist Party has its eye set

---

23. Zhangwu, "Shanshinian lai zhi Zhongguo Huijiao Wenhua Gaikuang," 385-405.

24. In the early 1990s, E. Huweidi, one of the leaders of the Egyptian Muslim Brothers visited large parts of China. His report is analyzed in my "Is There Shi'a in Chinese Islam?," In 1995, the Fujian Academy of Science in Xiamen, in collaboration with Oman, convened a large international conference on the Maritime Silk Road, to which hundreds of foreign Muslims were invited and all attended with enthusiasm in the mingling with Hui Muslims who converge on that event from all parts of China.

on the history of the militant sectarian Muslims in the country, which had contributed to bringing down the Qing dynasty.

The question of Islam in China and how it has survived for the better part of the millennium, isolated from the Muslim heartlands and frequently persecuted, is not easily answered. It is particularly interesting in light of the failure of so many other religions introduced on Chinese soil. Before the second half of the 20th Century, Buddhism was clearly the only foreign religion in China to have proved more vibrant and enduring than Islam, because it has undergone a far more thorough process of transformation and indigenization. Certainly, Islam's survival appears to be the exception in the history of religious minorities in China, unlike Christianity which disappeared at least twice before it gained a more permanent hold in the country, and Judaism that has almost completely vanished. Thus, understanding the nature of sectarian development in Chinese Islam, with the center of its activity in the remote Northwest, gives us a clue as to the reason of its remarkable survival. Two distinctive features of the Hui have marked the underlying success of this part of the Muslim world:

1. First, the establishment of the communities where the Muslims constituted either a local majority in the midst of its overall minority status, formed the basis for an ongoing and self-sustaining Hui society. The current clusters of Muslim communities in Europe (like Marseille in France, Molenbeek in Brussels, or Rosengard in Malmo and many others), tend to confirm that pattern of survival.

2. The constant reference to, and adoption of developments in the wider lands of Islam provided Muslims with a continuous renewal and update of their faith. New sources of cultural and religious identification have usually focused not on specific areas where they originated, but on the universal spiritual message they brought with them.

The continual process of sectarian development in Chinese Islam, based on events in Central Asia, Persia/ Iran and Arabia, perhaps suggests not an inherently factional society, but a continual need to reassert a separate identity. The ability of Sino-Muslim communities to draw inspiration from these sources has allowed the modern Hui to build an identity based on a connection with foreign lands. It is interesting to note that Donald Leslie has pinpointed the obliteration of communal identity in the ancient Kaifeng Jewish community at the time of their loss of the liturgical use of Hebrew, and with it, by extension, the sense of separateness based on a foreign-oriented identity. Barbara Pillsbury, together with many of the missionaries before her, documented the fragile and syncretic nature of Muslim communities in the coastal regions and in Taiwan. In these peripheral regions of Hui settlement, the Muslim presence has indeed been dwindling. For example, the Hui community of Hangzhou appears to be on the cusp of extinction. For, while 3,000 people are registered as Hui living in the city the Ahung estimated that no more than 150 worshippers are ever present at services, and then only at festivals, when many of the congregation are Turkic entrepreneurs from Xinjiang. Drawn from the twin lures of an assimilative Chinese society and the dynamic Protestantism of the Zhejiang Province, that ancient Muslim community may not survive much longer.

This situation is very similar to peripheral Jewish communities in New England, where Jewish congregations used to flourish until WWII, and are being liquidated when the majority of their congregants have moved to larger cities. Overwhelmingly, in Hui Linxia and Ningxia, if not demographically then spiritually, that sort of degeneration of Hui communities is much less likely to unfold in the foreseeable future. In sum, in areas where a "critical mass" of the Hui lives and maintains a link to the Islamic world, based either on Sufism or Wahhabi-style radicalism, or even modernist trends, or some other new form of Muslim expression, the Sino-Muslim community is expected to continue to bloom and grow within China's borders. Having survived the dark night of the Cultural Revolution and other pressures of Communist rule, the future of this outward-looking community will depend as much on developments in Iran, Saudi Arabia, Afghanistan and Kazakhstan as it does on developments in China itself.

Chapter Three

# The Ma Hua Long Heritage

Much of the restless nature of Islam in the Northwest today derives from its history of rebelliousness and indocility, best symbolized by the Ma Hualong great rebellion of the 19th Century, in which both the Muslim sectarianism of the Northwest, together with seizing the opportunity to shake off Chinese rule, came into play. Today, as the Muslim minority in the Northwest has been reduced to a few percentage points, save for some cities and "autonomous counties," like Linxia and Ningxia, the Hui are reluctant to dwell on that unhappy period when large portions of their coreligionists had been massacred by the authorities, and others were diluted in the massive Han settlement, especially in large cities like Lanzhou, where despite their visibility and apparent self-confidence, they were subdued and their rebelliousness compressed into the helpless, and at times hopeless, powder-keg of their existence. Bai Shouyi, the foremost scholar of Chinese Islam and himself a Chinese Muslim, wrote in the introduction to his monumental four-volume collection of documents relating to Muslim rebellions in nineteenth-century China:[1]

> It is incorrect to consider the Muslim uprisings as an ethnic movement; it is even more incorrect to consider Han-Hui interracial struggles [as the reason]. We must regard them as a form of class struggle and as part of the struggle of all China against the Qing....[2]

This view was also echoed by non-Chinese Marxist historians such as Imanaga Seiji, who wrote that "The [Muslim] Rebellion made clear the resistance against the feudal system, which manifested the emancipation

---

1. Shouyi, *Huimin Qiyi*.
2. Ibid., 1–2.

of Muslims in China"³. Fortunately, these Marxist analyses which were detached from reality and from a reliable understanding of Islam, were swept away with the winds of change in contemporary China. Muslims outside China continue to admire the heroes of those rebellions as "liberators," and even lament the lack of cooperation and collaboration between the three 19th Century rebellions in Gansu, Yunnan and Xinjiang, which might have ended differently. Conversely, they condemn in virulent terms turncoats such as Ma Rulong, who helped the dynasty crush the uprisings after he had split the ranks of the Muslim rebels. This attitude obviously ran counter to the Chinese nationalist dogma which seized upon the Tongzhi Restoration of the 1860s and 1870s as a model for reinvigoration of the Chinese social and political system. The Guomindang nationalists have in fact looked to the men of moral character and strength, like Ceng Guofan, Zuo Zongtang, Hu Linyi and others, who championed the cause of the Restoration, as a source of inspiration. In the 1930s, Chiang Kaishek took his stand not only against the Taiping Rebellion and the "communist bandits," but also against all rebels in Chinese history, going back to the Red Eyebrows and the Yellow Turbans. He proclaimed: "If we do not exterminate the Red Bandits, we cannot preserve the old morals and the ancient wisdom handed down from our ancestry." The Muslims of Taiwan, whose Association is part of the Nationalist establishment, find themselves on the one hand, glorifying their heroes who are deemed "bandits" by the regime and deprecating Chinese national heroes who had helped crush the Muslim uprisings on the other. Communist historiography in the Mao era did not desist, however, as the title of Bai Shouyi's Marxist-leaning seminal book suggests (*Huimin Qi Yi*-righteous Muslim uprisings) from theoretically supporting those "peasant revolutions" while at the same time oppressing any Muslim attempts to assert their identity or to celebrate their rebellious historical heroes.

In the post-Mao era, which is clearly reflected in today's narrative of that history, preference is lent to avoidance of this embarrassing topic among the Hui. While children and other innocent minds can still voice their admiration of their past heroes, the official Muslim establishment avoids any discussion of them, beyond mentioning their effect and lasting influence, so as not to contradict the party line, though they are aware of the inherent clash between the government's positive attitude to historical rebellions of minorities, and its fear from arousing unrest and antagonistic conduct among the emerging radicalism of certain Muslim groups in the Northwest in general, and in Xinjiang in particular. This paradox persists under the present nominally-communist regime, for despite its insistence on

---

3. Seiji, *Chugoku Kaikyoshi Josetsu*, 5.

a centralized unitary state, which allows no dissidence of minorities, either in Tibet or Xinjiang, it has endorsed the existence of "autonomous regions," where at least a certain amount of religious and cultural self-assertion is tolerated by the authorities, while at the same time giving to the "diluted" minorities a certain feeling of "independent" existence. Moreover, in view of the occasional eruption of violence, as in the 2009 Uyghur events in Xinjiang, the government takes concrete steps of "appeasement" of Muslims, by refraining from persecuting the aggressive among them and exhibiting gestures of "affirmative action" towards them, to the point of raising the wrath of Han who resent that reverse discrimination.

In 1958, official sources in China had acknowledged that:

> The meeting of the Gansu Nationalities Affairs Committee took the view that local nationalism among the Hui was not only widespread but also pronounced in Gansu. . . . Muslims denounced their fellow Muslim communist sympathizers as traitors to Hui nationality...
>
> The Hui declare that there is no living to be made in China, and even openly demanded emigration permits from the government so that they might return to Arabia to settle down. Some of them made it known that a government of clerics was a desirable target within an Islamic state.[4]

Those statements made during the harsh times of the Great Leap Forward (1958), followed by the tumultuous and chaotic decade of the Cultural Revolution (1966–76) were indeed fertile ground for such demands to rise, though it remains unclear how widespread they were. However, when the Communist state began to crack under the vigorous reforms of Deng Xiaoping in the post Mao era, the Hui launched open protests in Beijing and the Northwest, notably during the "Chinese Salman Rushdie" massive demonstrations of Muslims in Lanzhou, Xining and Beijing in 1989. Then, the already easing economic and cultural pressures on the Hui were reflected in their desire to protest to the Chinese authorities for the outrages committed to their faith, rather than against them.[5] Yet, the nudging question persists as to what was the root cause of the obsessive sectarianism and violent Muslim rebellions of the Northwest. Was it in the inherently rebellious nature of the sectarian movements to rise up, as did many other millenarian movements in Chinese history, or was it the ecological character of the Northwest on the rugged periphery of the Chinese Empire to cause or provoke such uprisings?

    4. Ghosh, *Embers in Cathay,* 81–82.
    5. Gladney, *Muslim Chinese,* 1–10.

## The Ma Hua Long Heritage

According to Lanny Fields,[6] Northwest China's geography and political situation must be discussed to illustrate the difficult problems Zuo faced and solved during his campaigns in that area to "pacify" the Hui rebellions, and to examine the causes of those uprisings which erupted there in the 1860s. The author claims that there was at that time, a general decline in the productive capacity of the region, which constrained the government to divert to Gansu and further West the revenue from provinces elsewhere. But then this assistance ceased, due to the devastation of China's economic heartland in the wake of the Taiping Rebellion. Thus, growing economic hardship, coupled with the usual discrimination by the Han bureaucrats against Muslims, and the usual occurrence of corruption and oppression that accompanied the Qing decline, provided the essential ingredients for rebellion. In addition, Sufi leaders and their movements, who seized the momentum offered by the inflammable situation, and kindled a series of revolts against government control, gave rise to the great rebellion in the Northwest, thus combining political, economic and religious factors for this great upheaval. We shall dwell here on the ecological and religious motives behind the unrest which as a matter of fact appeared in many uprisings.

As to topography, it is evident that the mountain ranges that separate Gansu, Shaanxi and Xinjiang from the rest of the Empire, and are penetrable only by narrow passes, have become strategic points for either defensive or offensive military purposes. In Gansu, a main water way is the Yellow River, which on one hand constituted an effective barrier for both contending rivals, but could be crossed when its waters froze in the height of winter. On the productive side, the River also constituted a network of irrigation canals in Gansu and Ningxia, and provided the defenders with an economic base, in the agricultural domain. In fact, Muslims used their strategic advantage as defenders to compel Zuo's troops, who faced difficulties crossithe Tao River (a tributary of the Huang-he) to negotiate with some of the rebels rather than using only brutal force against all of them with a view to either massacring or definitively subduing them.

Then too, the social and human make up of Gansu played an important part in the rebellion. According to Fields, under the Qing, the multifarious mosaic of minorities and group interests in Gansu, among them Mongols, Tibetans, Hui and others, also facilitated the unrest there. The Han bureaucrats were generally inclined to forestall good relations between the Tibetans and the other minorities by hiring the Tibetans as soldiers to fight against other restive minorities, resulting in the lack of cooperation between Muslims and Tibetans during the Hui uprisings. The Dongans,

---

6. Fields, *Zuo Zongtang and the Muslims*, 45.

were an important Muslim group which settled in the Northwest during the Yuan and the Ming, settling down in massive numbers in southern Gansu. They became politically active in the mid 19th Century, and Ma Hualong, the leader of the most important rebellion in 1862–1878 was himself a Dongan Muslim. The negative suspicious attitude of the Han officials vis-a-vis the segregated Muslims was reflected, inter alia, in the dog radical that they regularly added to the Hui character, to emphasize their contempt and hatred for that minority which kept increasing in numbers by marrying Han women and adopting Chinese children in times of famine. The author also believes that ethnic diversity promoted the divisions which underlay religious unity. In Gansu, for example, the Salar Turkic speaking Muslims lived in isolation from other Muslims and had a reputation for violent actions emanating from disputes within or without the community. They had converted to the New Teaching, probably the *Jahriyya* branch of the Naqshbandiyya, which was involved in many anti-government rebellions.[7]

When Fields turns to the religious aspects of the rebellions (Chap. V, pp. 62 ff), we discover the intimate link between the unrest and the various religious sects in Gansu. He locates the genesis of this development in the 1760s when Ma Mingxin founded the *Xinjiao*, a Sufi-oriented faction with Middle Eastern characteristics, whose many sub-divisions, appearing under various appellations, caused unrest in the provinces of Gansu, Shaanxi and Xinjiang, resulting in the death of millions of Muslims and others, in entirely desolated areas within a vast swath of Chinese territory. Ma had travelled with his grandfather from their Gansu residence to Central Asia where he visited major Islamic centers, but upon retuning home after several years, he began preaching his New Teaching among the Muslim Salars, developing rites such as the veneration of saints, meditation at tombs and miracle-working. The main distinguishing feature of the New Sect, however, was the loud recitation of the *dhikr* which classifies it as part of the *Jahriyya, which* provoked horror among the practitioners of the old established Islam (*laojiao*). When this religious dissension escalated into acts of violence at the end of the 18th Century, government troops intervened on the side of the Old Sect, their assumption being that it was the New Sectarians that caused the dissent, violence and the killing. When local officials arrested Ma, his incensed followers rose up, causing the threatened panicked officials to execute the founder, not realizing that they were turning him into a martyr. His most illustrious disciple was Ma Hualong, who was to head the sect in the 19th Century during the major Hui uprising. He also was eventually

---

7. Ibid., 60.

captured and executed and his HQ destroyed, crippling the sect for many years to come.

Viewed by the Chinese, the New Sect was heterodox, suspicious, and misunderstood. In many ways it became the scapegoat of anti-Muslim sentiment, a legitimate object of persecution, and by extension a legitimizing pretext for the persecution of Muslims in general, despite the self-righteous official Chinese pronouncement that they differentiated between «good» and «evil» Hui, not between Han and Hui people. But viewed by outsiders it was a confusing mixture of mystic sectarianism, popular millenarianism and Islamic revivalism, all lumped together under the *Xinjiao* heading, namely all the new accretions that had been recently added to the well-known and established *Laojiao*. Then, as now (2016), Chinese Muslims, both the followers of the sect and its rivals, were and remain silent about the whole issue, electing to avoid discussion, dismissing it as unimportant, or denying any knowledge of it altogether. It is equally true that the New Sectarians, whatever their specific factional affiliation, were more uprising prone than other Muslims, possibly indicating a compelling ideological thrust behind their rebelliousness. Indeed, both matters, ideology and discontent, can be related as two mutually reinforcing aspects of the same social phenomenon: discontent boosting the search for an alternative ideology, and ideology thriving on discontent.

Zuo Zongtang himself, trying to analyze the New Sect in his memorial to the Throne, wrote:

> Previously, in 1781, the Hui people, Ma Mingxin and Su Sushiher returned from Western countries and Arabia, where they claimed they had become aware of the secret of salvation. . . . They founded the New Sect and raised rebellions. . . Since Ma Hualong, the sect has become widespread. Under the cloak of tradesmen, they sent out missionaries to spread this evil faith everywhere. . . . The reason why the New Sect must be prohibited is that it claims its origin in God and indulges in preposterous prophesying. This sect's conduct is strange and often lures unthinking Hui into slavery. The followers of the sect are often unwittingly pushed into plotting rebellions, and they would be prepared, without hesitation, to face execution . . . which makes it a real danger to the Empire. . . . Some captured Muslims have testified to the effect that Ma Hualong knows the future, can predict the number of visitors who would come to see him from afar. . .Others testify that Ma often manifested his divine abilities, healed disease, accorded child-bearing to barren women. . .
> . Those who joined the sect confessed their sins before Ma, who

> whipped them and granted them redemption, after he intervened with God on their behalf. . . . Even though the Hui are usually skeptical, they change once they accept the New Sect teachings, and they seem possessed with madness. . . . Under siege, when the Hui suffered famine and had to eat human flesh, none of them came out to criticize Ma and his family, who availed themselves of large quantities of food supplies. Even when they were in hopeless situations, the idea that the Great Ahung would somehow save them, was comfort to them. . . . Even after Ma himself gave himself up, many Muslim leaders continued to flow to him, prostrated themselves before him, and would not redress themselves unless an order came from Ma himself. . . .[8]

Zuo's description of Ma Hualong did not differ much from that of other millenarian leaders, like Hong Xiuquan, the charismatic head of the Taiping, who also basked in prosperity while his followers starved under siege, and was also credited with miraculous deeds[9]. This description fits well, and can be identified as a Sufi depiction, and followed practice in Sufi doctrine. But the New Sect political activism, enthusiasm for warfare, readiness to suffer in the extreme, zealously following the leader-saint to the bitter end, has much in common with what is called Wahhabism, especially the Indian brand. True, some Sufi orders, particularly the Naqshbandiyya, also professed and practiced political militancy as well, but their work among Muslims and others was mainly missionary-propagandist (*da'wa*) in nature, not military coercive, like that described by Zuo:

> If anyone hesitated to join them, they all attacked him and threatened him with their weapons until he yielded. There are even cases when sons [of followers of the sect] would kill their fathers if they rejected them.[10]

In another memorial to the Throne of November, 1868, Zuo wrote :

> Numerous Hui people from Yunnan and Gansu having left their homes and being full of enthusiasm over their rebellion, are there [in Shaanxi]. Chinese who had been forced to convert to Islam are also there.[11]

---

8. Reported by Wendjang, *The Muslin Rebellions in Northwest China*, 156–58; see also Parker, *Studies in Chinese Religion*, 258–59.

9. See Shih, *The Taiping Ideology*.

10. Bai Shouyi, *Huimin Qiyi*, 9–10.

11. Chu, *Rebellions*, 129.

These firmly negative characterizations of the New Sect by such a great figure as Zuo have left their mark both in the Chinese record of history, as subversive groups who sought to disrupt the state at the height of what Mary Wright has termed the "Indian summer"[12] of the Qing before its final decline; and on the psyche of the Hui ever since. To be branded as a threat to the Chinese state is not something that can be easily dismissed or forgotten by the Han majority, hence the deep suspicion and the visible hostility towards Muslims on the one hand, and the desire of the reduced Hui community, on the other, to lower their profile minimizing friction within their environment, while licking their own wounds in an attempt to revive their prominent status in the Northwest, though under the less favorable conditions of today. One has also to always remember that the New Sect violence did not manifest itself solely against the Chinese establishment, which continues to resent it and entertain doubts about its loyalty and designs, but also against the old Muslim faithful (the *Laojiao*), which had regarded it with suspicion and ambivalence since its inception. This had applied especially when the rebellious New Sect, with such militant leaders as Ma Hualong, sought to impose itself forcefully on other Muslims who were not converted to their New Sect. Today, under the necessity to preserve the façade of unity between all Muslims, nothing blatantly negative is said about the Sect, but a sense of embarrassment and unease is still felt when one raises that issue in conversation.

In an edict of the Qianlong Emperor, this thesis found some roots which even preceded Zuo's times, as the term Old Sect was used to designate the "good " Muslims, as opposed to the "evil" New Sectarians. Moreover, the Old Sect people often collaborated with government troops against the New Sectarians, so dangerous must the New Sect trouble-makers have seemed to both of them:

Su Sushisan of Gansu belonged to a seditious sect, which has since been erased.[13] The Hui of the Old Sect are numerous in all provinces and particularly in Shaanxi. . . . Their prayers are traditional having nothing seditious in them. The outbreak of rebellion in Gansu last year resulted from a controversy between the New and Old Sects. . . . Where Su Sushan rebelled that year, the Hui of the Old Sect led the people in helping the government troops to defeat and catch the rebels, for which I commended and rewarded them.[14]

12. Wright, *The Last Stand of Chinese Conservatism*.

13. The Emperor referred to the Salar Rebellion of 1781, which had been suppressed.

14. Ford Documents. Joseph Ford has prepared but never published "Excerpts from Chinese Documents drawn from Wang Taiyu's *Chenjiao Zhenquan* and Liu Zhi's *Tianfang zhi-sheng Shihlu*

This means, that contrary to the pretense of unity and slogans of Hui brotherhood these days, in the time of the rebellions the New Sect must have been considered as a deviation from the True Faith. So much so as to justify the siding of the Old Sect with the government and fighting against their own coreligionists, given that under no circumstances are Muslims usually allowed to fight against other Muslims, unless they manifestly appear to have stepped outside the pale of Islam. Indeed, when there is infighting within the Islamic world today, the charge of "heresy" is often voiced to rationalize the Jihad war against the rival, given that this kind of hostility is only permissible against Unbelievers, while war between Muslims can only be a domestic affair within the Muslim realm which is termed *fitna*, i.e. internal unrest or rebellion. D'Ollone reported from Yunnan, soon after the Muslim rebellions were quelled in Gansu and Yunnan:

> The Muslims of Yunnan talked to us about Ma Hualong and his sect with an obvious horror, which indicated that some of those heretics had penetrated into this country as well, and. . . . I had the impression in many instances that I was prevented from meeting certain Muslims in the village of Huilong near Lingnan.[15]

D'Ollone, the first major Western field visitor to the Hui areas shortly after the Muslim rebellions, also reported about the mystical characteristics of the sect, which he related directly to Ma Hualong and explains the origin of the tomb worship which is an offshoot of the *menhuan* splintering among the New Sect, which had turned hereditary due to the charisma of the leaders that was transmitted from father to son:

> Xinjiao (New Sect) was also called Koumbejiao (or Gumbeijiao), namely the Tomb religion, which teaches the worship of deceased saints due to their continued preoccupation with the affairs of this world after their departure and the blessings they continue to bestow. Ma Hualong, who preached this doctrine, is considered by his followers as possessing supernatural forces which he inherited from his father. . . . But the adherents of the Old Teaching (*laojiao*) violently oppose these doctrine and practices. In the past, fighting had taken place between the two teachings, which are today swept under the carpet. My usual informants who belong to the Old Sect have adamantly refused to mediate between us and those whom they despise of the New Sect. It is perhaps because he knows of our good relations with

---

15. D'Ollone, *Mission d'Ollone*(1906–9), 275.

the Old Sect that the chief of the New religion refused to meet with us.[16]

At any rate, it is evident that the New Sect soon went underground, both because of its proscription by the government and its quarrels with other Muslims, and that New Sect missionaries, under one guise or another, reached Muslim communities as far as the Northeast and the great eastern cities of China.[17] Given that Ma Hualong had drifted from the Ma Mingxing teaching of three generations earlier, whose base had been in Lanzhou, and became much more mystical and rebellious, he also began operating from the city of Qiuzhibu on the right bank of the Yellow River,[18] inheriting his title from his father, Ma Erh, thus creating the succession line that became typical of the menhuan in China. He assigned to himself the title *Zong da Ahung* (the General Grand Ahung), indicating his status as the supreme "Guide" of the New Sect.[19] After his execution in 1871 a schism resulted from a battle over the succession, for it was his son in law, Ma Dashi and his grandson Ma Erxi, who contended for the sacred heritage. Ma Dashi, who was 55 in 1898 had the majority on his side and his home became an important religious center.[20] Two of Ma Hualong's successors, Ma Yuanzhao and Ma Yuanzhang, were brothers, but there is no clear indication that they were descendants of the founder. During the 1930s the leaders of the New Sect in Gansu were the third and sixth sons of Ma Yuanzhao.

What separated Ma Hualong from the founding master Ma Mingxing was that while the latter became a venerated scholar by his reforms and learning, to the point that when he was taken by the Chinese authorities to the city wall, all the Hui who looked at him dismounted their horses and prostrated themselves on the ground and cried out of emotion[21]; Ma Hualong was considered by his sect as a Prophet, and a few decades after his death he became idolized as a holy man (*Shengren*), equal or even superior to the Prophet of Islam. According to writers on this extraordinarily charismatic man,

> Ignorant members of his following held the belief that a visit to their sheikh was more important than pilgrimage to Mecca, and that he could issue tickets to Paradise. Therefore, other Muslims

16. D'Ollone, *Mission d'Ollone*(1906–9), 216–17.
17. Shouyi, *Huimin Qiyi*, 46–47.
18. Bales, *Zuo Zongtang*, 218.
19. Israeli, *Muslims in China*, 169.
20. Hartmann, *China*, *The Encyclopedia of Islam*.
21. Shouyi, *Huimin Qiyi*, 9–10.

were so exasperated that they almost came to take up arms and they severed all connections with them.[22]

It was quite noticeable that the backs of the worshippers were toward Mecca, for lower down the mountain I had seen a company worshipping in a field the opposite way toward Mecca... The tomb of Ma Hualong is an imposing affair of carved brick... but it only contains his head, and his body is at Qinqi Xian near Ningxia. The Saints' worship is denounced by the *Laojiao* together with the practice of kneeling before human leaders.[23]

Both Ma's were dubbed as saints by their followers who after their deaths worshipped them and attributed miracles to them, much as in Hassidic circles the *Rebbe* is adulated during his lifetime and after his death many supernatural feats are attributed to him. But unlike Ma Mingxin and his Jewish counterparts who were quietist in their conduct, Ma Hualong was also a militant activist who led a rebellion against the Chinese state. That was the reason he was resented, persecuted and fought both by the authorities who had a stake in eliminating him, but also by other Muslims who feared that their reputation and standing in Chinese society might be tarnished by his acts which threatened them. That is the reason for the reluctance today to talk much about him among the Hui and especially when addressing foreigners. These extremist practices, which were and are still shunned by the rank and file of Sunni Islam in general and among the Hui in particular, are reminiscent of some branches of Isma'ili Shi'ites who indulge in the deification of their Imam, which may also produce the abandonment of law to the point of practicing a ritual violation of the law. Thus, Ma Hualong's followers turning their back to Mecca may have been one manifestation of this millenarian extremism. For, if people are relieved from the duties imposed by Shari'a, that means that in a millenarian period of change, all believers must turn to God and relinquish the rites of religious law that had been devised, first of all, to guide the believer on the path to Allah and keep him on the right track.

Ma's followers and descendants had occasionally turned their backs on Mecca, and in so doing may have also forgone several of their fundamental duties that are recognized in Islam as the five pillars *(arkan)*, which serve, in a way, as the daily validation of one's belonging to the universal *Umma*. There is no trace of those deviations today in the semblance of Muslim unity which appears to dominate the Hui daily life throughout Gansu, unless, of

22. Zwemer, *Moslem World*, 69. Cited by Israeli, *Muslims in China*, 170.
23. Saunders, "Chinese Muslims."

course, secret practices remain hidden from the eyes of other Muslims, and even more so to foreign visitors and inquisitive researchers. When these practices were valid, esoteric and symbolic interpretation was given to the Five Pillars to wit, that Prayer (*salat*) meant loyalty to the leader (*Imam*); pilgrimage (*hajj*), is substituted by a visit to the Imam-saint tomb; and fast (*sawm*) meant refraining from divulging the secrets of the Sect. In the case of the Ism'a'ilis, Bernard Lewis, explained how their deviations from the norms of Islam were understood, as every bit as reminiscent of Ma Hualong's crowd:

> A personal, emotional faith, sustained by the example of the suffering of the [Shi'ite] Imam and the self-sacrifice of his followers—the experience of passion, and the attainment of truth. To the discontented, they offered the attraction of a well-organized, widespread and powerful opposition movement, which seemed to provide a real opportunity of overthrowing the existing order, and establishing in its place a new and just society headed by the Imam.[24]

One cannot help also being struck by the similarity of the secretive atmosphere of the New Sect, in all its many manifestations, to the principle of *taqiyya* (secrecy, simulation) that is current in the Shi'a in general and among the Isma'ilis in particular. The Qur'an recognizes the necessity of Muslims to hide their religion in times of danger,[25] just like the hidden Spanish and Portuguese Jews (Maranos), during the Inquisition, or the early persecuted Christians, or the members of any other oppressed minority or faith. Islamic law, however, prescribes that under circumstances such as the threat of death, or when Muslims cannot live openly professing their faith, they are called upon to migrate to other places, for "Allah's world is wide"[26]. Women, children and invalids and their dependents are permitted connivance (*muwafaqa*), but a normal individual is not justified in simulation, nor bound to migrate as long as the compulsion remains within endurable limits. Thus *taqiyya* is at most permissible, not recommended and certainly not mandatory, and stories of noble martyrdom of those who proudly refused to conceal their Muslim faith, are often cited as the proper conduct of paradigmatic believers. Some Shi'ites say that *taqiyya* (or *kitman* in other words) is a form of Jihad, but with the understanding that this Jihad is fought against

---

24. Lewis, *The Assassins*, 44.

25. Sura XIV, verse 196: "If anyone is compelled to confess Unbelief with his tongue, while his heart contradicts him, in order to escape his enemies, no blame shall fall on him, because Allah takes his servants as their hearts believe."

26. *Shorter Encyclopedia of Islam*, 561.

other Muslims, because in the standard Jihad against unbelievers, the overt message of Islam cannot be hidden. The Isma'ilis, who were the masters of taqiyya, sometimes concealed themselves under the cloak of Sufi orders or else, when they were hard pressed by enemies, to mislead their opponents as to their true beliefs and intentions, in order to gain a breathing spell. We recognize all these elements in the New Sect's conduct then and now.

The fact that so little is known about Ma Hualong and his successors, while other Chinese Muslims have left behind a considerable volume of writings, raises the suspicion that, like extreme Shi'ites, the New Sectarians kept their "secrets" and did not then, as they are reluctant to now, divulge much information about their beliefs and rituals. Like the Isma'ilis, they were organized as a secret society and regarded by outsiders as nihilists, troublemakers or even unbelievers, much like ISIS today, and other extremist Sunnis, who treat other Muslims as Unbelievers and the Shi'ites as "worse than Jews." Again, as their status in China today commends a façade of Muslim unity, their dissent from the mainstream has been concealed under the slogans of "all Muslims are the same," that one often hears in field surveys and talks with both clerics and lay leaders of the Hui community in the Northwest. However, they like other Shiites, consider themselves to be the custodians of sacred teachings, through which they will attain salvation. In effect, we know of Ma who led his rebellion that he also was

> Making it appear to the government that he was friendly and on the side of the Imperial cause . . . just what he hoped to accomplish by playing both sides in such a manner, was one of the most mysterious features of his great and bloody rebellion.[27]

In effect, Chu Wendjang cites numerous cases of Ma's and his followers' contrived friendliness and even helped the Manchu to rule while they were conniving war and preparing for it. Ma accepted, for example, a government appointment as an official but did not seriously obey orders; he sent token supplies to government troops to show his loyalty, but at the same time delivered food and money to Muslim rebels[28]. Of course, one may argue that any sensible strategist or leader would act in this fashion to secure his objectives, but if we add to this evidence the contradictory reports of Ma's allowing prayer in the ordinary mosques of other Muslims at times, and forbidding it at others, the reluctance of the New Sectarians to talk about their creed, and the inability of anyone, so far, Chinese Muslim or otherwise, to pin down exactly what this New Teaching was all about,

---

27. Bales, *Zuo Zongtang*, 227–28.
28. Chu, *Qing Policy, etc.*, 347–51.

all this adds up to a suspicion that some form of concealment, *taqiyya* in religious terms, was at work underlying all these phenomena. In the present day, the strategy may have been reversed by letting the New Sect current merge into the general flow from Hui Islam, namely, instead of being salient, prominent and noticeable by their dissidence, cultivating differences and even rebellion, they have opted to hide their true nature by making it part of the general and seemingly docile and peaceful Muslim community. That is perhaps the reason why a Chinese Hui Ahung "laughed at the notion that anyone, even a Muslim, could get all the sects tabulated and pigeonholed."[29] Or the experienced missionary who conducted field research for years and finally confessed that: "the more one heard, the less one was inclined to know."[30]

As shown by Lipman and others,[31] eruptions of Hui rebellions in the Northwest had predated the Great Rebellion of the nineteenth century, under such appellations as the Salar and then the Dongan Uprisings. The Ma Hualong unrest, which has left its traumatic mark on the Chinese Hui until today, was only part of what Lipman termed the "multifocal rebellions" of Shaanxi and Gansu which had broken out in the 1780s. In Gansu, due to its large size (nearly the area of France and larger than the United Kingdom and united Germany), its distance from the major bases of the Dynasty in the East, and the rate of growth of Muslims in that province, the Qing Dynasty could not hope to inflict the swift, massive annihilationist defeat as it did in neighboring Shaanxi, nor had the rebellious Muslim population any nearby place to retreat for their lives. For even neighboring Xinjiang, where most inhabitants were still Muslim Uyghurs, did not seem an attractive alternative to them. Therefore, the Chinese strategists, notably Zuo, tried at first to pacify the rebellion through diplomacy and the traditional *divide et impera* policy which had always seemed suitable to placate the minorities and other barbarians by separating between their varying foci of power, so as to eliminate or pacify them as the situation required. Thus, after achieving quiet in Shaanxi in 1868, Zuo turned his attention to Jinjipu, the fortress of the *Jahri* New Sect under Ma Hualong, who had deviated so far from the more quietist Ma Mingxin, it is doubtful that the two could be considered links in the same apostolic order.

It is true that Ma Hualong had also engaged in negotiations with the authorities since 1962, but in view of the secretive, discreet nature of the

---

29. Saunders, "Chinese Muslims," 69.

30. Ibid.

31. See Lipman, *Hyphenated Chinese*, 103–66; and Lei, *The Hui Minority in Modern China*, 123–32.

sect it is doubtful whether he ever intended those discussions to come to fruition, as the name he had taken, Ma Chaoqing (Ma who sought to serve the Qing Dynasty) might have falsely indicated. In the meantime, while the Chinese command was debating whether or not Ma was sincere in his offer to surrender, the latter continued to reinforce and fortify his bases and even to aid the defeated and banned Muslims of Shaanxi to retrieve their homes. Finally, in 1869, as Lipman describes it,[32] Zuo resolved to send three columns into eastern Gansu, reaching Ma's HQ in 1870 and capturing defeated Ma in January 1871. Thereupon, the entire leadership of the *Jahriyya* New Sect in neighboring Ningxia and Ma himself, including members of his family were seized and executed, while thousands of other adherents of the sect were pitilessly massacred. True, neither Zuo nor any other Chinese official had ever succeeded in eliminating the Sect entirely as they had planned, for after its followers were massacred their ideology survived; but that trauma of massive executions, addressing first the leaders and then the rank and file of the Sect, left its post-traumatic mark for ever on the psyche of Muslims, both locally and county-wide. As a consequence, it also contributed dramatically to the thinning out of the Muslim population in the province and its vicinity, and to lowering the profile of the rest to the point of concealing their identity and religious affiliation, and pretending to belong, as anyone else, to the extant Hui people.

Since the Great Rebellion and the lasting trauma suffered by the Hui in its aftermath, a century and a half have elapsed. The big question is what happened in the intermediate period between then and now, which has on the one hand metastasized the rebellious Hui into a quietist submission, yet crystallized the Ma Hualong legend as a martyr of lasting memory with the ambivalent burden he continues to impose on the history of the region which remains unalleviated over the years. Perhaps the missing link of this progression is suggested in Wan Lei's narration of the Muslim unrest in the Republican era, which bridges over the gap between old Imperial China and the Communist era, and now the post-communist epoch, when more relaxed policies of the Chinese government have been adopted, coupled with great economic development, greater leeway in communicating with the outside Islamic world, and improvement in the standard of living, at least in the urban areas (e.g. Lanzhou and Linxia in Gansu). He relates, for example, the story of Ganzhou, (now Zhangye), which used to grow opium right after the Daoguang Emperor (1821–51), i.e. the period that immediately preceded the Great Rebellion of the 1860s and 1870s. Local officials were corrupt, as usual, and they often levied taxes on that illegal fruit of the earth.

32. Ibid., 125.

In 1911, just before the collapse of the imperial rule, 3,000 people, including the Hui population, refused to pay taxes, but the Governor of the province suppressed the movement and exiled its leaders to the Heilongjiang border area in the Northeast.

Gansu, as Wan Lei narrates the tale, delayed in those circumstances establishing a republican government, mainly due to the employment of Hui, Ma Anliang, by the Governor-General of the provinces of Gansu and Shaanxi. The faltering Qing government urged Ma to quell the newly established republican revolutionary government in Shaanxi, and even elevated Ma to the rank of Chief General of the Imperial government in Gansu and Xian. Ma, who originated from Hezhou in Gansu, was the eldest son of Ma Zhan'ao who had surrendered to the Qing at the end of the Great Rebellion in 1873, therefore being loyal to the Manchu government, he was in turn appointed to a high military position in his provinces. At the same time, however, Zhang Yunshan acted as one of the commanders of the revolutionary army, who was confronted by Ma and his troops. After the Qianzhou battle of January 1912 between the two rivals, a military stalemate emerged where no one party could overwhelm the other. To overcome Gansu, the republicans, under Ma Yugui, the Governor of Shaanxi and also a Hui, did their best to drag Ma to their side and soften the hearts of the fighters by shouting: "a Hui does not kill a Hui," much as during the Afghanistan war of 2002–12, when Muslim radicals attempted to discourage the Muslim believers among the Western troops from fighting the Muslim Taliban.

In the heat of this indecisive battle, in which the government troop white caps (the standard Hui headgear of Muslims in the Northwest) tempted their rivals to switch sides, the Governor wrote to his opponent:

> The battles between Shaanxi and Gansu would cause the troops of both parties to suffer enormously on the frozen battle-fields. In these battles, no matter who is defeated and killed, they will sadden Allah and our people, both the Hui and the Han. I am hoping that you will manifest your magnanimous heart and maintain the peace of [the area], and grasp the opportunity of declaring your neutrality [in this confrontation].[33]

To precipitate a settlement to the government's liking, the renowned distinguished Imam from Beijing, Wang Kuan, who was credited with the foremost innovations and reforms in the Hui educational system of modern China, was mobilized to call upon Ma Anliang to surrender. He indeed wrote to Ma Anliang urging him "not to fall into the trap of some wicked man," and not to elect one name and neglect the needs of millions." This

---

33. Cited by Wan Lei, *The Hui Minority in Modern China*, 124.

message by Wang may have contributed to breaking the resistance of Ma Anliang, who had in any case, come under strong pressure of Yuan Shikai's republican administration, which had begun to direct troops from Henan in support of the republican forces in Shaanxi. But when word reached Gansu that the last Emperor had abdicated in Beijing and there was no longer any Imperial cause for which to fight, the stalemated battle between Gansu and Shaanxi had become irrelevant and the war was ended. In March Zhang and Ma met, and from their former antagonistic attitude emerged a new sense of brotherhood, cordiality and reconciliation. Ma declared his support for the Republic.

As to Ningxia, which was then part of Gansu and the HQ of Ma Hualong during the great rebellion, after the suppression of the rebellion it became a new outlet for settlement of many of Zuo's soldiers, who had originated from Hunan, but now due to the thinning out of the population as a result of the massacres and the desolation of large swaths of land, they found an opportunity to remain in place and thrive on the lands they had seized. The new settlers brought with them many branches of the *Gelaohui* and *Tongmeng Hui* who also settled in the extended Gansu-Ningxia expanse. During the attempts to pacify the many uprisings that broke out in Xian in and around the area, which Han, Hui, Manchus and others helped to pacify as part of the activities of those two republican societies (*Gelaohui and Tongmenhui*), a new republican-nationalist spirit emerged that was fueled by the common hatred against the bygone Imperial regime, and the new spirit of brotherhood between all parts of the nation that were recognized by the Republic as constituting the same nation, each represented by one of the five colors of the new national flag : Han, Hui, Manchu, Mongol etc. . . . That era of collaboration between the various political, ethnic and religious groups towards the establishment of a healthy national entity, served as a model of coexistence in the years to come, and somehow mitigated for a time, the strong enmities which had pitted one group against another as the decline of the dynasty began, and everyone had acted for himself in order to save oneself from the reigning chaos.

Chapter Four

# Xidaotang

One of the most intriguing aspects of Islam in China in general and its sectarian fragmentation in particular, is the emergence in Gansu, at the turn of the 20th Century of such a thoroughly assimilated Islam in its midst as to cast serious doubts about its continued inclusion within the pale of the faith. In some ways, indeed, the Xidaotang, the most acculturated sect in question, is the parallel of the *ghulat*, those Shi'ite splinters of Islam which have travelled so far from the trunk of Islam they can no longer be considered one of its branches (e.g. the Druze, the Alawites or the Bahai's). Conventional scholarship, for the most part Chinese-Muslim, has anchored the Xidaotang solidly in the Confucian tradition, with its roots going back to early Chinese- Muslim apologetic scholars versed in the Confucian as well as the Muslim traditions, such as Wang Daiyu and Liu Zhi, but with separate characteristics of the sect appearing only during the lifetime of Ma Qixi, the legendary founder from the beginning of the twentieth century, whose native city of Lintan, and the religious center of the sect that was erected there, I was subtly prevented from visiting in my 2016 field trip.

Ma Tong, himself a Hui scholar from Gansu, devoted his major study[1] to the many different menhuan that were spawned by the four major Sufi orders that took root in China: the *Jahriya* and *Khufya*, themselves the two branches of the Naqshbandiya, and the smaller Qadiriya and Kubrawiya. But he classified the Ikhwan and the Xidaodang as "Islamic teachings" or schools, to distinguish from the menhuan which are usually based on genealogical descent. However, unlike the Ikhwan who sought to purify Islam from foreign accretions, Xidaotang, on the contrary, allegedly wished to absorb Chinese elements of the Chinese soil where it grew and was

---

1. Ma Tong, *The Origins of the Islamic Sects and Menhuan in China*.

nurtured. The *Xidaotang* (the Western Way Hall), also previously known as the *Jinxingtang* (the Golden Star Hall), arguably basing itself on the work of the great Islamic scholar Liu Zhi, was in fact founded at the beginning of the twentieth century by Ma Qixi, from Lintan, Gansu, and was sometimes also dubbed as *Hanxuepai* (the Han Teaching), demonstrably indicating its Chinese orientation and creating this syncretic faith which today claims unity with normative Islam. Ma Qixi, born in a family of Ahong, embarked quite early on a Confucian course when he took the state examination, achieving the title of *Xiucai,* a state degree in Confucian doctrine, which he used to pave the road gaining recruitment into the prestigious elitist state bureaucracy.

But Ma had also studied the classical Chinese Muslim masters, like Liu Zhi, Wang Daiyu, Ma Zhu and others, and came to believe that the combination of both Confucian and Muslim traditions was the key to understanding both. Apparently due to his *Jahri* instruction and upbringing, his *Khufi* rivals dubbed him a "heterodox" or "heretic" Muslim, which in Muslim society can justify capital punishment. Nonetheless, he went on the *Hajj* to Mecca in 1905, probably as "proof" of his Muslim orthodoxy, but due to travel difficulties he was stranded in Samarkand and remained there for three years of study with Sufi orders. In 1909 he and his disciples retuned to Lintan, where he opened the Xidaotang. Our acquaintance from the Gansu rebellions, Ma Anliang, who himself followed the *Khufya* branch of the Nashbandiyya, persecuted this novel faction which was also known as the *Xinxinjiao* (the New New sect) to distinguish itself from the *Jahri* New Sect, but according to some Christian missionaries who worked with Muslims in China, he termed himself *Ersa*, namely, *Isa* in Arabic, the name of Jesus Christ in the Qur'an. Some westerners dubbed him "Prophet Jesus"[2]. These illusory appellations existed when some Christian missionaries, who despaired of a rapid conversion of Chinese to Christianity, turned to the Muslims, hoping that they were closer to the knowledge of one God, and therefore more likely to yield to their *mission civilisatrice.* In any case, Ma Anliang's troops seized Ma Qixi in 1914 and executed him along with seventeen members of his family.

Ma Qixi's crowning in Confucian, Christian, Arabic, Hui and Sufi terms and titles, may indicate the extent to which his doctrine had integrated many ideas that were alien to normative Islam. It is reminiscent of the Chief of the Taiping rebels, Hong Xiuquan's confused dreams, which many missionaries interpreted as Christian at the outset, hoping he would help them convert all China to the teachings of Christ. Wan Lei claims that

---

2. Zwemer, "Islam in Gansu," 381.

the Xidaotang embraced what was to later become the central model of organization of the Communist party, placing its head (*murshid*—guide, a term borrowed from the Muslim Sufis, and later borrowed by the Egyptian Muslim Brothers) at the apex of the pyramid, and that it arose as a result of a Muslim-Confucian dialogue in the wake of the preceding Hui revivalism represented by Liu Zhi at the end of the Ming and the beginning of the Qing Dynasty. The Guide was the religious head and the lay manager of his congregants. Wei emphasizes that the Sect was not considered a *menhuan*, in that it pursued secular activities encouraging its followers to engage in business and farming, especially along the river Tao near Lintan. At one point, and again similar to the Taipings, the followers experimented from 1901, with communal living, sharing private property with every member, which was to last officially until 1958 as "the big family organization"[3]. It is conceivable that when the forced collectivization campaign started in China, after the dismal failure of the "Great Leap Forward," the Communist Party under Mao could not tolerate "competition" or positive challenge from any other sort of communal life that might have dwarf ed its own.

The Xidaotang placed an emphasis on education, encouraging studies by both boys and girls, in both the Chinese and Islamic domains, and promoted harmony between the Han and Hui as well as with other minorities. The communal households were located in Lintan county, where the agricultural ideal, similar to the *Kibbutzim* in Israel, promoted farming, various local light industrial enterprises, and physical labor. The communal units counted about 400 households, in total encompassing some ten thousand people in Gansu and the adjoining Qinhai, Xinjiang and Sichuan provinces, where each community lived separately and independently from the hub in Lintan, though the latter remained their spiritual center where they could turn in time of need. Some Xidaotang members, striving to exhibit a façade of harmony with the Han, have claimed that when the People's Republic imposed collectivization, their organization had nothing to change or to adapt to, since it was the very same idea they had pioneered and practiced. However, in the Deng Xiaoping period, subsequent to Mao's death in 1976. when the communes in China were disbanded, Xidaotang clung to its own organizational system, in that it did not completely disappear, and in fact, when China opened up to the world, though it adopted other names such as "bonded corporations," namely voluntary communes, again like the *Kibbutzim*, as it had always been, and not by fiat of the Communist party. Until today, while not revealing openly a communal system of living, both some

---

3. Lei, *The Hui Minority in Modern China*, 271–72.

Xidaotang members and other Hui mention that they were "always living together."[4]

Ma Qixi and his faction liked to think that their commune system was a "pioneering" social invention. But both the Taiping precedent within China, and the beginning of the voluntary movement of Kibbutzim in Palestine around that time, would indicate that a more precise investigation is required as to the possible links between these ideas. At any rate, the ideal of communal living appealed to many impoverished minorities (Hui, Salar and Baoan) in Gansu, who sought refuge in the Xidaotang in large numbers, thus populating its ranks and transforming it into becoming the "most flourishing of all Sufi orders and sects in Lintan and its vicinity."[5] The sect also extended education between 1917 and 1949 under the leadership of Ma Mingren, who established a Sino-Arabic school in Lintan, as well as a girls' schools, and since the 1920s has sent its students to universities across the nation, at a time when over sixty percent of its membership attained a primary school education, a record in those days of tumult, bigotry, in-fighting and illiteracy. Wan Lei nonetheless stresses, speaking only reluctantly, that despite all these efforts at integration, until the present, the hatred between the majority of the Hui and the minority Xidaotang in Lintan did not recede. The Hui people I met in Linxia in March 2016, who spoke about that sect, despite the presence of some of its mosques in town, did dissuade me from traveling to Lintan under all sorts of irrelevant pretexts, and despite the fact than in our talks, they insisted that "all Muslims are the same." An historical reason is cited for this hatred, that goes back to the 1929 massacre of the *Laojiao* people in Lintan, where the Xidaotang allegedly played a significant part. Some Hui members of the *Gedimu*, and the *Khufya* menhuan of *Huasi*, all of them still maintaining their own mosques in Linxia, had been victims of that massacre which was occasioned not only by tension between Xidaotang and the rest of the Hui, but also by contradictions among Tibetans, Hui and Han, and by the contemporaneous Ma Zhongyin Rebellion.

Major questions are raised by this schismatic chronology, the most important of which are:

1. Is the anchoring of this essentially modern sect in the writings of those early impeccable Muslim scholars, due to the sect's and other Muslims' desperate attempt to plaster over what appears to be a schism from Islam, and perpetuate the facade of one, indivisible Islam?

---

4. Ibid., 272.
5. Ibid.

2. Is there any substance to the prevailing claim that Wang Daiyu and Liu Zhi were indeed the spiritual fathers of the sect, or only the great Muslim names that can be invoked to rationalize the schism? It is noteworthy that a contemporary of Ma Qixi, Kang Yuwei, the giant Chinese figure at the end of the Century, who attempted to reform China in the name of Confucius, may have been the source of inspiration for this way of thinking.

3. Were the founders of the sect aware of the connection that was made between them and their great apologetic predecessors, or is this a concoction of later scholars?

4. Is the Xidaotang Islamic? If it is, and considered to be so by other Muslims, why is it that the animosity of other Muslims towards it seems much less than the standard levels of hatred and violence that are customary among indisputably Muslim sects in China? If not, why is it that other Muslims do not push it beyond the pale?

5. In the post-Confucian society that is China today, what has allowed this supposedly Confucian-Muslim sect to perpetuate itself when half the construct of its identity is no longer relevant?

According to conventional wisdom as laid out above, the Xidaotang is emphatically considered "one of the Chinese-Muslim sects (*jiaopai*).[6] Its initial name was The Golden Star Hall (*Jing Xingtang*), and later re-baptized The Western Path Hall (*Xidaotang*). We are told that due to the fact that famous Chinese-Muslim scholars, such as Liu Zhi, "used Chinese culture as a base" to develop the Pure and True Faith *(Qing Jen jiao)*, the sect is also dubbed the Chinese Teaching Sect (*Hanxue Pai*).[7] We are also told that the sect was established at the beginning of the twentieth century by Ma Qixi (1857–1914) in Jiu Chengjen (the Old City), Lintan County, the Province of Gansu.[8] These events are stated, often repeatedly in Chinese-Muslim sources, without critique or interpretation, although they certainly merit some attention and explanation.

First, to what extent is the appellation *Jiaopai* used as a generic term for any sect, in a schism-ridden Islamic society which has invented the very unique term of *menhuan* to depict the numerous sub-orders in each of the major Sufi orders, which had fragmented Chinese Islam for centuries? The Xidaotang itself had its origin in the Huasi Menhuan, which typically split, as in Shi'ite Islam, over the question of the legitimacy of succession to the

---

6 Ma Tong, "Xidaotang," 600–601.
7. Ibid.
8. Ibid.

leadership. Its founder, Ma Qixi, certainly did not use the term *Jiaopai* to designate his new creation, since he was aware of the divisive, and therefore derogatory, connotation of that term, much as *Dang* (faction, later political party) was in Confucian Chinese society. For him it was simply Jing Xingtang, and then Xidaotang (the Western Path Hall), exactly as the menhuan he had originated from was called Huasi (Flowery Mosque, or Flowery Temple), a Chinese appellation of a Chinese-Muslim teaching, or splinter group, that regarded itself as the truest manifestation of Islam. That Chinese-Muslim scholars should have chosen the term *Jiaopai*, in order to demarcate its boundary with the *menhuan*, and yet signal that it was within Chinese Islam, is a question that seems to concern them more than it troubled the founder himself. Incidentally, the Sunnite-Shi´íte poles of the great divide of Islam, in which neither considers the other as a sect, are also termed by Chinese-Muslim scholars as *pai*.[9]

The initial terminology of the Golden Star Hall, that was converted into the Western Path Hall, also begs a clarification, exactly as the unexplained conversion itself. Why *tang* (hall), when the Muslim communities throughout China regularly referred to their *si (or ssu)* as their hall of prayer, or mosque? Is it not significant that the founder of a new Muslim teaching, which insisted on its Muslim identity, should resort to their general term of hall? The Golden Star is the Chinese version of the Northern Star which had a certain astrological quality in Chinese cosmology. Thus, the construct: Golden Star Hall seemed to have had a totally Chinese, non-Muslim connotation in the eyes of the founder. But then, why change it without apparent reason? Names of institutions, especially when they had a well-thought out symbolic import, were not altered at the whim of anyone. Something must have happened to occasion this shift. Why should Western (*xi*) replace the Northern (star)? Was that an allusion to Islam that came from the West? Not likely, because had Ma Qixi wished to insist on an obvious Islamic quality to his group, he could have retained the universally accepted term of *Qing Jenjiao* (the Pure and True Teaching); but he was manifestly of the opinion that he could not abide by this term, which applied to Islam in general, and yet justify the creation of a new teaching. After all, there could not exist many "Pure and True" faiths at the same time. Moreover, had Ma been truly concerned about the justification of his sect in the eyes of his fellow Muslims, he would have also, on the occasion of this rarely occurring change, replaced *tang* by *si (ssu)*.

*Xi* (West) also happened to have been one component of Ma´s first name (Qi-xi), and one cannot discard the possibility that the founder wished

---

9. Ibid.

to leave his personal imprint on the name of his creation, by attributing it to himself (Xi´s Faith). This theory can be corroborated not only by the fact that one of the Sect's girls schools in Lintan was called *Qi-xi xiao* (the (Ma) Qixi School )[10], but also by the examination of the term *dao*, which is perhaps the most value-loaded and the most pregnant with ambiguities in the entire construct of the name. The easiest way to dispose of it would be to use *dao* (path) as the Path of Allah that is repeatedly referred to in the Holy Qur´an and which fits exactly the translation of these passages from Arabic into Chinese[11]. However, in the original Arabic language, the *Sirat* (the Path) is associated, as in the *Sura al-Fatiha* (the Opening Chapter of the Qur´an) with the attribute *al-mustaqim* (straight), as against the tortuous ways of the non-Muslims. Therefore, it is hard to think of *Xi-dao* (the Western Path) as the Straight Path of Allah mentioned in the Qur´an, much less when it is preceded by its restricting epithet of Western which limits the universality of the Qur´anic term.

Thus, we must explore the avenue of Ma´s borrowing from the Chinese cultural milieu: exactly as he substituted the generally Chinese *tang* for the specifically Chinese-Muslim *si (ssu)*, he also adopted the Chinese culture-loaded *dao,* to replace the current Chinese-Muslim Straight Path connotation. Here *dao* would acquire its wide philosophical significance as one of the three recognized Paths (Daoism, Buddhism and Confucianism) in Imperial China. However, since some Islamic elements had survived in Ma´s teaching, it was (Ma Qi-) xi´s particular *dao*, one that might be conveniently thought of, or interpreted as coming from, the (Islamic) West (*xi*), an ambiguity for the sake of apparent humility, which nevertheless, serves the two purposes of Ma´s self-attribution of his sect, and at the same time reflects the originality of his creation. For, in this Islamic-Chinese amalgam, as it was indeed to be, both elements remain unmistakable.

The historical development of the sect is usually periodized into three successive eras which significantly, in a Hui society that kept fragmenting along leadership lines and legitimacy of succession, coincide with the three successive leaders who shaped it and lent to it its modern characteristics:

1. The Period of the Founder—Ma Qixi (1902–17)

    Ma was born in 1857 during the turbulent period of the Taiping Rebellion which tore China apart and threw it into total chaos for more than a decade (1850–64). Through the examination system he earned the scholarly title of *xiu-cai*, which enabled him to enter the

---

10. Ma Tong, "Xidaotang," 601.
11. See Israeli, "Translation as Exegesis," 81–103.

privileged and highly regarded gentry class though he did not gain any bureaucratic appointment. In 1891 he, like others of his rank in other places, opened a private academy in Xifeng Shan, in the Old City of Lintan County, under the name of Golden Star Hall where he taught, in addition to the Confucian Four Books and Five Classics, the works of Chinese-Muslim masters, like Wang Daiyu, Ma Zhu and Liu Zhi, who had written in Chinese[12]. It is also related that taking the works of those masters as a base, Ma diffused the faith and simplified its rituals and ceremonies, while ridding it of its "old fashion rules and stupid customs" *(cheng-gui lo-xi)*.[13] It is hard to imagine anyone within the tradition of Islam dubbing established customs as "stupid," and accepted rules as "old fashioned," and professing their eradication, unless one claims that they were *bida'* (innovations, Allah Forbid) that had accrued to Islam and bastardized it, following the accusations against other Muslims by the Wahhabis and fanatics like ISIS today, as well as other puritanical Muslims. But from what we learn about Ma Qixi's reforms, such as advocating universal education for both boys and girls, they were, quite the contrary, anti-puritanical, truly innovative and in that sense "un-Islamic" for their time. Therefore, whether those goals were stated by Ma Qixi himself or imputed to him by Ma Tong, or merely judged to be so by the latter, we are talking about ideas that take us far afield from the accepted norms of Islam.

We are told that Ma's local followers greatly increased in numbers and they supported his educational reforms. It was then that he established a "prayer hall" or the Hall of the Dao (*dao tang*, not *li-bai si*, or *qingzhen si*, as is customary with Muslims), and renamed his organization Xidaotang,[14] whose significance was discussed above. The ambiguity which may have combined with the founder's ambition to appropriate to himself his creation (his name *xi*), with the Western (also *xi*) Path, was enriched by yet another meaning which drew from the name of the village where it all took place—the Western Wind Mountain (*Xi-feng Shan*). The sect could now be understood to mean: the Hall of the Dao of Xi (the founder, or the village), the Hall of (Islamic) Path of Xi (again the founder or the village), the Hall of the Western Dao (or Islamic Path). It is within these ambiguities that the Muslims of Lintan and other places in Northwest China, reputed for their rifts and fragmentation, could all be accommodated. Ma Qixi

12. Ma Tong, "Xidaotang," 600.
13. Ibid.
14. Ibid.

also introduced another element of self-sustenance that had nothing to do with religion or doctrine, but helps explain the attractiveness of the sect, and that is communal production, which was perhaps borrowed from Taiping ideology. Under this remarkable system of collective sharing, contemporaneous with the Israeli *kibbutzim,* but the antecedent of the communes in Communist China, the members of the community engaged in agriculture, husbandry, trade and miscellaneous occupations, yielding all their produce to the common treasury of the Xidaotang. Within a relatively short time they attained a successful income and profits which in turn allowed them to expand their activities further, thus increasing both the prosperity of the community and Ma Qixi's renown, but also earning them the scorn and persecution by others, with ensuing outbreaks of violence and litigation.[15] Ma Tong does not specify who those "others" were who persecuted and attacked the successful Xidaotang, beyond dubbing them as "other sects" (*qita jiaopai*), but learning from the Hui experience in the Northwest, those were probably other Muslim groups identified with the Sufi *menhuan,* or some elements of the more conservative Muslims like the *Ikhwan,* who either shunned the revolutionary reforms of Ma Qixi, or were concerned lest his success and popularity impact their own constituencies.

In 1914 there appears to have occurred a major upheaval in the fortunes of the sect when the local warlord, Ma An-shi, falsely accused Ma Qixi of collaborating with another warlord, and in consequence he ordered the massacre of 23 members of his family, seized the Hall of the Dao and confiscated the property of the sect. Those events drove the Xidaotang into a deep and protracted crisis as well as interminable law suits. It was not until 1919 that the warlord fell ill and died, and the legal proceedings were discontinued.[16] Ma Qixi, having died either as part of the onslaughts against the sect or as a result thereof, new leadership was required, to collect the shattered pieces and re-launch the entire enterprise along the lines set by the founder but under completely new circumstances.

2. The Era of Ma Mingren (1918–46)

The successor to the founder, Ma Mingren, who for almost 30 years shaped the sect and brought it to its peak, was born in 1896 and served until his death in 1946. A capable and cultivated Muslim of Lintan, the county where it had all begun, who had a special talent for

15.. Ibid.
16.. Ibid.

management, in fact took over in 1918, when the immediate successor of Ma Qixi, Ding Quangong, was assassinated by the warlord Ma Anshi, to become the third in the line of succession. He summoned the widely dispersed survivors of the massacres to return, settled them and rekindled the faith, using his extraordinary organizational skills to perfect the rules and regulations, recreated and managed agriculture, commerce, animal husbandry, and established other auxiliary branches of subsistence. After 20 years of strenuous activity, the sect had not only completely recovered, but had established trading stations in Beijing, Zhang Jia-Kou (in Hubei), Guangzhou, Bao-tou (Inner Mongolia), A-ba (on the Tibet-Sichuan border), Kan-ding (west Sichuan), Lhassa (Tibet) and other areas, and a network of ambulatory trade that covered all the major cities across the land[17].

This second Ma is credited with establishing agricultural farms in 12 different locations, on a total area of more than 7,000 *mou*, and taking over vast areas of grazing in 5 locations where over 5,000 cattle heads of all kinds could feed. He also appropriated to the sect 13 forested lands and workshops in more than 10 locations. He amassed funds amounting to more than 1,000,000 silver taels, thus lending to the Xidaotang a solid economic foundation. He also established primary schools for girls and boys, one for each in every area, and ran a selection process for the best graduates among them to be sent to other places for high school and further education with a view of preparing the future leadership of the Xidaotang. This is the reason why his period of leadership is rightly regarded as the heyday of the sect[18]. Ma Mingren can then be considered the Joshua, the Paul, the 'Umar, the Stalin, and the Deng Xiaoping who followed with deeds, stamina, enthusiasm, practical talent and imagination, in the footsteps of their great spiritual founding predecessors: Moses, Jesus, Muhammad, Lenin and Mao, respectively.

3. The Tenure of Ming Xuecheng (1947–1957) Onward

Ming was born in 1882 at Zuo-luo near Lintan. He was a Muslim with some education, honest and sincere. After the death of his predecessor in 1946, he inherited the title as the 4th Master. But since he was physically frail and often sick, the actual power devolved to the middle class who amassed private property thus weakening the collective economy which was at the base of the sect´s success. Moreover, the oppression of the sect by warlord Ma Bufang imposed limitations

17.. Ibid.
18.. Ibid.

on its economic development and gradually led to its decline[19]. Thereafter, the Xidaotang which had long passed its climax, settled into a shrunken pattern of existence which preserved some of the characteristics of its glorious past, but in a much more held-back stance, a more subdued style with a lower profile.

## The Question of Theology, Beliefs and Ritual

Ma Tong considers the Xidaotang as part of the legal system of the Hanafi School of law *(Hanafei Xue-pai jiao-fa)* of Sunni Teaching of Islam *(Su-ni pai Jiao-yi)*, whose beliefs and rituals are marked by several characteristics, that will be discussed below. The fundamental beliefs of the sect, according to him, are: the unity of God *(rang zhu dou-i)*; obedience to God and the Holy Man *(xun-zhu, xun-shen)*; obedience to the Classics and following the Teachings *(zun-jing, i-xun)*; practicing the Heaven-ordered Five Principles *(tian-ming wu-gong)*; and using the writings in Chinese of Liu Zhi and others as the base of the faith. In the pursuance of the faith, one had to advocate coexistence of the religious conveyance *(jiao-cheng= shari'a)* with the Dao conveyance *(dao-cheng=tariqa, or the Sufi Order)*. "Prepare the body by ritual, clear the heart through the dao, educate yourself to go back to nature with your whole heart *(jin-xing fu-ming)*, return with all your body to the truth," such were the supreme tenets of the followers. As to the aspect of religious ritual, they were encouraged to "join together the characteristics of both factions *(pai)* of the Qadim ( *gedimu)* and the Jahriyyah *(jehelinyeh)*, such as the 16 prostrations of the Friday prayer *(juma li)*, like the *Gedimu*; and to lend full attention to the Holy Record *(shen ji)* and observe strictly the Days of Fasting *(jiri)* of the Lord *(Jiao-zhu)*. Besides the Qur'an, the believers must read other classics which praise the Lord *(Zhu)* and the Holy (man), just like in the *Jahriyyah*." But they did not build Tombs *(Gong bei)* for the Masters of the faith over the generations, and in this they are totally different from other *Menhuan*. At the same time, except for the founder, Ma Qixi, who strongly maintained that one had to sit silently, the Masters *(Jiaozhu) of* later generations did not lend too much attention to the strict conveyance of the dao *(dao cheng= tariqa)*[20]. This meant he heeded more the normative Shari'a than his particular Sufi *Tariqah*.

First of all, we have the question of the terminology for the Supreme Being—Allah. Since the rite controversy under Emperor Kangxi (1660–1720), when the Jesuits and their Christian opponents struggled to find the

19. Ibid.
20. Ibid.

equivalent of their Christian God[21], there has hardly been a conclusively and universally accepted rendering of the monotheistic God. While in the standard translations of the Qur'an into Chinese, Allah is rendered as *Zhen Zhu* (The True Lord),[22] in Ma Tong's essay about the Xidaotang He is referred to as simply *Zhu*, a term easily confounded with the Master of the Faith in each generation (*Jiaozhu*). Indeed, when the followers are enjoined to obey what the *Zhu* has ordered, it is very difficult to tell whether it was Allah, for whom there exists the appellation *An-lah* in Chinese if one wishes to avoid ambiguities, or the living Master of the sect. Maybe the departure from the accepted *Jen-zhu* (the True Lord) in Chinese Islam, which also signified the True Lord of the True Faith (*Jenjiao*), in itself carries the message of distancing the Xidaotang from conventional Islam, something that is implicit in the interchangeable use of *Zhu* for both God and the Master of the Sect, an honor that even the Prophet of Islam was not found deserving (he is referred to in the sect as *Shen-ren*, the Holy Man).

*Zhu* (the Lord or Master) lends itself to this ambiguity because it could means a human master, like the Master of the Faith, as we have seen, or a divine master, like the Master of Heaven (*Tian Zhu*), or Master of the Universe as it is used in monotheistic religions. The term *Zhu* is not frequently used in Chinese religions, but rather in Christianity and Judaism, and here in Islam. That in itself posed a problem to all of those foreign religions inasmuch as that usage could lead the non-initiated Chinese to confusion. For example, the term for Catholic Christianity is *Tianzhu Jiao* (the Teaching of the Lord of Heaven), which could perfectly apply as an adequate descriptive to any of the other monotheistic faiths. Sometimes Buddhism used the same term, and Emperor Song of the Southern Dynasty (AD 420–589) is reputed to have called himself *Tianzhu*, a title that would put him in contradiction with the Confucian Emperor who never claimed to be Heaven itself, but only the Son thereof (*Tianzi*). Therefore, for the Muslims in China to claim that their Lord is *Tian*, or *Tianzhu*, would have implied that their Emperor was the Son of God, a notion that they could not entertain lest it be tantamount to the irreparable sin of *shirk* (that is the association of the only God with other deities), precisely the offense that Muslims everywhere attribute

---

21. This debate in which various Christian denominations have been in disagreement, centers around the question whether existing Chinese words and concepts should be borrowed, with all the attendant problems of inter-cultural exchange of idioms, or new terms be coined. The existing terms: *Shang-Di* (the Supreme Ruler), *Tian* (Heaven) and others, had profoundly different connotations in the Chinese mind and would easily be misapprehended by new Chinese converts. The first translations of the Bible into Chinese, preferred the term *Tianzhu* (Lord of Heaven).

22. See Israeli "Translation as Exegesis," 90–91.

to the Christian God who also has a divine Son, a notion that is patently rejected by the Qur'an, which determines that "God was neither created nor gave birth, He is One."

Interestingly enough, while mainland translations of the Qur'an into Chinese use the *Jenzhu* (True Lord) construct, in Taiwan the appellation *An-lah* is the rule, in order to steer clear of all those other loaded translations which may be controversial in themselves. However, the choice of the syllables to transliterate *An-lah* can also be problematic. In the usually accepted construct, *an* means quiet, stable, benevolent; and *la* has the meaning of "to pull," "to destroy." An *An-lah* who can both impose peace and tranquility and also wreak havoc, would be quite in accordance with a Muslim conception of Allah the Omniscient and Omnipotent whose compassion and wrath can be expected in the world, depending on the Believers' conduct. For the Xidaotang, their diminished, however unique, God is no more than an ambiguous Zhu (master) of the world and perhaps of their sect too.

Additional references to *zhu* in the standard translations of the Qur'an into Chinese can create even more confusion. In the *Fatihah* (the Opening Surah of the Qur'an) for example, the Master of the Worlds (*rabbi'l 'alamin*), is rendered in Chinese as *Quan Shijie de Zhu*, meaning the "*Lord* of the entire world," in singular as compared to the plural worlds in the Arabic original. In this sense, it is much closer to the Chinese concept of *Tianxia* (everything under Heaven), that is the physical universe ruled by the Emperor, the Son of Heaven. This contrasts strongly with the traditional Islamic exegesis which encompassed under the plural worlds everything relating to man, to the Devil underground as well as to the angels in Heaven. However, in the Taiwan translation of that same verse there is an ingenuous attempt to skirt the confusion by rendering *rabb* not as *zhu* but as *yangyu*, in the meaning of "to bring up," "to foster." The translator deduced from his translation that the Lord not only created the world and is its Master, but is also bent on perfecting its character. He cites the Qur'an 43:84–5 to emphasize that Allah had created heaven and earth and everything between them, including human beings, hence His desire to rear them[23].

In verse 5 of the *Fatihah* of the Holy Book, *zhu* comes in yet another context: the Owner of the Day of Judgement *(malik yaum a-Din)*. The Taiwan translation again found a way to express the meaning without resorting to the much loaded *zhu*, by substituting to it the term *Zhi-zhang* (in charge of, in control of). The writer explains that *malik* had two different pronunciations: *ma-li-ke* in the sense of "owner," "master," and *mai-li-ke*, meaning "monarch," in this case opting for the first. This "difference" of course exists

---

23. Ibid., 94–95.

only in the two various ways of transliterating the same Arabic word; by establishing this artificial bifurcation of the same word into two different transliterations, the author was obviously seeking to transmit to his readers the two variants of meaning of the Arabic original[24]. Be that as it may, it is difficult to gauge whether the author wished to avoid loading the term *zhu* with too many significances so as to obscure its original rendering of the Lord and He alone, or that he lent more importance to reflecting the richness and plurality of the Qur'anic text than to the consistency for the sake of clarity that the Mainland translators have chosen in order to avoid ambiguities and confusion.

But the problem inherent in translating religious terms into Chinese is not fully exhausted in the confusion around *zhu* and its derivatives. The unity of God, whoever it is, as well as obedience to God and the Holy Man, however we identify them, are straightforward enough, but when we turn to the injunction to follow the Classics (*jing*) and the Teachings (*xun*), the issue gets more complicated. The question is what Classics and what teachings are meant? *Jing* applies to both the Chinese Classics as well as to the Muslim Qur'an (and the Bible for that matter). Moreover, Chinese Classics could be Confucian, as in the *Wu Jing* (the Five Classics) or Daoist as in the *Dao-de Jing*). Even more complicated is the tenet to practice the Heaven-ordained (*tian-ming*) Five Principles (*Wu Gong*). What renders things more nebulous is that the notion of *Tian –ming* may also refer to the Mandate of Heaven, the legal and philosophical Confucian term which lends legitimacy to the rule of the Chinese Emperor. Are the Five Principles coterminous with the Islamic Five Pillars (*Arkan*), or a totally syncretic amalgam? Maybe these ambiguities, and others, were calculated by the Masters of the Xidaotang to leave the ultimate power of interpretation and instruction in the hands of the autocratic ruler of the Sect in each generation?

Then, according to Ma Tong, the followers of the Xidaotang are enjoined to "use as a base the Chinese writings of Liu Zhi and others." Who are the others? Presumably Wang Daiyu and Ma Zhu. But why leave it to the followers to decide? And in any case, it is doubtful whether even the Masters of the sect who were no scholars, either in the Chinese or the Muslim tradition, could understand the intricacies of Liu Zhi's writings, part of which are presumed lost anyway. What is the difference between *Jiao-cheng* (the conveyance of the religion=Shari'a) and the *dao-cheng* (the conveyance of the Dao= Tariqa). *Cheng* is, generally speaking, a Buddhist term which means to convey the Truth to men and help them. What does it mean in an Islamic context? Is the coexistence between the *Jiao-cheng* and the

---

24. Ibid., 96.

*Dao-cheng,* prescribed to the followers of Xidaotang, clear to them? What religion or teaching is the *Jiao,* and which is the *Dao*? Is the *dao* a generally recommended way of being virtuous, is it the *dao* of Daoism, or is it the Path of Allah? Or does *Jiao* refer to the theory and theology while the *dao* addresses itself to the more practical aspects of the ritual and daily deeds, a notion that would be very close to the Path of God?. Moreover, to prepare oneself through ritual and *dao,* does not give a clue to the believer as to what he or she ought to do, in a religion which is essentially one of deeds, unless of course, it is assumed that the *dao* is coterminous with the prescribed Five Principles which are the necessary baggage for the Believer to engage in the Straight Path. If so, then the Shari'a, which prescribes the deeds, is seen as different from the *Tariqa* which is supposed to represent the practices of the Path of Allah.

This question is further compounded if we refer to the normative translation of Verse 6 of the *Fatihah,* which begs Allah to guide the Believer in the "Straight Path" (*al-Sirat al-Mustaqim*). In most of the translations of the Mainland Qur'an, the word *lu,* the mundane term for "way" or "road" is used. But in the Taiwan version, the Path of Allah is rendered as *dao,* again with all the attending confusion that can derive therefrom, especially in a sect where the word *dao* is such a central component of its constructed name. The Qur'anic text elaborates in Verse 7 on the meaning of the Path: it is the "Path of those whom You have favoured, not those who earn Thine anger, or those who go astray." This, once again, would open the way for innumerable interpretations, since any group or splinter-faction can claim that they are the favoured ones, much more so the Xidaotang who have chosen *dao* (may be interpreted as the Path of Allah), to advertise their very denomination. The Qur'anic *an'amta 'alayhim* (those favoured by Allah) was rendered in the Chinese translations as *you* (assistance, help), interestingly the same word used to translate the previous verse *iyyaka nasta'in* (Thy help we seek), though the Arabic idiom was different. In the original text, of course, this could mean that those who are meritorious enough to seek Allah's help, and to receive it, are the Muslims; but in the Xidaotang's context, especially in the period of Ma Mingren when it was eminently successful and prosperous, that meaning could be narrowed down to signify that the followers of the (Xi) *Dao* (Tang) were the meritorious ones who won the favour of their God *zhu,* whoever that was.

Perhaps the most intriguing tenet of the Xidaotang, as reported by Ma Tong, is the injunction to amalgamate together the practices of the *Gedimu* with those of the *Jahriyya,* a seemingly unfeasible endeavor. *Gedimu,* is the Chinese transliteration for the Arabic *Qadim* (ancient) and it refers to the established Islam that had settled in China over the generations before the Sufi orders began their penetration into the land in the 15th Century. Since the new accretion of the Sufi Naqshbandiyya was regarded as the New Teaching *Xinjiao),* the existing non-Sufi followers of Islam became known as the Old Teaching (*Lao-jiao, or Gedimu, or Lao Gedimu*). Later, when the Naqshbandiyya was split between the *Khufya* (the quiet *dhikr)* and the *Jahriyya (*loud *dhikr),* the *Khufya* who wished to differentiate themselves from the *Jahriyya,* called themselves the Old Teaching, while their rivals became the New Teaching. Hence the confusion in this terminology as to who is old or new. But in Ma Tong's discussion of the Xidaotang he suggests that the sect was enjoined to combine between the conservative Old Teaching-*Gedimu* and their restive arch-rival New Teaching- *Jahriyya*, something almost unheard of in the Sino-Muslim sectarian line-up, especially when the founder, Ma Qixi, had originated from the *Huasi* Menhuan known for its *Khufya* leanings. Unless he was led by his conviction to reduce the tensions, indeed hostility and open enmity, between the various factions by synthesizing two of the most variants of the Faith into one peaceful and harmonious Xidaotang.

Clearly, the tenets of the Xidaotang contained in an eclectic rather than a syncretic fashion, the elements in each of the two otherwise incongruent factions, which are to be followed. On the *Gedimu* side, the believers were to observe the *Zhu-ma li,* namely the rituals of the Arabic *Yaum al-Jum'a* (the Day of Assembly—Friday), with the attending 16 prostrations, as they would have it. Incidentally, we have here yet another use of the same *zhu* (God, Master) in the *zhu-ma* compound, with all the possible interpretations that one could append thereto. Secondly, the followers were to pay full attention to the Holy Record (*shen-ji),* something that may be coterminous with the Arabic *Hadith,* the collections of the life of the Prophet which describe his deeds and utterances and make up the Muslim tradition *(Sunna).* For Sunnite Muslims, of all schools of thought, the Qur'an (in Chinese *Shen Jing* or *Gu- lan Jing,* the Holy Classic or the Qur'an Classic) and the *Hadith* are the main basis for the Shari'a (Islamic Holy Law). The Holy Record, as differentiated from the Holy Classic, clearly refers to some extra-Qur'anic text, presumably the *Hadith.* As to the "fasting Day's of the Lord *(Jiao-zhu),"* the ambiguity does not permit to determine whether it is the Ramadan, or some day of abstention observed by the founder of the Xidaotang.

On the *Jahri* side, the believers are enjoined to also read, besides the Qur'an, some difficult to identify Muslim writings. Interestingly, enough, since the second important source of Islamic Law (the *Hadith)* is not mentioned here, is it possible that the *Jahriyya* in China does not heed it? On the other hand, the other extra-Qur'anic texts recommended as representing the *Jahriyya,* include the *Mau-lu-de,* perhaps a transliteration of the Arabic

*Maulid* (birth) which may be a biography of the Prophet or some other holy man in the history of the sect; *Mai-da-i-ha* , probably a work of praise ( the Arabic *mada'ih*) of God and/ or the Prophet; and the *Mu-han-mai-si*, perhaps from the Arabic *Muhamasa* (ecstasy, great enthusiasm), which is descriptive and typical of the loud-*dhikr* Sufis ( such as the *Jahriyyah*) who have the propensity to be swept by ecstatic trances while they whirl around pronouncing the name of Allah. It is noteworthy, that the first two syllables *Mu-han* of the latter recommended reading are identical with those commonly used to transcribe the name of the Prophet—*Mu-han (mo-de)*. It is evident, at any rate, that the prescribed books are all written in Chinese, either in the original, or are old translations of Arabic texts into Chinese. For it is inconceivable that members of the Xidaotang, whose very founder was not an Imam (*akhund*) and had received no particular religious instruction, should be able to read any Arabic writings of any significance, certainly not a religio-philosophical treatise of this calibre and depth.

Finally, Ma Tong tells us that unlike the *menhuan*, the Xidaotang did not construct Tombs (*Gong-bei,* probably a bastardization of the Arabic *Qubbah= dome*) for their Masters who became saints after their death. Those menhuan, which sometimes won the attribute of *Gong-bei Jiao* (the Tomb Religion), often turned the saint worship into a major tenet of the faith, to the point of sometimes substituting it for the *Ka'ba* in Mecca as the site of their religious pilgrimage. In those cases, the tomb could also become a nucleus around which a new *menhuan* was created, at times on a hereditary basis. However, unlike the founder, Ma Qixi, who preserved the quiet *dhikr* he had inherited from his Huasi (*Khufya*) background, the rest of the sect did not care much about the way their Dao (whatever that meant) was conveyed. It is noteworthy, however, that during the 2016 field visits to Lintan, several domed mausoleums were seen and described in detail above, something which can indicate that those are either remnants of some other New Sect groups of Hui, or that some vestiges of the New Sect Gunbeijiao traditions have survived within the XIdaotang. In either case, there was not much eagerness among the present day Gansu to admit or talk about those possibilities.

## The Question of Organization and Practice

Ma Tong determines that the organizational structure of the Xidaotang is much like the menhuan in that the Master of the sect wields autocratic powers, inasmuch as he is not only the leader of the sect but also manages its daily lay affairs, be they pertaining to the collective or to the family units[25]. As we have seen above in the biographies of the founding masters of the sect, much emphasis was laid on collectivization of life within the community, not only to enable the leader to tightly control daily life, indeed the fate, of the followers, but also to create cohesion within the community, and a united stand towards the Chinese externally. The fact that the sect was prosperous economically not only allowed it to spread its message in various places wherever its trading stations brought it, but also attracted other Muslims who were less fortunate economically and wished to secure a base of subsistence for their families, and even non-Muslims who were attracted to the welfare provided by the sect. The emphasis the sect put on the tenet of the *zakat* (alms), which had allowed the Prophet Muhammed in his time to build and sustain his congregation *(umma)* of the first Muslims, was adopted by the Xidaotang as a way to bolster its economic viability.

Much can be said about the communal way of life that the Xidaotang may have derived from the recent, though abortive, precedent of the Taiping. Like the *Kibbutz* in its heyday, the ideology which drew the people together to a life of spirituality and sharing, was from every individual's point of view superior to personal gains and economic enhancement. The autocratic powers of the Master of the Sect can be easily compared to the Rabbi's in the Hassidic way of life, where the spiritual leader, who is inherited by his descendants, exerts a magic influence on his followers, not only in their rituals and religious lives, but also in all their activities be they within the family, with other individuals, the community, business deals etc. The blessing of the Rabbi is necessary to undertake any new venture, to apply any new idea, to run any new connection, or to manage the existing properties. However, the Xidaotang leadership differs in that it is not hereditary, though the Master exercises a powerful authority in dealing with the affairs of the community, assumes much responsibility in so doing, and makes his own living from the fruit of his labour and management talent. The Hassidic Rabbi, by contrast, remains wholly spiritual, inasmuch as he only dispenses advice and blessings, but bears no responsibility for either, and lives off the support of his followers.

Organizationally, the Xidaotang was divided, from its inception, between families, sharing collective living, and individual families which kept to themselves. The latter were spread across the Northwest, lived autonomously and were self-reliant, but in times of difficulties the sect offered assistance. The collective was based in the Old City of Lintan and collectively ran its agriculture, animal husbandry, forestry and other auxiliary trades. Their production as well as income in cash was managed and distributed by

---

25. Ma Tong, "Xidaotang," 600.

an overseer; they had a general manager for the entire collective, and a person in charge of every branch of the economy. Their needs in food, clothing and funerals were all paid for by the collective[26]. This is so strikingly similar to the structural bifurcation of the patterns of settlement of the Zionists in Palestine at the turn of the 20th Century, that it would be worth inquiring whether there were some degree of contact or inspiration between the two, or was it simply a parallel discovery of the human mind in similar circumstances. For in fact, the Jews who went to settle the harsh land of Palestine established two types of communal life: the most renowned is the *kibbutz* where all the production and consumption is made in common and all the property belongs to the collective, which is managed by a secretary, while all branches of the economy are entrusted to "responsibles" in their trade. The only difference is that the *Kibbutz d*oes not recognize hierarchy, and all the officials and persons in charge are elected democratically for a fixed term of office. In the other type of settlement, the *Moshav,* all households are basically independent, but a system of mutual help is available for the cultivation of the land, marketing, transportation, services etc.

As to the educational system, besides the girls school named after the founder (Ma) Qixi, there were two more schools in Jiu-Cheng (the Old City) plus a middle school, where children of the Sect as well as of other groups were encouraged to enroll for the study of culture (*xue-xi wen-hua)*. Moreover, the sect chose among its youth promising talent to pursue high school and higher education, thus achieving a degree of learning for all members of the sect. At the end of the 20th century, according to Ma Tong, there remained only about a thousand followers of the Xidaotang, most of whom were in Jintan, Gansu, in the Old City, and other places in Qinghai.[27] If there is anything that can keep alive this tiny community, which is not particularly looked upon with favour by other Muslims, it must be the educational system. But what they teach within that system which can perpetuate that tiny group, is another issue which has to be addressed separately.

## The Canonic Source and its Problems

It is assumed that Ma Qixi, the founder who was neither a scholar nor a cleric, left behind no writings nor crystallized any systematic doctrine, hence the many ambiguities that we saw above when attempting to unravel the bits of information pieced together by Ma Tong, probably one of the foremost contemporary Sino-Muslim scholars of Chinese Islam. We have

26. Ibid., 601.
27. Ma Tong, "Xidaotang," 601.

a manuscript in Chinese, attributed to Ma Qixi's son, who supposedly summed up his father's thought (or thoughts) and utterances. The book was written by someone who had either come from, or at the very least visited the West (pilgrimage to Mecca?)[28], and is entitled " The Origin of Purity and Truth"[29]. Although it is signed, not on the cover page but after the preamble, by one Gui Liangqin, a descendant of Islam himself, in the 13th Year of the Republic (1925), namely some ten years after Ma Qixi's death, it does not purport to have created a new book. Rather, it claims to report on the work of the Great Master Jing Yiqi, which carried that same title *The Origin of Purity and Truth,* that means *the Origin of Islam*. A measure of the deep respect that Gui felt towards the work of the Great Master is he reported he duly bathed before he undertook his holy task.[30] Another more likely version imputes this book to Qi Daohe, one of the sons of Qi Jingyi, the founder of the Qaderiyya in China.[31]

The book is replete with esoteric symbols and mystical allusions, which besides underlying the non-systematic thinking of its author, and the rather confused *melange* of a multi-cultural eclecticism, does not make any serious effort to synthesize the whole into a method for understanding the world, or for tracing a clear path for the followers of what was supposed to be a comprehensive Dao-Path-Way of life and social organization. Let us glean a few central messages from the text and attempt to make some sense of them:

1. First and foremost one is struck by the "naturalist," perhaps Daoist, leanings of the writer of the preamble, something which may deepen the mystery of his identity if he came from the (Islamic) West and was completely foreign to Daoist ideas, unless during the 27 years of his stay prior to the writing of the book, he absorbed some of its influences. He is full of admiration for the amount of "purity and truth" (*qing jen*) he found in the universe[32], but does not emphasize those

---

28. The writer says: "It has already been 27 years since I came here from the West. At first, I found shelter in a mosque. It is worth mentioning that both northern and southern communities showed profound concern for me during this period. Then I built a house in the western part of the city with the help of dozens of families."

29. *Qing jen geng yuan*. No author, publisher, date or place is mentioned. The manuscript was handed by a Muslim scholar in Gansu to Adam Rush, from Canberra, Australia, in 1995.

30. Ibid., 5.

31. I am indebted for this information and for other identifications of some other transliterated names and terms to Wang Jianping, a researcher at the Institute of World Religions at the Chinese Academy of Social Sciences in Beijing.

32. Ibid., 2.

attributes were used precisely for Islam in China (the Pure and True Religion). He writes:

> Nothing is worth longing for but nature with green hills and water, and nothing is worth esteeming more than the custom of honesty and simplicity. I do not deserve the compliment that I have made after careful and deep observation, I simply wish for a world of peace and tranquility. . .According to previous generations, you could have a longer life and more descendants tomorrow if you have mercy on others today; you could enjoy remarkable favors from others tomorrow if you give in and offer convenience to others today; you could avoid regrets tomorrow over what you have said, if you keep silent for a while today; and you can save more physical and spiritual power if you try not to lose your temper. . . Probably he who can endure the utmost insult and wipe his face clean by himself when he is spat on, is sagacious; and he who keeps his spirits and goes through the time of hardship is distinguished. . .
>
> It is no use for you to compete harshly with each other because you follow your own fate of prosperity and decline, and there is no need to complain because everything, good and bad, is arranged by Heaven's will. Remember to keep your three-inch tongue idle and that you own nothing in this world but a six-foot body. A bird occupies no more than one branch in a wood no matter how much resting space it scrambles for, a mouse drinks no more than one stomach of water no matter how hard it competes with others drinking by the river, because its need is rather limited. At the very end, life comes to be fantasy, and hard work comes to be emptiness. Don't you see how fast the young dark hair turns to grey and how soon a new baby becomes old and dies. . .?[33]

2. Now, besides the one mention of God's will, in this preamble, the rest is either Buddhist-inspired (life as a fantasy) or, more emphatically, Daoist-like. God, is the same *zhu* that we encountered above, and the Islamic idea of pre-destination is evident, inasmuch as everything is pre-arranged by His Will and cannot be altered by human choice. But the longing for nature, the parables that draw on natural metaphors, the contradictions in positing one thing against its reverse, the emptiness that life amounts to, the philosophical thoughts about life that the old author, who was nearing his death[34], is uttering with the tone

33. Ibid., 2–3.
34. Ibid., 3.

of resignation of the author of the Biblical Proverbs, all attest to some intake from Daoist, perhaps also Buddhist, sources. He compares his failing health to life in a frail boat in the heart of the ocean, with the lightest breeze likely to throw him into the water. He also urges people not to be too attached to their properties, lest they leave behind much regret and criticism. And for a faith of Islam in which the Believer is urged to praise Allah and the Prophet incessantly, at least during the five daily prayers prescribed by the Shari'a, it is quite unsettling to read the summons of the author to his followers to keep their mouth shut, because "one scatters his spirit when he opens his mouth, and one brings about trouble when he moves his tongue."[35] This sounds particularly contradictory if indeed the Xidaotang had *Jahri* roots where the followers are urged to utter the loud *dhikr* with their mouth.

3. For the author, there appears to have existed one great transcendental Truth which he calls the Holy Teaching (*shen jiao*), from which all faiths and religions derive, something like the Bahai and the Daoist beliefs. In his words:

> From ancient times, when true and superior sages wrote a book or created a theory, they had always tried to reveal the principles and meanings of the Holy Teaching, and clarify the comprehensiveness and profoundness of the Great Path (*Dao*), looking for its origin and exploring its source, thus proving that all varieties share the same roots. Hence the logic that the exploration of the essence will make known the nature (*xin*) of things, and the latter will make known Heaven (*Tian*). Since the True Belief- "Clear and True" (*Qing Jen*) was introduced by our Great Grand Master Hua Zhe Er Bu Dong Na Xi ( Khoja Abdallah, the Arabian Qadiri missionary who went to China to introduce his order), it has been the belief for more than one hundred generations and will carry on that way of eternity, revealing mysterious meanings and observing the heavenly secrets. He knew there would appear a perfect man in the Eastern Land, Hehuang (probably Khokand in Central Asia which is, in relative geographic terms, east of the heartland of Islam in the West) and so he came to the Central Plains three times to teach Grand Master Jing Yiqi (Qi Jingyi, by reversing the order of name and surname), by instructing him both orally and mentally, exposing him to the refinement of the Purity and Truth, and repeatedly administering to him lessons of cultivation. The Great Master He Qi (=Qi Daohe one of the sons of the founder and the putative author of

35. Ibid.

this book), who lived during the reign of Emperor Tong Zhi,[36] feared that all those things would be lost or be distorted, therefore he wrote his book about the Origin of Purity and Truth (*Qing Jen*), and recorded in detail the Great Noble's trip to the Eastern Land (=Central Asia).[37]

4. We shall address ourselves below to the identity of all those masters, who appear to be related to the history of factionalism among Chinese Muslims. But we can immediately refer, once again, to the notions of *zhu*, in the double meaning of Allah and also the Master or Head of the sect; *xin*, the nature to which the followers of the Xidaotang were urged to return; and *Tian*, Heaven, which may be Confucian as in *Tian-ming* (the Heavenly-ordained) Five Principles discussed above, or the Abode of Allah, a construct that is assiduously avoided by the Xidaotang by qualifying God as *Zhu*, instead of the normative *Tian-Zhu* (the Lord of High). Moreover, by declaring that the True Faith in question had been valid for "more than one hundred generations and will endure forever," he declares it not only universal but also eternal, detached from history and from the persona of the Prophet. The latter is not credited for his mission as the founder of the faith, but that honor is reserved to Hua Zhe Er Bu Dong Na Xi. The Perfect Man is not the Prophet, as Muslim tradition would have it, but someone who "came to the Eastern Land, Hehuang" whose task was to instruct Jing Yiqi. And it was not until the dusk of the Qing Dynasty (1644–1911) we are told, under the reign of Tong Zhi, during the era known as the "Tong Zhi Restoration," (1862–75) when the last valiant effort was made to arrest the decline of the Empire, that the Great Master He Qi(= Qi Daohe), sat down to write his *Origin of Purity and Truth*, in order to avert the total loss of the Faith. He is also credited with recording the details of the Great Noble's trip to the East.

5. We are talking of late developments in Chinese Islam, three centuries or more of Sufi activity in China and at least one century of *Jahriyya-Khufya* enmity within the prevalent order of the Naqshbandiyya. In the preface to the book, signed by Ma Fengle, also in 1925, as contrasted with the above preamble, the author identifies his roots with the *Ge de le* faction, which is identified with the *Qaderi* Order, and described as the "religious sect of purity and truth which inherits the past and

---

36. There may be a confusion of dates here, since the Tongzhi Emperor reigned from 1856–1875, while Ma qixi lived 1857–1914, so his son could have hardly been born during that Emperor's reign, unless his father married very young.

37. Ibid., 3–4.

ushers in the future," that "takes a neutral stand and is easily comprehensible, instead of holding extreme views or being eccentric"[38]. This description accords well with the non-partisan stand taken by the *Qaderiyya*, in the bitter controversy between the two splinters of Naqshbandi Sufism. The teachings of the faith were established, according to the author, by Hua Zhe (bastardization of the Arabic *Khoja*, a religious Master in Central Asia who claims descent from the Prophet) Er Bu Dong Na Xi (apparently Abdallah) who originated in Arab lands, "was born a mystic and adopted the Great Path *(dao)* early in his life[39]. This description accords with Khoja Abdallah, who moved to China from the heartland of Islam in order to bring the Qaderiyya there. Later, it is said, it was Grand Master Jing Yiqi (= Qi Jingyi) from He Huang (Khokand in Central Asia) who inherited the theory and developed the sect, and his mantle was inherited from generation to generation by a successive line of masters. Jing Yiqi (=Qi Yingqi) is credited with the founding of the Qaderiyya in China as he learned it from Khoja Abdallah. However, unlike the sources cited above, which clearly identify the Xidaotang with the Naqshbandiyya, particularly the *Jahri* branch thereof, the book under discussion speaks clearly of the Qadiri origins of the faith, something that immediately raises the suspicion that perhaps there is no link between the book and the Xidaotang. Another possibility is that the historical memory has lingered of the merger of the Qaderiyya and Naqshbandiyya, as has been the case in Java, where the Naqshbandi-Qaderi Order has survived to this day under that combined appellation.

6. Then Lord He Qi, or Qi He in reverse order, who was probably one of the founding father's descendants (son or grandson) wrote the book under the late Qing period, about his ancestor, Grand Master Jing Yiqi, and distributed it among Muslims, in spite of the difficulties. In the book, the miracles performed by the Master are detailed. A certain teacher La, an authority in the sect, had the manuscript printed in Fuzhou in the 1920's so as to ensure its mass distribution among Muslims in China. The author explains that at La's demand, he summarized the main ideas of the book and put them as an introduction, but due to his own poor knowledge of Islam, he did not dare to make any rushed commentary beyond describing the virtues and teachings of the Great Master, the original writer of *The Origin of Purity and Truth*.[40]. This

38. Ibid., 6.
39. Ibid.
40. Ibid.

admission by the writer explains perhaps the many oddities that we will encounter when accounting for its contents. In other words, what we have here is an interpretation by an anonymous author Gui, compounded by a self-deprecating author Ma, and written in response to the urgings of teacher La, about the book that Master He supposedly wrote on the life, virtues and teachings of the Great Master Jing Yiqi. It is doubtful whether such a chain of transmission, where some links are not exactly sound, can be taken as an authoritative account of the great master to whom the roots of the sect are imputed. In consequence, our understanding of the Xidaotang gets ever more blurred.

7. Be that as it may, it is evident that the above course of events, as well as the succession of great names who are accredited with the perpetuation of the Faith, relate to the main strokes of the coming of the Qaderiyya into, and its later sectarianization within, the Middle Kingdom. The Great Khoja corresponds vaguely to the first teacher of the Qaderiyya who came to Central Asia from the Islamic heartland some time at the end of the Ming (1368–1644); the founder of the Qaderiyya in China, Jing Yiqi, himself originating from the *Gedimu*, followed shortly thereafter and taught the faith in China; then, towards the end of the Qing Dynasty, Muslim rebellions were rife (1850′s-1870′s) and threw most of Northwest and Southwest China into chaos, and large scale massacres of Muslims ensued, notably by Zuo Zongtang's formidable armies of the post-Taiping era. There was a tangible danger then that the Faithful might be completely eliminated in those parts of China where sectarian Muslims, especially members of the *Jahriyya*, who provided the core and the ideology of the rebellions and were dubbed *Hui-fei* (Muslim bandits) by the authorities. Hence the fear articulated by Master He Qi that the Doctrine might be lost, and his keen concern to write the book on Jing Yiqi, the Master-founder in China.

In sum, if the book is indeed linked to the official founder of the Xidaotang, Ma Qixi's son, of whom we know nothing, the latter must be identical with either Gui Liangqin who wrote the preamble, or more probably with Ma Fengle[41] who contributed the preface, or more remotely with Teacher La who urged the printing and diffusion of the book. They were all contemporaneous with the end of the Qing Dynasty and the first years of the Republic, they all suffered from the high-handedness and persecutions of the warlords, and they were all eager to preserve the sect by referring back

---

41. The identity of the family name may be an indication, though the surname Ma is so widespread among Chinese Muslims that it does not necessarily attest to family relationship.

to its founding masters and perpetuating their writings. This is the reason why the members of the Xidaotang are not merely enjoined to respect and live by the tenets of the traditional Islam of the *Gedimu*, based on the Qur'an and the Hadith, but also to study and heed the writings of the other Masters, like Liu Zhi. It remains to be seen whether any of the latter are identical with the founding fathers of the sect described in the book, namely the Khoja, Jing Yiqi and He Qi, who had preceded the writers of the extant text we have by centuries, in the case of the first two, and decades in the case of the latter.

## The Doctrinal and Cosmological Enigma

As we have seen, the book renders Allah as *Zhen-Zhu*[42] (The True Lord), a terminology that is more in tune with the conventional rendering of that concept by Chinese Islam in general, both to differentiate it from the Catholic *Tian-zhu* (the Lord of Heaven) and to emphasize the pertinence of this God to the True Religion (*Zhen-jiao*) of Islam. But at the same time it borrows the Chinese notion of Heaven and Earth (*Tian- Di*) as the twin dichotomy nurturers of man and all living things, which are also proof of the omnipotence of God, because He preceded their creation. He did not proceed with the Creation until He first created a Bright Pearl which was transformed into water, and some of the water into fire. The fire, in turn, generated air, and some dust was produced in the water. As the light and the pure rose up and took the shape of heaven, the heavy and obscure sunk down and became earth. This was the Great Being (*tai-ji*). After the Great Being, there appeared two parts, distinguished from each other. God showed the light of nature and principle in the non-being (*Wu-ji*) which embodies subtlety of invisibility. *Tai-ji*, and by contrast, showed the principle of visibility. With his light of nature and principle, God created life first and then nature came into being. . . .[43]

In this Creation story, we have the element of the pearl which split apart to allow heaven and earth to derive therefrom, a far cry from the world Allah created by decree and stages. This is somewhat reminiscent of the Chinese creation legend of Pang Gu, that mammoth creature whose limbs and body functions were the origin of the universe, and his head broke into two parts which constituted the foundation of heaven and earth. The creation of life preceded that of nature according to this book, while in the Qur'anic narrative, following the Biblical one, the creation of man was the pinnacle of Creation and came at its final stage. This story also affirms

42. Ibid., 9.
43. Ibid., 8–9.

the principle of a created world (*makhluq*), which means in effect that Allah the Omnipotent existed before anything else, therefore everything was created by Him. In this extraordinary Creation story the Prophet Muhammed takes an active part. For after the visible was created out of the invisible, the Prophet shattered down the pearls of light from his spiritual light, thus creating the spiritual consciousness of 120,000 Holy Men. He also created out of the pearls of light Ar Le Shi and Ku Er Xi (probably the bastardization of the Arabic '*Arsh* and *Kursi*, (both denominating the Throne or the Chair of the Lord), mountains, rivers and all other objects, again similar to the unending partition of the body of the legendary Pan Gu in Chinese mythology. Interestingly enough, the Prophet shares his status of sanctity (*shen*) with all the 120,000 holy men he created. True, in this book as well as in the literature of the Xidaotang, Muhammed is often dubbed the Most Holy (*Zhi Shen*) to differentiate him from all other saints, but here he is referred to as one of them[44], thus opening the way towards a "democratic" view which regards the Pantheon of all saints as a pluralistic forum rather than one subjected to the monolithic prevalence of Muhammed, something unthinkable in normative Islam where the Prophet maintains his undisputed primacy as the most perfect of Allah's creatures.

This ambivalence towards the persona of the Prophet comes to the fore in this book when one thinks about the fact that he is elevated, on the one hand, to the level of a partner with Allah in the act of Creation, but on the other hand he is assigned the role of Holy Man, one of many. Obviously, this has far-reaching implications inasmuch as within those 120,000 other Holy Men many of the sect's leaders could be counted, thus contesting in their life-time the traditional Islamic assumption that the generations are in the process of diminishing, in direct relation to their remoteness in time and space from the era and birthplace of the Prophet. The latter is cited in the treatise under consideration as conversing with Allah:

> The Prophet: The first thing that Allah created was my life and my soul
>
> The Lord: I would not have ever created the world and everything in it if it had not been for your sake.[45]

The conclusion of the author of the book is that the spiritual light of the Holy Man, that is the Prophet, was before the manifestation of everything, meaning that the other Qur'anic Prophets, beginning with Adam and Noah, and then Abraham, the Friend of Allah (*al-Khalil*), are not only demoted in

---

44. Ibid., 9.
45. Ibid.

comparison with the Messenger of Allah, but are said to exist thanks to him and for his sake. Once again, not only is the Prophet almost deified, but his "spiritual light," a notion susceptibly Shiʻite, becomes a source of Creation, a far cry from the created human Prophet that the Sunna has cultivated. On the other hand, the title of "Imperial Envoy" that the author confers on him[46], makes him subordinate to the Chinese Emperor, who can confer titles and sanctity that comes close to the common sanctity that the Prophet is made to share with others in the Xidaotang ethos. We are told that God had three reasons to create heaven, earth and mankind, this trio in itself constituting a basic tenet in both Confucian ritual and heterodox sectarians in China such as the Triads, whose influence was rife during times of rebellion and devolution of power. The reasons are: to show His supreme power, to demonstrate the paramount prevalence of Muhammed, and to guide the Believers (*Mu-min*)[47] to acknowledge Him as their God.[48]

Then come stories elaborating on the Creation that we find in other Muslim and Sino-Muslim sources:[49] it took God six days and nights to create heaven and earth and everything in them, and another forty mornings to create Holy Adam. Thus, not only do we revert to the right sequence whereby man was the apex and conclusion of Creation, but his birth took 40,000 years, because each morning of his creation lasted 1,000 years due to the complexity and perfection of his nature. God "personally" made Adam of mud and then blew His own life into the body of the newborn. Holy Man Da-Wu- De[50] (the Biblical and Qur'anic David/ Dawud), one of the Prophets of Islam, is cited in a dialogue in which he engaged with God about the nature of the creation of man. God emphasized that the reason for the creation of man is that in the latter's very existence is inherent the recognition of the Creator. Then, the treatise attempts to settle the contradiction between man at the beginning and at the end of the process of Creation, by citing the Holy Man (probably the Prophet ) who allegedly asserted that first Allah created his nature (*xing*), so as to enable him to recognize the Lord[51]. Thus, the nature of the Prophet preceded all creation, while Adam, the father of all mankind, came at the end of Creation. This odd depiction of the

---

46.. Ibid.

47. The character is the same used for Mu (-han-mo-de= Muhammed), and Min simply means people, thus creating a transliterated compound for Mu'min (Believer, in Arabic), meaning literally the "People of Muhammed."

48. Text of the Treatise, 10.

49. See Israeli "Translation as Exegesis etc. . .," op. cit.

50. The Chinese characters mean "reaching the Five Virtues," and sound almost Confucian.

51. Ibid., 10.

"nature of the Holy Man" which pervades this entire treatise is somewhat reminiscent of the Christian Holy Spirit, and leaves the primacy to Adam as father of all humanity, with historical Muhammed as part of that progeny.

According to this book, after *Huo Da Yi Tai Er Liang* (must be a transliteration of one of the names of God) created heaven and earth and all things in them, he told the Angel Gabriel (*Zhe Bai Yi Le*) to go to the heavenly garden in *Tunya* (probably the Arabic *Dunya*- the real world), pick up a sample of soil and bring it back to the Holy Presence. Gabriel picked up 5 grams from a white, clean and fragrant soil, and brought it back to God who proceeded to make Adam. Here too we have a Pan Gu—like myth of creation how God made each one of Adam's limbs from different natural elements like flowers, incense, water springs. When the body was ready, God mixed some earth and water into a small ball and ordered Gabriel to travel to all seven spheres of heaven, including the *A Er Shi* (the Arabic *'Arsh*) and Ku *Er Xi* (the Arabic *Kursi*), and seven layers of earth, leaving no place untouched. The other angels who saw that light inquired about its nature, to which Gabriel answered that it was the light of Muhammed the Sage who belonged to God[52]. Here we have the light of the Prophet born simultaneously with the physical creation of the first man, but prior to the breathing of life into Adam.

Following that, we are told that Allah covered that ball with light for 1,000 years, then placed it under His Throne (*Kursi*) for 1000 years, under Nuo Ha (probably Biblical and Qur'anic Noah) for another 500 years, and then under *Qian Nan* (?) for yet another 500 years. Finally, the ball flew and came to rest in the water of *Nai Ha Mai ti* (?). It is from there that Allah took some of the light of Muhammed and put it on the forefront of Adam, thus breathing life into him[53]. Thereafter, after having eaten the forbidden fruit, Adam was sent from the Heavenly Paradise to the earthly world (*Dunya*). But the angels continued to stream to visit him because they wanted to see the light on his forefront, which was the Prophet's. Upon Adam's request, who yearned to see that light for himself, Allah instructed him to arrange his fingers in a prayer setting[54], and reflected that light in his fingernail. Adam immediately greeted the Holy Light with *Salamu* (from the Arabic *salam*—salute, peace), and Allah responded similarly. Therefore Adam prayed to Muhammed. Thus, when even Holy Adam prays to Muhammed, how much more so regular mortals who sin and need to seek salvation with

---

52. Ibid., 11–12.
53. Ibid., 12.
54. Fingers of both hands are joined together in a prescribed way for the Muslim prayers.

the Holy Man, under the specific guidance of "wise teachers" (presumably the masters of the sect).[55]

Typical of sectarian Islam (and for that matter Judaism as well), the wise teacher is key to the attainment of Allah's and the Prophet's favor. Hence the pivotal position of the head of the sect as the appraiser of the Believer's situation (*Ha-Lu*= the Arabic *Hal*). The treatise determines that already at the moment of the creation of the Holy Light, the Four Meritorious ( Xi Pei) had already been in existence. The first of them was Ai Bu Bo Ker , probably Abu Bakr, the first of the Four Rashidun Caliphs (1632–34)[56] the second was Wu-Mo-er ,namely 'Umar, the Second Caliph (634–644); the third was Ou Si Ma-ni= 'Uthman (644–56), and the fourth- Ai-Li=Ali (656–661). After Allah created the light of Muhammed, and implanted it on Adam's forefront, 51 generations elapsed until the Holy Father (*Shen Fu*) was born. He was called Er Bu Dong Na Xi (the spiritual founder of the Sect discussed above) and the Holy Mother was A-Mi-Na (probably the Arabic Amina). It seems quite surprising that the simultaneous, predestined birth of the Four Righteous Caliphs is placed at the very moment of the creation of the Holy Light which itself preceded Adam and certainly the Prophet. Maybe the explanation lay in what is to come, namely the appearance of the founder of the Sect and his wife 51 generations later. The implication is clear: it is not the chronology of the physical and historical existence of holy men that counts, but their early spiritual ordainment by Allah at the moment of Creation. The Founder and his wife Amina could then, potentially, become the equals of the Prophet, Adam and the Rashidun, for they are also Holy, with Amina joining that exclusive club as the only woman, even before Khadija, 'Aisha and Fatima, respectively the wives of the Prophet and his daughter.

Then comes an exercise in hagiography in the form of a discussion of the Prophet's and his descendants' and holy followers' biographies. His birth was situated exactly in the thirteenth day of the sixth month in the fifth year of the reign of Emperor Zhong Da Tong (AD 529–534) of the Liang Dynasty (AD 502–557), that is the year of AD 534. When he was 40, he was awarded holiness by means of heavenly designation. He lived 63 years in virtue, and passed away, according to this account in 597, that is 35 years short of the official biography. Three thousand years after since the creation of the Holy Light and 3,500 after the Creation of Adam, the Holy Man of the Sect was born in the "Western Regions." Before the Holy Man was born, there were in those Western Regions four schools of preaching: the first

---

55. Ibid., 13–14.
56. Ibid.

led by Ai Er Zhan Jiao fa(= the greatest religious law, probably that of the founding Hanafite Imam) from Ke Fa (Kufa in southern Iraq); the second was Sha Fei Er ( = the Arabic Shafi'I) from Mu Tuan Le Ge (?); the third was Ma-li-ke (= Malik Ibn Anas, founder of the conservative Malikite School) from Sha-Mi (= al-Sham, or Damascus, or Syria in general); and the fourth was Han Ba Li (the strictest Hanbalite School). From this one can deduce that Ai Er zhan was the Hanafi School. The author asserts that "Our religion dates back to the Emperor Wen (ca. 589) of the Sui Dynasty (581–618).[57] That brings us closer to the times of the Prophet (probably 570–632), but leaves open the baffling statement that the Four Schools which succeeded the Prophet, in fact preceded him.

Only now does the confused author come to the founding of Chinese Islam, which according to his and to the accepted Sino-Muslim myth,[58] began by the embassy of Wan Ge-xi, presumably the Prophet's uncle- Sa'ad Ibn Waqqas, who is believed to have been sent by Muhammed for a mission to China. He built a Mosque in Canton and began spreading Islam throughout the land. He introduced the Five Pillars of Religion: *nian* (= reading or recitation, presumably the declaration of the *Shahada*, the first of the *Five Arkan*); *li* (=ritual and worship, reference to the *Salat* or prayer); *Zhai*, that is fasting, reference to the Ramadan; *ko*, literally a lesson or a task or a levy, probably the paying of alms, *Zakat* in Arabic; and *chao*, the pilgrimage to Mecca. The Believers were supposed to meet every seven days, obviously referring to the Friday communal Prayer, and hold two assemblies every year, probably alluding to the two most important festivals of 'Id al-Fitr, marking the end of Ramadan, and *'Id al-Ad'ha*, the Festival of the Sacrifice, which celebrates the end of the *Hajj*. The two assemblies are justified by Allah's "fear" lest the Believers forget the truth. A conscientious implementation of the Path (*dao*) is conducive to the fulfillment of the *She le Er-te* (=Shari'a Law).[59]

That was the level of the external law and the cultivation of the concrete body. Then comes the inner way that is attributed to the *Tuo Lo Gai-ti* (the Arabic *Tariqa*= Sufi Order?) which addresses itself to the highest degree of the merger between man and Heaven. The term of *Mo Er Fei-ti* (probably the Arabic *Ma'rifa*=knowledge, the high degree of the knowledge of Allah in Sufi Islam), is invoked as well as *Ha ge Gai-ti* (*Haqiqa* = the Truth).That is considered the supreme way of worshipping God. The Believer is required to follow the 12 commandments, the 12 rituals and the 28 holy behaviors, to

57. Ibid., 15–16.
58. See Israeli, "Myth as Memory."
59. Ibid., 16.

practice 5 prayers daily, to attend the weekly (Friday) assembly, and the two annual festivals, and honor the Five Pillars. The morning prayer is *Bang Buda(?)*, which originated from Adam and includes 4 prostrations; the noon prayer, which began with *Yi bu na Xi-mo(?)* is *Pie Sheng(?)*, with 10 prostrations. The afternoon service is *Di Ge (?)*, has its roots with You Nusi ( the Arabic Yunus= Biblical Jonas), and consists of 4 prostrations; at dusk, the prayer goes back in its origins to *Er Sa (*=the Qur'anic *Issa*= *Jesus)*, includes 5 prostrations *and* is called *Sha Mu* (?), interestingly reminiscent of the Jewish *Shema*; alternatively, it reminds *al-Sham*= Syria, at one time the seat of the Umayyad Dynasty); the evening prayer, called *Huo Fu-dan(?)*, with 6 prostrations, originating from *Mo Sa (*the Qur'anic *Mussa*= Biblical Moses*)*, the Holy man; and the night prayer, originating from Muhammed, the Holy Noble, consists of 3 prostrations and is called *Wei Tai-er(?)*.[60]

All five prayers, collectively called *Lai Mazi* ( Perhaps from the Arabic *Lazim*= obligatory?), total 32 prostrations, 17 of which are *Feile ze (?)*, 12 are *Sun Nai-ti* ( Customary, according to the *Sunna*?), and 3 are *Wa zhe-bu (*the Arabic *Wajib*= compulsory duty). They are all designed to cultivate the inner self *(li)* and to realize the foundation of God. Conversely, the human body reveals four features: the True One ( *Zhen yi)*, namely God; the one body (*Ti yi)*,that is the Cosmos; one source (*Shu yi)*, that is the original seed; and all-mightiness (*Wan you)* which represents the omnipotence of God. When one knows oneself one knows God, and when one unites all those four elements in one, through study with enlightened masters, one can retrieve his unity[61]

## Sufi Genealogy

And here comes the crucial issue: the cultivation of life is not discussed in the classics, according to the author, and therefore cannot be transmitted in writing. Only oral teaching from the Master and direct understanding, a clear reference to the Sufi orders' *silsila* (chain of transmission) of saints who build their congregation around their charismatic figure and dispense their teaching orally, thus lending more emphasis to their own transmission than to the written texts. The author recognizes that while in the Central Plains of China there is a large variety of Muslim sects, in the Western Regions, that is perhaps Gansu, Xinjiang and Central Asia, there are four major denominations ( *Men-hu)* headed by Sheikhs, each of which has its own Prayer Hall *(Dao tang)* which served as the base of their missionary work. This

60. Ibid., 17.
61. Ibid., 17–18.

appellation resolves, of course, the question of the name of the Xidaotang itself, not only the use of *Daotang* as a prayer hall, instead of the traditional *si*, but also as a denomination originating from the west (*xi*). The four Halls are enumerated as *Zhe he le ye ( Jahriyya), Ruo bu le ye (Kubrawiyya) , Ge de le ye (Qaderiyya)* and *Hu fei ye (Khufya).*[62]

Of course, the author is himself of the Qaderiyya, and he elaborates on it: it was founded by Sheikh Mu hu Yin din Ni (Muhyi a Din), and special attention is given to transliterate the first syllable *Mu*, in a Chinese Character different from that used for the Prophet (Mu han Mo de). The Prophet's fourth assistant, *Na Mu Er li*, also entitled as *Mu Er Tai Zhan (*perhaps the Arabic *Muazzin=* who calls the Believers to prayer), passed the celestial seal of Islam directly from its founder. The evidence lay in the Holy Scripture which recounts that when the Holy Man (the Prophet) went on his *Mi Er Na Zhi (Mi ́raj=* the Prophet's Nightly Journey to Jerusalem), there stood a lion on the fourth level of *Ar Si Ma Ni ( Sama'=* Heaven?) who at the entrance gate asked the Holy Man for *Mu lu Wai ti* ( maybe *mutawalli*, a delegate, a man in charge), whereupon the Prophet took off the ring from his finger and tossed it down the lion's mouth. Then the Holy Man got to the graveyard of *Lue Hu ti,* still finding the gate closed due to his arrogant identification when called upon to do so, and was refused entrance, until he adopted a more modest self-effacing identity, and then he was let in. There he greeted the 40 *effacing ge er* he encountered, and *Han Ge* was straightened out

When the Prophet returned to the people of *Mai Si zhi* (Mecca), a *Sa Ha bo* (Sahaba= the Companions of the Prophet) stood with him in *So lai Wa ti (Salat=* Prayer), then the Prophet saw that the ring he had given up in heaven was on the finger of *Ai Li* (Ali, the Prophet ́s cousin and son-in law, extricated from the Prophet the exclamation: «Oh, Ali! I am you and you are me!!!). Thus Ali inherited the mantle of the Prophet, and became the fountainhead of many Sufi chains of transmission (*silsila).* The question here remains unanswered whether Ali, who is here mentioned by name, and was to become the fourth Caliph, is identical with the aforementioned Na Mu Er Li, the fourth assistant of the Prophet mentioned above. The author relates this story to his former account about the creation of the holy light, where the "fourth assistant" was mentioned.[63]

So far, we have the universal story of Islam, but now the author becomes specific in his pazochialization, namely Signification, of the story, much in the vein of the tradition of myth-building by Chinese Muslims.[64]

62. Ibid., 19.
63. Ibid., 21.
64. See Israeli, "Myth as Memory."

For example, a well-known Chinese historical base or event would be borrowed by Muslims as an anchor to deliver their own myths, thus lending to them credibility. Here, the author claims that the place where Hezhou (now Linxia) is today, used to be a lake without any outlet. Then Ali came in from *Man Ke* (another transliteration for Mecca?), stood on the mountain north of the lake, made his *Du Wa (Da'wa=* preaching, sermon*)*, causing the north east corner of the mountain to open and to drain the lake, making room for today's Hezhou and the adjoining Xiehu Valley.[65] On that place the city of Hezhou, now Linxia, which is repeatedly mentioned in the description to this author's 2016 field visit, was built during the Tang Dynasty (7th-10th Cent AD). However, the city wall was breached in that northern corner every time the Chinese attempted to complete it. And then appeared a white-haired sheikh, who originated from the *Dao tang* of the *Ge de le ye* at *Man Ke*, namely the religious Hall of the Qaderiyya in Mecca or some other place in the Western regions. He proclaimed to the local Chinese who prayed to Islam that his sect, the *Ge de le ye*, would be revived in a thousand years. His name was Ali and he mentioned his Order, begging God to complete the building of the city.[66] In one stroke, this myth attains two goals: the first, to make the Chinese indebted to the Muslims for the construction of Hezhou; the second, to explain how and when Islam came to the Hezhou area, in the period of the Tang which is particularly rich in mythical stories about the opportune arrival of the Muslims to the Empire, either at the request of the Emperor, like in the An Lushan Rebellion which they helped quell, or in self- initiated rescue missions to the Emperor[67].Furthermore, the book relates that the religious forefather of the Qaderiyya, *Mu Le Tai Zhan (?)*, once appeared for three hours and surprised all the people of Hezhou who cheered him.[68] This is to say, that the Qaderiyya under this interpretation, far from constituting a mere negligible splinter group of the tiny minority Hui group in China, is acclaimed here by all the people of Hezhou, "old and young," as if it were a universally irresistible and sweeping faith. The people of Hezhou also built the old Muslim graveyard at the city corner, thus also lending legitimacy to it, though no attempt is made in this story to settle the lack of logic of founding a Muslim cemetery in a new city which not only did not have any Muslim population as yet, but had hardly any population at all at its onset. But the story certainly explains why and how the Qaderiyya was first implanted in China, specifically in the city of Hezhou by the roving

65. Qing Zhen Gen Yuan, op. cit. p. 21.
66. Ibid., 22.
67. See Israeli, "Myth as Memory."
68. Qing Zhen etc..pp 22–3.

Master who covered thousands of *li* to get there twice, all the way from Mecca and back.⁶⁹

## Master Qi- the Founding Father

When the Great Grand Master completed the building of the city during the Tang Dynasty, he predicted that 1000 years after him the Qaderiyya would be established in China, thus exactly foretelling the appearance of Master Qi, who was born, according to the book on 19 September, the 13th Year of the Shun Zhi Emperor⁷⁰, namely the founding Emperor of the Qing Dynasty who ascended to power in 1644, thus- 1657. Unlike the myth of the ancestor who helped build the city and performed some miraculous feats, Master Qi is solidly anchored in history and has a birthday that one can account for. According to the book, his parents died when he was young and he was raised by his grandmother. He was schooled from age 7 and learned the classics (could be Chinese or Muslim). Since he was extremely gifted, he was quick to learn, followed Heavenly orders (*Tian Ming*, the Confucian term for the Mandate of Heaven assigned to the reigning Emperor, but here probably meaning Divine Grace), practiced daily the Five Rituals ( *Wu Li*), here probably meaning the Five Pillars of Islam, because of the inclusion of fasts observance of the Friday prayer *(Zhuma)*⁷¹.

Qi sought enlightened teachers to instruct him in Islam until he was satisfied he had found that for which he had been searching. He also encountered a fellow student in Huajiachang, who was the Fifth Great Master. One day someone said that a Sheikh from the Xining area had arrived, bearing the name (and title?) *Xi Da Ye* (Sayyed?) *Tong La Xi*, who had originated from the Western regions. He preached the Khufya ritual (of the Naqshbandiyya), in association with *Ai Bu Bo Ke (?)'s* Sect *(Dao Tang*= Religious Hall), and he had many followers. Hearing that, the Fifth Great Master, Master Qi's bosom friend, came to him and said that instead of dreaming to go abroad in search of learning, they might as well hurry to Xining, and they made their way there together. Upon arrival they settled down in the *Daotang* (Religious Hall, an indication that the Xidaotang's use of that terminology as discussed above, was by no means original) of Wei Liang Ye ti. The door of the venerable Sheikh was well guarded by his disciples, and it was difficult to approach him, but he decreed that the two young *Halifa* (=*Khalifa*, the term used in China for lower clerical status than the Akhund

69. Ibid., 23.
70. Ibid.
71. Ibid., 24.

or Imam) from Hezhou would be given priority to see him, especially the younger among them, who was Qi *Man-la* (= *Mulla*, clerical trainees in Chinese Islam)⁷².

The venerable Sheikh, upon seeing young Qi prostrating before him in prayer, helped him back to his feet, absolved him from praying for Islam (*Yi Si la mu*) and assured him that there was nothing he could teach him that he did not already know because he wa (the Ramadan) and prostrations (the prayers) therein, especially the s , "an appointed man, whose *Wu Si Da* (= the Arabic *wasat*, an intermediary?) was coming, and therefore he urged him to return home the next day. Then came the Great Fifth's turn to enter the room of the Sheikh. The latter let him hold his right leg and inquire about *sai zhi dai* (?). Thereupon, the Sheikh transmitted the Islamic Khufya to the Fifth Master and also ordered him to return to Hezhou to spread the teaching there.⁷³ All this means that in the eyes of the author of the book, the founder of the Qaderiyya in Hezhou, Master Qi, and in consequence the Qaderi order itself, took precedence over the founder of the Khufya and his order. For though the two had come from Hezhou and were intimate friends, Qi He had no need to be initiated or taught anything, while the Fifth Master was initiated by the Sheikh who also ordered him to spread the faith there. This also explains the developing proximity between the two orders of the Naqshbandiyya and the Qaderiyya, which, in Indonesia for example, came to be combined together in a joint Qadariyya wa Naqshbandiyya Order.⁷⁴

Master Qi was then said to have been illuminated by the spiritual light during the time of Mi Sa Geng, and to have received the visit of the Great Grand Master Hoja Er Bu Dong Na Xi, who came to Hezhou for the third time now, in the 13th year of Emperor Kangxi (1662–1722) that is 1675, when young Qi was barely 18 years old. It is noteworthy that in an Islamic tract like this book, both the birthday (1657) and the third visit of the Great Grand Master are denoted in terms of the Chinese Calendar (the 13th Year of two successive Emperors), not the Muslim one, and both fall, respectively, on the same 13th year of the Emperor's reign. The Great Grand Master this time said he was from Mai Di Na (=Medina). He came from Ali's Religious Hall (*Daotang*) in order to spread the Qaderiyya sect (*Jiao men*, not *Jiao pai*), and stayed at the home of Mu Youlin in a corner of the city. Many people from all over Gansu rushed to see the Hoja. Only three months after his arrival did the Great Grand Master ask his host about the *Man-la* called

72. Ibid., 25–26.
73. Ibid., 26–27.
74. Bruinessen, "The Origins and Development," 150–79.

Qi, alias known as Xi Lianli, and wondered why the young cleric did not come to see him as yet. Through the intermission of Mu Youlin, a meeting was finally arranged between them on the bank of the Ci Shui He. The Hoja noticed that Qi was trembling and he interpreted that as a manifestation of Allah's promoting the young cleric, as stated in the scripture *Mo Ge Suo De* which says that there are four categories of Huo da Wai-li (various categories of Wali), of which the first is *Mai zhi Wu bu Sali ke*(?), which is granted to novices before they attain cultivation; then, the second rank of *Sa Li ke Mai zhi* which is awarded after man attains perfection. These two first categories allow the *Wali* to accept disciples and guide them. The third rank is *Zhong zhong de Mai zhi wu bu,* also dubbed "pure promotion," which one attains through Allah's grace, without need for cultivation. The fourth is *Zhong zhong de Sai li Ke,* in which man reaches perfection but does not get Allah's promotion. This is reminiscent of the concept of the *Buddhisattva*, a holy man who has attained *nirvana* but remains in society to help others to reach his spiritual status. These last two categories do not allow their titulars to guide others[75].

The conclusion of the author is that Master Qi was of the first category and that at the time of *Mi Sa Gong (?)*, that is the day the Master was appointed, the Hoja was eager to "unload" the charisma onto Master Qi during their meeting on the river bank. He urged young Qi to move to the Hanzhong district in the Shaanxi province and to wait there. He set off, accompanied by Ma Wu Man La (the Fifth Great Lord) on the 14th Year of Kangxi (1676). They were ordered by the Great Grand Master to approach *Mai Si Zhi (?)* every morning and evening, to wait in place for him and to worship Allah incessantly. They performed the *Sai zhi dai* and were on their way. When he arrived in Hanzhong, he settled down and did the *Le ye ma ti* (the prayer?) every day, five times daily, in peace. This must refer to the five daily prayers prescribed to Muslims[76]. In view of the strong impression he made on the local Muslims, they invited him to settle down in the preaching room of the Great Mosque so that he could perform his *He li Mo ti (?)* often. They wrote the characters *Yi Qi Shi* on the entrance of his door, and he sat there to wait for the return of the Great Grand Master for three years. His companion, the Fifth Great Master Ma, began doubting whether the Great Grand Master would fulfill his promise to come back to meet them.[77]

The next day, the Fifth Master Ma rose early, did his *Pang Bu Da ( wudu'* = ablutions?*)* and went out to the street where he encountered the

---

75. Qing Zhen etc, pp. 27–30.
76. Qing Zhen etc. p. 32.
77. Ibid., 33.

Great Grand Master and led him to meet Master Qi. The meeting resulted in sending Master Qi to meditate and cultivate himself on Mt Purple Pines, and the Fifth Master to the Qingyang Place in the city of Chengdu (Sichuan) where two *er ji zi* (disciples ?) were waiting to get the Hoja's instructions. He was warned not to sit on their cushion and he should just warn them that there was no impending instruction forthcoming for them and therefore they should leave. That cushion was *Ya xi ni (?)*, the other was *Mu li ke* (the Arabic *Mulk*= Kingdom, Property), and the messenger was to wear a *Zhong ba*(?) cloth on his back. When invited to sit on that cushion he duly refused[78]. But Master Qi went to the mountain where he was assigned, and his reputation became as widespread as that of the Great Grand Master and attained the rank of *Wali*, and also the attending capacities to perform miracles[79]. He reached his rank after he was initiated by the Great Grand Master, meditated attentively and "merged truly man with Heaven, life with nature". His process of self-cultivation took three years (1670–3), then he was dispatched by the Great Grand Master to another location where he also sat in meditation and nominated some of his followers as *Mu er shi di* ( the Arabic *Murshid*= spiritual guide or instructor in Sufism). His peregrinations brought him to other places, as instructed by the Great Grand Master, to perfect himself in meditation.[80]

Finally, Master Qi was made a Holy Man after he presented *Sai Zhi dai*(?) but he was told that since the great seal of *Fe Le Ze* (?) was not vacant, he had to persevere in his constant contact with God. So, after he had spent 10 years of cultivation, he was released from the Great Grand Master's tutorship. The latter moved to the Iron Pagoda Mosque in Sichuan, to Ma Ruyuan as a disciple, in preparation of a "new generation of Qaderiyya," then he died in 1690 and was buried in Baoning[81]. Grand Master Qi rushed to the place to mourn his death and built there the Pavilion of the Eight Diagrams in his honour and memory. Thereafter, he asked the Fifth Master to remain there and lead the worship, while he himself returned to Xixiang where he established three meditation halls outside the western city gate. The Great Master performed miracles, such as producing water during a drought year, so much so that the local official Kang became his disciple until he (the official) died and was buried there. Father Wang, one of the disciples, followed self-cultivation until he reached the second rank of *Wali*, performed

78. Ibid., 34–35.
79. Ibid., 36–37.
80. Ibid., 37–40.
81. Ibid., 42–44.

miracles in Mount Guangzi, and after his death the local Muslims built the Frozen Green Mosque in his memory.[82]

Great Master Qi returned to Baoning in 1692 and purchased a large patch of land from the Wang family for his tomb site, close to where the Great Grand Master had been buried. A year later, in 1693, the Great Master Akhond, Ma Tengyi from Heiqianqing, took up the study of the Scripture in Baoning, where he had 16 *Hal Li Fa* (*Khalifa*—disciples) and 360 *Er Ling* (students). One day he took 10 *Mai Sai Lai(?)* from the Scriptures to the Great Master to test his *er bu* (knowledge?). But the Grand Master who detected the Akhond's intentions, reprimanded him and made his pardon conditional on the Akhond's fulfilling three conditions: to stop studying the Scripture; to leave family and urban dwelling; and to go into the mountain for meditation. Upon which the Akhond swore allegiance to the Great Master, dismissed the Scripture, divorced his wife and became an ascetic at his Grant Master's side as his fifth disciple. Then, the Akhond wrote to his 360 *er ling* to show, based on the scriptures, the validity of the Qaderiyya. The stone tablets at his tomb in Hezhou are evidence of his metamorphosis, as is the tomb of Magistrate An who left office and followed the Great Master's instructions for self cultivation and ended up buried in Houhaoxi[83].

In the winter of 1693, the Great Master moved back to Hezhou. There, he reprimanded a local Akhond for being unable to return his *Ling de Ti(?)* to its proper place. Under him Father Ge Sude also reached the second rank of *Wali* through self-cultivation and then returned to the Red Mountain where his tomb is to be found and worshippers continue to flock. Then the Great Master moved to Gaizi in Sichuan where he set up a cottage where he meditated and instructed the masses. In the meantime, Great Akhond Ma in Hezhou who had been meditating in solitude for a long time, but could see no miracle happening. Therefore, he decided to go back to learning the Scripture. The Great Master knew instantly of the Akhond's intentions, so he went down to Gaizi. There he met the Sect's (*Dao*) Forefather Mo Ni Jing, in Arabic Nu Le, at the Ke Tuo Garden, and also *Mu Han Mo De She Mu Song De Ni* (= Muhammad Shams-a Din), and *Nu Yan xi Na (?)*. The Forefather said that he came to warn about the instability of heart of the Akhond, but he deferred to the Great Master who already knew of that development. Thus the Grand Master brought food to the Akhund and urged him to go back to the Scripture because his flesh was too weak to resist desire. Only after the Akhond's begging did the Great Master forgive him, taught him the secret of the Qaderiyya and entrusted him with the task of propagating

---

82. Ibid., 44–45.
83. Ibid., 47–49.

its doctrines[84]. These accounts of the passing of authority from the Hoja to Master Qi and then to Akhond Ma, are significant in that they underline the precedence of charisma over scripture, because the latter is the law which binds the weak of flesh and the hesitant of heart, while the former signifies the highest stages of purity and *wilaya*, when self-cultivation makes the law redundant.

In 1716 the Great Master went back to Xixiang for meditation, and four years later, on 11 September 1720, he "ascended to Heaven and became immortal." A tomb was built next to the meditation room where he died and was baptized "the Pavilion of Eternity."[85] This tendency to immortalize the founding father or the charismatic leader of a sect, which can also be seen in Hassidic Judaism, comes closest in Islam to Twelver Shi'ism's core belief in the immortality of the Hidden Imam, who will return eventually to usher in the era of universal justice. Other than that, Sunni Muslims do not uphold the idea of any human, except for the Prophet in his time, to ascend to Heaven, and even then he went during his lifetime for his *Mi'raj*, while his death and tombstone were this-worldly. True, folk religion in Islam, as in Judaism, recognizes saints and practices saint worship, but the idea of placing a deceased charismatic leader in Heaven is quite extraordinary. In January 1721, the Master's coffin was moved to Hezhou, but he continued to be credited as the "first man who had achieved complete reception, complete returning and complete truth"[86]. A tomb was erected on the site where his body was finally put to rest, known as the Great Tomb or the Qaderiyya Mosque, and that became "the only gate for thousands of creeds to unite and reach the same goal by different routes"[87]. This statement, which is very similar to the Chinese basic belief that one can pursue different routes to get to the *Dao,* elevated the Qaderiyya from a parochial, local and sectarian call to a universal one. The status of immortality that the Great Master achieved made him the equal of the Great Grand Master, who had also ascended to Heaven, and possibly of the Prophet himself. All in all, he had preached the faith for thirty years and died at age sixty-three.

After laying the Great Master to rest, the book undertakes to put him in context and establish the genealogy of mystic orders in Sino-Islam. It is said that the Great Grand Master (the Hoja) had cultivated six disciples:

1. Great Master Qi Jingyi (1657–1720) who was born in Hezhou, ascended to Heaven and became immortal as described above;

84. Ibid., 50–53.
85. Ibid., 53–54.
86. Ibid., 55.
87. Ibid., 56.

2. The Great Fifth Master Ma Chunyi (d. 1685), also from Hezhou, who died and was entombed in Songxi. He too ascended to Heaven and became immortal.

3. Old Great Master Ran Jingyi from Xining (d. 1719), who ascended to Heaven and became immortal at Sand River Bank in Xixiang County where he is entombed.

4. Old Great Master Ha Huiyi from Xinjiang (d.1714), ascended to Heaven and became immortal at the Northern Mosque in the Hanzhong county;

5. Another Great Fifth Master, Ma Shengyi (d.1718), from Guyuan. He ascended to Heaven [no mention of becoming immortal like the others, but perhaps this is implied when one dwells in Heaven]. He is entombed in the county of Baoning;

6. Yet another Great Fifth Master, Ma Sunyi (d. 1714), originally from Hezhou, but ascended to Heaven in Jiujing where he is buried.

Having established the list of the founders of the collateral chains of transmission of Master Qi Jingyi's contemporaries, presumably all the disciples of the Great Grand Master, the book turns to list Master Qi's recognized five main disciples, but does not account for "dozens of others":

1. Great Grand Ancestor, Ma Ruyuan (d. 1745), from Hezhou, who also ascended to Heaven [again, no claim to immortality, perhaps to differentiate Master from disciple], entombed in Hezhou;

2. Senior Great Master, Sha Mingqing (d.1689), from Hezhou, but was entombed and ascended to Heaven at Xixiang County in Xining;

3. Senior Great Master Wang Zaiqing (d. 1689), from Hezhou, who ascended to Heaven and was entombed in Xixiang County.

4. Senior Great Master Ma Changqing (d.1684). from Hezhou, ascended to Heaven from his tomb in Baoning;

5. Great Master Ma Tengyi Akhond, born and died (1759) in Hezhou, ascended to Heaven.[88]

---

88. Ibid., 57–58.

## Spirituality and Mysticism

Man, according to this treatise, undergoes four stages of being and becoming in his lifetime. At first, he is flesh and blood in his mother's womb, and that is life; then he is able to move in his cradle and acquire consciousness; when he grows up and learns to know and speak, he embraces the spirit; and after age fifteen he gradually opens himself to enlightenment and embraces the Principle. Finally, all features come under the True One, thus attaining the unity of nature and life. Therefore, even though the nature of God is beyond description, when a Muslim introspects into himself he is the very evidence [of God's reality], and is not far from realizing the *Dao*[89]. Significantly, He Qi, the main author of this treatise, signs off at this point under the name Qi Daohe (again a rearrangement of the order of the surname and name), with the addition of *Dao* in between, which was to become part of the name of the Xidaotang. This author, who lived during the Tong Zhi (1862–75), as explained above, was probably a descendant of Grand Master Qi Jingyi who lived during the Kangxi reign (1662–1722), some 150 years, or six generations earlier.

Now come two additions to the text, which provide some insights into the Xidaotang. The first is by La Yonggui, an undated brief text about the nature of the faith, which is significant mainly because it provides, perhaps, the missing link between the Qaderiyya and the Xidaotang. Unlike the title of the book which proclaims "The Origin of Purity and Truth" *(Qing Zhen Genyuan)*, the addition by La states "The Original Dao of Purity and Truth" *(Qing Zhen Yuan Dao)*. The insertion of *Dao* reflected, in the eyes of the later author, not only the syncretic nature of the Xidaotang, which had assimilated Daoist (and Buddhist) elements into its creed, but also the precursor of the name of the sect as it was to crystallize by the lifetime of its founder- Ma Qixi, possibly one of the remote descendants of He Qi the main author of the treatise, who was himself probably related to Grand Master Qi Jingyi, the founder of the Qaderiyya.

The True Way *(Zhen Dao)* is, in this addition, the essence of the Faith while the religion is merely the outer skin of the *Dao*. Since Adam, there have been 120,000 Holy men, and the holiest of them was Muhammed in the 51st generation after Creation. He was born on the 13th day of the seventh month, the fifth Year of the Datong Emperor of the Liang Dynasty . After him there were only sages who interpreted the righteous way, until the advent of Great Master Qi Yingyi who carried Allah's will for about ten years, from the end of the Ming (1369–1644) and the beginning of the Qing

---

89. Ibid., 59.

(1644-1911) Dynasties, when he "inherited the past and enlightened the future" and connected with Hoja Abdallah. The implication is, of course, that those great luminaries found the righteous interpretation of the *Dao*. His enlightenment with the *Dao* made him prefer visiting famous mountains and beautiful landscapes, to render the Principle complete and nature perfect. The Hoja, who lived in seclusion in the West, made three visits to the Eastern Lands to seek ways to teach the *Dao*. When he met Great Master Qi, they immediately became intimate friends and both explained the Way of nature, the mysteries of Creation and transmitted the practice of the Great Way (*Da Dao*) of Purity and Truth.[90] Here, the traditions of Islam and the legacy of the Prophet, known in China as the Pure and True Teaching (*Qing Zhen Jiao*), combine together in the Chinese Great Way (*Da Dao*), to create the amalgam of the Great Way of Purity and Truth *(Qing Zhen Da Dao)*, which is what the Xidaotang was all about.

Both of those masters are credited with the propagation of the *Yi ma ni* (the Arabic *Iman*= Creed, Faith) of Purity and Truth throughout the Eastern Lands ( Central Asia and China), as if the Islam that had implanted itself in China several centuries before had been non-existent or not pure and true enough for them. This text explains that it was while wandering around mountains and remote resort areas at a young age, that Master Qi practiced meditation and discovered the *Dao*[91]. This appears like a Daoist narrative, but then the second, much longer, textual addition to the treatise, imputed to Akhond Ma Tengyi of Hezhou in Gansu, brings us back to Islamic tradition. If it is the same Akhond (d. 1759) mentioned above as one of Master Qi Jingyi's disciples, then his text must be more authoritative than what the main author of the treatise, He Qi, wrote much later. Furthermore, the claim that the original text was written in Arabic, the language of the Prophet and of the Word of Allah, lends to it not only more authenticity but also more authority. The text is supposedly an epistle written by Ma to the 360 Akhonds in Qinchuan[92]. While the epistle (*risala*) is a recognized genre of writing, geared to religious instruction, practiced to this day by heads of mystical orders and Muslim revivalist leaders, the figure of 360 Akhonds seems exaggerated for an area and an era in China which suffered from a permanent dearth of adequately trained clerics.

The fact that the letter was allegedly in Arabic and necessitated not only a working knowledge of that language but also an understanding of the intricate terminology involved, makes it improbable that the 360 recipients

---

90. Ibid., 60-61.
91. Ibid., 61.
92. Ibid., 62.

in question could have merely been clerical trainees, who would have been, in any case, referred to as *Man-la*. It is evident that the translator, who added the text in 1982, on the occasion of the renovation of the Tomb and the adjoining Mosque of the founder, did not master Arabic. He leaves many blanks which he transliterates into awkward Chinese characters, and directs his readers to refer to skilled instructors in order to understand the original meaning. The translator also explains that the text had been copied from a stone tablet which had been destroyed during some disaster, and therefore its translation into Chinese was appended to the latest printing of *Qing Zhen Genyuan* in order to preserve it for the coming generations.[93]

After a lengthy narrative of mystical metaphors and transliterated names that can only be partly deciphered (Muhammed, Jesus, Solomon, Ali etc.), the epistle is essentially a monologue of the writer with Allah: "Oh Allah, you look after me. I suffer thirst and hunger because I try to follow you. I suffer all sorts of bitterness because I accept you. . . I expect to pass in ease in your path. . . . I expect to reach your world. . . . I expect your facial complexion to illuminate my face. . . I have, from Mt. Ai Bu Hai Ya Ti now arrived at your feet. . . . Please lift your eye-cover from my eyes. Oh, all *Duo Si Da Ni(?)* are my affair. . . This is not the *Er Mai Li* of *Ba Tui ni* (=batini?), but the *Er Mai Li* of *Na Xi Er*. The *Er Mai li* of *Ba Tui ni* is completely secret. I cannot express it too much with my tongue . . . etc."[94]

The Prophet is cited as saying that it was not his *Wen mai ti(* destiny?) to be a man of religion, a phrase that no one in Islam could utter. The man who does not like to nestle in *Ha ge gai ti* (= *Haqiqa*, the Sufi Truth), can settle with intimacy in his place, because his heart is still linked to mundane life. One ought to follow *Na Fu xi* (=*nafs*, the soul) and *Hai wa* (= *Hayat*, life), where there is no trace of *Yi ma ni* (=*Iman*, faith). *Ai Xi wo fa(?)* and *Ge Lai bu* (=*qalb*, heart) are transferred from *hai wa i hai* (?) scripture. Man is a confused creature wandering here and there, and that is not good. Your heart is distracted by lots of thoughts. According to *Die wa ha xi mu (?)* scripture, *Wa wu* and *Mi mu* (the letters *waw* and *mim* in Arabic) come from the same place. Religious people do not know about this secret.[95]

This exercise in interpretation of letters (and numbers) is current in mystical writings. However, the intensive use of transliterated mystical terms which are hard to fathom, make this part of the text almost impossible to penetrate. For example, a sentence like : Due to all *Ya er, Duo xi da*

---

93. Ibid.
94. Ibid., 66.
95. Ibid., 67.

*ni, Ye ge ni*'s *Zha xi ni* that are transmitted to me from *Lai ma er ti* scripture[96], is any one's guess. However, clear precedence is given in this text to mysticism over the regular worship of God: the scripture of *Mi er sa de (Mirsad=* observation post?) is more significant than glorifying the name of Allah for one million years in the Flower Garden of *Gu dusi (=Al Quds,* namely the Holy Place or Jerusalem). Much of the rest remains enigmatic, except for the recurring mentioning of *Ha ge gai ti (Haqiqa=* the Truth) and *Ge ya mai ti (Qiyyama=* the Resurrection of the dead at the end of time).[97] Here ends the text of the book.

The final part of the book was written in 1982, on the occasion of the restoration of the Spring Moon Mosque and the Great Tomb, when the text underwent a second printing. Perhaps from this late introduction/ prologue one can learn about the cumulative knowledge, interpretation and scholarship that have occurred in the 70 years or so which separated the original *Qing Zhen Genyuan* from more recent times. It seems natural that during Communist rule in China, and especially under the commune system, the alternative organizational model of the Xidaotang, should have been dismissed by the authorities in favor of the uniform and controllable system that was enforced throughout the country. Hence, the existence of the Xidaotang could only be maintained on the religious level, no longer on the organizational and economic levels which had provided its strength and viability. Under the excesses of the Cultural Revolution (1966–76), even the religious aspects of the sect suffered setbacks and were exposed to a high degree of jeopardy. It was not until the 11th Communist Party Plenum in 1981, that the new policies towards the minorities allowed the Xidaotang to breath anew[98]. The period of relaxation under Deng Xiaoping's aegis[99] is what permitted the restoration of the mosque and the tomb, and the second reprinting of the book.

The text of this summary is clear: *The Origin of Purity and Truth* is about the story of the Qaderiyya in China, something that brings to the fore the most important question we have raised so far, namely is the Xidaotang of Qaderi origin, or if there is no link between the two, then why is this book imputed to Ma Qixi and his son? In other words, why is it that all those writing about Xidaotang mention its Naqhbandi, specifically *Jahri*, attachment, while here the Qaderiyya is prevalent? Unless, of course, we can show that either there was a merger between Qaderiyya and Naqhbandiyya in China,

---

96. Ibid., 66.
97. Ibid., 67–68.
98. See Hong, "The Pattern of the Xidaotang," 50.
99. See Israeli, "Muslims in the People's Republic of China," 901–19.

as already hinted above, or that the Xidaotang drew from both. If yes, then what exactly from which? The text indeed refers to the "military catastrophe of the 17th Year of the Republic" (1928), then to the year of 1958, namely the Great Leap Forward when repression prevailed in China, and the Cultural Revolution when "people suffered oppression and a great many classics were burned"[100], which correspond to the events described above with regard to the Xidaotang. The text also refers to the 1980's when "freedom of religion was adopted . . . and Islamic authority was re-established," as a result of which "Muslims have become more pious. . . ." That was the rationale for compiling the book once again and republishing it.[101]

The text concedes that because of "poor learning" and vague passages in the original book it had become imperative to attach to it the new interpretations discussed by the writer of the Prologue. The author states the beliefs of the Qaderiyya in a nutshell: self-recognition, or self awareness (*ran qi*), because the "true knowledge" (*Zhen zhi*) is by definition limited. One is enjoined to follow the most basic laws that are not written down, because "one may lose one's enlightenment when one engages oneself in the study of old books"[102]. The Holy Man, i.e. the Prophet, is the embodiment of the unwritten scripture. The true Path does not live in words, and the perfect religion does not lie in the classics. The Prophet is the origin or Creation and the life artery of the faith (*Yi ma ni*= *Iman*). The Holiest, that is the Prophet, is quoted as having said that he existed before Heaven and Earth, before Adam the first man, and that "He who sees me sees Allah."[103] This is a far-reaching statement, coming dangerously close to the Sufi extremists like al-Khallaj, who at the height of their ecstasy regarded themselves as one with God, and were chastised by execution.

The Faith consists of seventy-three sects according to the author, much in the vein of the "70 sects" evoked in Islam, but only one is the true root, raising the question of how to detect it among the lot. Here the Holy man of the order plays the key role, because recognizing him is tantamount to identifying the true path. Man's body is the successor of Adam's, but his soul is inherited from the Prophet. Human life is the divine light that is called *Yi ma ni* (Faith). The Faith is in the human body like the fragrance in the musk or the sound of the bell. Like the light which comes out of the pearl and in turn illuminates it, so is the soul for the body. A citation from Mencius makes the point of the relationship between man and Heaven through

---

100. Qing Zhen etc. p. 70.
101. Ibid.
102. Ibid., 71.
103. Ibid., 73.

self-cultivation.[104] This is one of the rare explicit references to Confucianism to explain Islamic concepts to the Chinese-grown Muslim public, and under a Communist regime to boot. If this is Confucianism, what about the Daoist statement "existence comes from inexistence?" and the harking back to the Chinese creation story in which one original egg produced heaven and earth, sun and moon, the Eight Trigrams, thunder and lightening?[105] And then, a whole discussion of the human essence (*qi*), consisting of the dual elements of Ying and Yang, and the Buddhist lamentation about desire that controls the body.[106] Finally, breathing sessions are recommended as a way for self cultivation.[107] A truly intricate eclecticism where one finds what one wants, without however any attempt to systematically elaborate any new syncretic whole.

Nevertheless, the footprints of Sufism are well recognizable, with death identified as the ultimate *Fu ai na* (*fana'*= the final dissolution and merger of the soul), in which "one must relax spiritually and physically without any desire or worry. The self and the world become united, at which moment it is equi-distant from Heaven and also from Hell"[108]. More concretely, the author claims that Qaderiyya was founded by none other than Ali, who had inherited the most intimate knowledge from the Prophet in person. Furthermore, through Ali, who "enjoyed Allah's favor" and was "the column of religion"[109], he was enjoined to keep to "his own *ka'ba*," namely to substitute his own locus of pilgrimage, as is sometimes done in Chinese sectarian Islam, for the central object of *Hajj* in normative Islam. Here Ali himself replaces the Prophet: he himself had taken the ride on his horse to Heaven, and became the most intimate with Allah's secrets and the most amazing among His people. He was given charge of the Qaderiyya Seal in Heaven, and from him stemmed the uninterrupted link to the Great Grand Master who went three times to the Central Plains to teach the faith. The latter had arranged for the appointment of Grand Master He Jingyi and attained the degree of *wali*[110]. That is the reason why "the end of the road for other religions is the starting point for our honorable religion"[111].

This epilogue ends as a truly Daoist scripture:

104. Ibid., 74.
105. Ibid., 75.
106. Ibid., 77.
107. Ibid., 78.
108. Ibid., 83.
109. Ibid., 84.
110. Ibid.
111. Ibid., 85.

> The religious sect of *Ge de le* ye (Qaderiyya) has profound secrets and significances which are impossible to describe with a sea of ink. A heavy strike produces a big sound, and a light strike produces a weak sound. In an unrighteous man no sound is produced even after many heavy strikes. It is impossible to talk about the ocean with a frog in the bottom of the well... There is no way to know about the universe through a pipe. Little learning cannot cause a great deal of knowledge. A stupid man should not talk about philosophy. Preserve silent praying (a *khufya* feature, contradictory to the alleged *Jahri* base of the Xidaotang); be careful with your speech and do not make rash and careless remarks....[112]

## Conclusions

This seminal text, which has not been referred hitherto by most scholars of Chinese Islam, both native Chinese and foreigners, Muslims and non-Muslims, potentially contradicts many of the accepted generalizations said and written about the Xidaotang. Maybe the new thorough ethnographic study of Marie-Paul Hille, published as a PhD dissertation by L'ecole des Hautes Etudes Sociales, Paris in 2014,[113] holds the key to the many enigmas that persist in an understanding of the Xidaotang. Most conventional wisdom rests on Ma Tong and Western scholars like Gladney and Lipman, who have conducted prolonged fieldwork in the Northwest[114] and came up with hitherto almost indisputable conclusions. For example Lipman cited an event in Gansu in 1914, where Xidaotang women proved to possess an extraordinary knowledge of orthodox Islam, not found today even among ahungs of the mainstream Hui communities in China[115]. Lipman's survey added that after the death of Ma Anliang in 1919, the Muslim general Ma Lin brought the Lanzhou authorities and Ma Qixi together, thus legalizing the Xidaotang, who had been pitilessly persecuted by Ma, an adept of the Huasi menhuan which held Ma Qixi and his group as "heretics." Now, the Xiodaotang was recognized as a legitimate Muslim group rather than a "renegade gang."[116]

112. Ibid., 87.
113. Hille, *Le Xidaotang*.
114. Ibid., 186–99.
115. Ibid pp. 186–7
116. Lipman, *Hyphenated Chinese*, 195.

However, without digging deeper into the Xidaotang doctrine, which had been the real reason for its estrangement from the rest of the Hui in Gansu, Lipman recounts how the persecuted maligned sect tried to make it back to normalcy as a part of the mosaic of the Hui sects in the region, against the background of the much impoverished and opium-stricken population under the tyrannical rule of local warlords. Lipman notes that in spite of the general decline, the Xidaotang prospered religiously and commercially, and their membership in Gansu amounted to some 3,500 souls out of a total membership of 5,000. Nonetheless, in the fighting in which it became involved, the sect lost much of its wealth, as its HQ moved to Tibet while continuing to maintain businesses in Gansu and elsewhere. They allied for a while with the Guomindang, which allowed them some leeway in conducting their business, and provided precious products to the Nationalist troops which had moved to Chongqing during the Japanese invasion. At that point, around 1946, the sect reached the height of its prosperity, maintaining shops and agents as far as Beijing, Shanghai and inner Mongolia. In southern Gansu, it possessed 2,000 draft animals and over 1,000 acres of land, five ranches with thousands of livestock, a forestry station, water-powered mills, brick and tile kilns, oil presses and workshops for making leather, sugar, flour and vinegar. In 1927 they founded a joint venture with a Beijing firm to sell borderland goods in Beijing and import the Capital's goods to Gansu[117].

Lipman also reported that the daily religious activities of Ma Qixi and his followers did not differ from other Muslims, an indication, which was confirmed in my 2016 field trip to Gansu, that following the torments it had undergone, the sect had practically come back to the Islamic fold, at least in public. He identifies the Sect's religious beliefs as centering on and deriving from what he called the *Han Kitab* (the Han Book, or the Chinese Canon), that is the corpus of Islamic writings that were dipped in the Chinese style and revealed the very special amalgamation that Xidaotang has achieved between the two cultures. He says that the *Mirsad* (the Observatory) a 13th Century text that was imported to China, and we have seen cited in the sect's "book" analyzed above, had been brought in by Wu Sunqie, a Chinese Muslim scholar who undertook the translation of the *Mirsad* into Chinese. He traces the use of the notion of *Iman* (faith, creed), which we have also encountered in the "book" as mentioned above, indicating that all these sources, writers and vocabulary had served as ingredients in the concoction that the Xidaotang had created in the final analysis, mainly deriving from Liu Zhi, Wang Daiyu and Ma Zhu, the latter claiming descent from

---

117. Ibid., 197.

Sayyid Edjell, who was also mentioned in the "book." Lipman's summary[118] of the work of these three masters certainly contributes tremendously to our understanding the sources of the vain attempt of the Xidaotang to combine Confucianism and Islam, as has become evident in the almost total dilution of the sect into normative sectarian Islam in all its manifestations.

118. Ibid., 74–102.

# PART II

Chapter Five

# The Yunnan Pattern of Muslim Settlement

Like Beijing, Gansu and Qinghai, which generated and participated in the largest Hui Muslim protest in the post-Mao era, so did Yunnan, though on a much smaller scale, in what came to be called the "Chinese Salman Rushdie Affair" in May, 1989,[1] an indication of the still vigorous Islamic sentiment that survived in that southwestern province of China, which had been almost depleted of its vibrant Hui population during the Du Wenxiu (Panthay) Rebellion (1856–73) that ran paralell with its counterpart in Gansu and also ended equally tragically. Unlike Gansu, listed second (after Hebei) in the number of townships that are under Hui "autonomous" administrations (21 and 24 respectively), Yunnan has "only" 14 "autonomous" townships and two "autonomous" counties, while Gansu has only one "autonomous" county but also one "autonomous" prefecture, which is higher, larger and more populated in the administrative hierarchy of the People's Republic nowadays[2]. In many of those "autonomous" counties or townships the Hui are no more than perhaps the largest minority, often not attaining even 50 percent of the entire population, which in the entire province does not surpass 2 percent of the total. In any case, and surprisingly, what had been considered as "Muslim country" is now far behind the major provinces and cities of the East Coast, like Beijing, Shandong and even the Northeast, where the largest masses of Muslims dwell.[3]

Like the Muslims of Gansu, those of Yunnan have located their sources in the common myth that is recounted all over China by the Hui. It is

---

1. Gladney, *Muslim Chinese*, 1–64.
2. Wan Lei, *The Hui Minority in Modern China*, 69.
3 Ibid., 4.

reported that a Muslim notable from the border town of Momien, between Yunnan and the Burmese land, stated that the forefathers of the Muslims had arrived there from Arabia a millennium ago during the reign of a Tang Emperor, who had dispatched his Chief Minister to ask for help against the rebellion of An Lushan. When the 3,000-man contingent completed their duty, their compatriots refused to accept them back, because they "had been defiled by their residence among the pork-eating Infidels, so they settled in China and became the progenitors of the Chinese Muslims.[4] This story is basically the one told by many Muslims all over China, but here it acquires the sense of a self-indictment, by not only accusing their ancestors as irremediable sinners, but by also accusing themselves of being the descendants of Muslims who were unable to keep the rules of the *Shari'a*, and perhaps of being contaminated by "pork-eating," an abominable crime in Islam. For, if they were rejected by their coreligionists, that meant that they persisted in their sins, and who can guarantee that they had remedied their grave deviation from the Law in the intervening years?[5]

Anderson further claims that, according to his Muslim informants, while insisting on their Arab descent, they clearly stated that their more immediate ancestors had migrated from Shaanxi and Gansu to Yunnan some 150 years earlier, which would mean ca 1700, adding that in China Muslims were known as Hui, while their local appellation as Panthay (or Pansee) was of Burmese origin. Citing Garnier, a French explorer of Indochina in those years, he says that the word *Pha-see*, which was corrupted into *Pan-the*, actually depicted Parsis or Farsis, the common word in adjoining India for Muslims. Sir Wade, the famous China scholar, was claimed to have opined that Panthay derived from the Chinese *Puntai*, signifying the aborigines of the land, and in effect there was a people called *Penti* who were found on the eastern side of the Dali Lake and in the plain extending north of there, precisely the domain of the Du Wenxiu state of the 19th Century, that was contemporaneous with this description. Those people were described as a "mixed race, descended from the first colonists sent into Yunnan by Mongols after the conquest of the province by Kublai Khan." But it was also asserted that Chengis Khan's conquests had caused a considerable movement of the population of Uyghurs from further west into Shaanxi and Gansu, thus spreading the Muslim faith among those people before the Mongol conquest of Yunnan.[6]

4. Anderson, *Mandaly to Momien*, 228.

5. The entire elaborate story was reported by Colonel Sladen, in Appendix II to Anderson's book, 456–57, which purports to be the translation of a Chinese official document accounting for the coming and establishment of Islam in China.

6. Ibid., 225–26.

Then came the seminal eye-witness reports by Marco Polo and then Ibn Battuta, who stayed in China for a long while and was able to investigate Muslim affairs. Marco Polo noted during his long stay in China (1271–95) that in addition to the Arab contingents who settled in China, Arab traders and migrants from Gansu and Shaanxi also settled in Yunnan, making up a considerable proportion of the foreign population. He also emphasized that under the rule of the Yuan Mongols (1279–1368), especially during the reign of Kublai Khan, the provincial governments of the western provinces were entrusted to Mongols (Tartars), Christians and Muslims, the latter also filling high positions of trust, both civil and military, so it can be conjectured that after the conquest of Yunnan, Muslim soldiers and traders established themselves in the new colonies. Ibn Battuta, who visited China in the mid-fourteenth century, found in the large towns rich Muslim traders, and within each town they had their own neighborhoods with a mosque, market place, a refuge for the poor, and a *Sheikh al-Islam* (a Muslim cleric in charge). He even made a tactless remark that would be taken as "racist" or "Islamophobic" today, when he wrote that "in some districts they were exceedingly numerous." The reference here was made to all China, but it certainly also included the towns of Yunnan, where using their wealth in time of famine, Chinese traders purchased starving Chinese children and raised them as Muslims.[7]

H.K. Davies attributes the large variety of ethnic and linguistic groups in Yunnan primarily to the great geographic features of the country. For the high mountain ranges and the swift-flowing rivers have created the differences in customs and languages and the innumerable ethnic distinctions. He illustrates: a tribe that has increased in numbers comes down from the Himalayas and settles down, but when its numbers grow again, parts of it emigrate again, and having surmounted pathless mountains and crossed unbridged rivers on rickety rafts, they found a place to settle down and felt no inclination to undertake such a journey again to revisit their old home. Being without a written language to perpetuate their traditions, cut off from the influence of any other civilization, and busy with cultivating crops to survive, their ties to their own cultures and ancestors died out eventually, ending up identifying themselves as a new and separate ethnic group from their ancestral roots. The hilly nature of the country has also militated against the formation of any large kingdom with effective control of the mountainous areas. Conversely, in a flat country, where communications are available, heterogeneous groups can easily be welded into one country and people, speaking one language. However, in the past, a great part of Yunnan had

---

7. Ibid., 228–29.

been ruled for many centuries by what is known as the Nanchao Kingdom under the Shan tribal dynasties, although it is doubtful whether that unified rule could influence the customs and languages of the many hill tribes that retained their separate identities[8]. To this day, when one circulates around the large Dali Lake (*Ehr Hai*) or in the provincial Capital, Kunming, one realizes the smooth passage from one group's country into the other (Han, Hui, Dai, Miao, Shan, Lo-lo, etc) under the unifying Chinese Communist strong Unitarian state which no one seems willing or able to challenge.

In this maze of nationalities and ethnic groups, not only were the Hui people able to find their place and survive, but at some point, probably based on the Nanchao precedent, to carve for themselves a sultanate in the nineteenth century, based on the same Dalifu which used to serve as the Nanchao Capital, and even to seek in vain, for a while, to secede from the then declining Chinese Empire. Only recently was the origin of the Yunannese Muslims investigated and solid historical foundations obtained. For example, Wang Jianping,[9] who specialized in the Hui in that particular area of China, conducted the most thorough investigation to date on that complex topic and came up with a series of all-encompassing findings dating back even to the pre-Mongol era. He locates the outset of the long process of Muslims trickling into Yunnan in AD 801, in the battle between the Nanchao Kingdom and the Chinese Empire under the Tang Dynasty, in which soldiers from the Muslim Abbasid armies and Samarkand participated. Those Muslim soldiers had possibly been part of the war prisoners taken by Tibetan forces in Central Asia, and then forced to fight for them against the Nanchao and then China, thus tracing back the origins of Islam in Yunnan to the ninth century. Wang himself believes that due to the slave status of the prisoners of war, they were probably distributed among tribal chieftains as war booty, and were then assimilated into their environment over the years.[10]

The long hiatus in historical record between those events and the Mongol conquest in the 13th Century has remained anyone's guess, but consensus among scholars has regained a firm basis when it was agreed that Islam had its historical and verified roots in Yunnan when Muslim Central Asian soldiers who served in the Mongol armies arrived in the process of the Mongol conquest of the crippled south Song Empire and much of the Abbasid Caliphate, after they had taken over Central Asia, and settled there. The advancing Mongols waded through the upper reaches of the Yangtze

---

8. Davies, *Yunnan*, 334–36.
9. Jianping, *Concord and Conflict*, 39–60.
10. Wang, "Islam in Yunnan," 41–42.

and occupied the Dali Kingdom south of it, whence they continued their march eastward to take over China. In other words, while various barbarians had previously attacked the Middle Kingdom from the sea or from the northern and northwestern desert borders, the Mongols invaded from the West, not only establishing the Western route as another possible gate into China, but also using it as a springboard for occupying the rest of the country. After the conquest of Dali, Kublai Khan established it as his military HQ, and made Hugechi, one of his commanders, Prince of Yunnan, who administered his fief according to the pattern of the six ministries of the Chinese central government. The central Asian Muslims became officials in the administration. Kublai then appointed Sayyid Adjall Shams a-Din Umar, one of his most trusted officials, as the governor of Yunnan in 1274, who was recorded as a "descendant of the Prophet of Islam," hence his accompanying title of Sayyid. He ruled the province until his death in 1279, but his genealogy, which establishes his links well back in Chinese history, has determined that his ancestor of six generations earlier (*Safir*, meaning Ambassador or Envoy) had first arrived to China in 1070 to give tribute on behalf of tribes from Bukhara. After the famous Sayyid died, many of his descendants continued to fill central positions on the level of the province, the prefecture or the various counties.[11] Thus was forever established the link between the Hui and Yunnan, not as a guest culture of migrants, but as builders and participants in turning Yunnan into part of China, in addition to having brought it into the Chinese Empire in the first place.

In addition to many Turkic tribes, including some Uyghurs, which were brought into Yunnan during the Mongol reign and remained, Wang tells us of Muslim Central Asian troops who were recruited into the Ming and Qing armies and settled there. One should recall, that since the evacuation of Mongols from China took place under the Ming in reverse order of the conquest, Yunnan remained their last stronghold where they made their last stand, supported by indigenous tribes which refused to submit to the new rulers. The Ming Emperor then sent two of his Hui generals, Lan Yu and Mu Ying to Yunnan to liberate the area from the retreating Mongols, and after they accomplished their mission they were asked to remain, with the latter as Governor. Thus, the pattern was established in the local Hui lore that Yunnan was not only brought into the Kingdom with the help of Muslim soldiers during the Yuan, but was also liberated from its Mongol occupiers by Muslim generals, who later stayed with their troops, thereby augmenting the Muslim population of the Province, once again as aggressive partners and fighters for the Chinese cause, not as diffident hosts who

11. Ibid., 43–47.

had no stake in the nation, and were merely begging as a favor to stay. Thus, what became known as the Yunnan Expedition of 1383, with Muslim troops and their Muslim chieftains, was registered in the Yunnan chronicles as a Hui victory, which could only enhance the status of the Muslims in the Province.

Under the Qing Dynasty, itself an alien rule which took time to acculturate and assimilate into the Chinese landscape, the previously advantageous relations with the Hui soured, following the initial recruitment of Hui soldiers and officials in the struggle of the novice dynasty against the Ming loyalists. Many of these Hui personnel, who helped quell local tribal rebellions in Yunnan, remained there during the pacification process. Among them was Ye Daxiong, a Hui from Sichuan, who was appointed as military commander in the Province in the early 19th Century, and settled with his Sichuan and Shaanxi Hui troops in Yunnan. As did many others, who followed his example. Most of those Hui who eventually settled in Yunnan, had strong though distant roots in Central Asia and West Asia, and through intermarriage they were thoroughly Sinicized, and their interaction with the preceding Muslim generations who had settled there earlier, helped create a self aware Hui community that could boast not only of its ancient roots in the land, but also of its renown as the ethnic group which had repeatedly come to the rescue of the Kingdom when in danger. Since most of the Hui enclaves in Yunnan today are located on the route of the Mongol conquest, and then on former military farming settlements which were found scattered across the province along the routes of the Mu Ying's and Ha Yuansheng's expeditions to quell the local tribal uprisings, the pattern of the various waves of Hui settlement in Yunnan supports that history. Moreover, Hui villages in Yunnan have retained such words in their names as *ying* (barrack), *shuo* (stronghold, like Fort Lauderdale in Florida or Fort Worth in Texas) or *wei* (garrison) or *pu* (courier post station, that had been established during the Yuan to link the provinces with the Capital). There is no better indication as to their origin.[12]

Apart from the Du Wenxiu Rebellion in the 19th Century, which led to the trauma of outright secession, resulting in a massive massacre and flight of millions of Muslims from Yunnan, which will be discussed in detail in the coming chapter, perhaps the most memorable and impactful event in Hui modern history, both in Yunnan in particular, and in Hui China in general, has been the Shadian Incident, which chronicles what was done to the Hui during the abuses of the Cultural Revolution (1966–76). It is natural that people, especially minorities, should remember the suffering the host

---

12. Ibid., 57–58.

culture inflicted upon them despite their total "innocence" and "peaceful intentions," rather than reflect over their own trouble-making past and their attempts to undermine the country that gave them shelter, to the point of jeopardizing its security and very existence (watch for example the Muslim migrants' complaints today against the European countries that have generously absorbed them). Nonetheless, despite the horror of the events of the Shadian Incident, one cannot help wonder at the great trauma this caused among the Hui of Yunnan. The Muslims tend to dismiss their great rebellion of the 19th Century as an episode in the past, and remain reluctant to discuss its details. No doubt this relates to the fact that these events decidedly diminish their inflated history as the local heroes to disloyal rebels who were intent on destroying what they had built and in which they had previously taken great pride.

The Shadian Incident, which began unfolding in 1967, was indeed most instructive in illustrating the background behind the violent Muslim eruptions in Post-Mao China, and its relationship to the past. The most widely accepted account of the Incident was illuminated by Ma Shaomei,[13] although it is evident that due to censorship, some critical elements in this description were omitted. Ma, himself a Hui leader and participant in the events, narrowly escaped death as he was evacuating elderly women and children outside the affected Hui villages before they were destroyed by the Chinese authorities. He suffered arrest and torture but was later rehabilitated and promoted to the Secretariat of the Shadian District Party branch of the Gujiu city Shadian Town, in the southernmost prefecture of Yunnan (Honghe Hani and Yi Autonomous Region. The population at the time of the Incident included some 7,200 inhabitants, most of them Hui. According to Ma's authoritative account, many of the Hui had responded to Mao's appeal during the Cultural Revolution (1966–76) and joined the Red Guards against Liu Shaoqi and his followers. They closed down mosques and burned religious books in their drive to wipe out the "Four Olds" (Old Ideas, Old Culture, Old Customs and Old Habits). Obviously they had not volunteered to uproot their own culture, but under the social and political pressures of the Cultural Revolution, the most zealous communists among them saw no escape from supporting the general trend of the time. However, other conservative and loyal Muslims countered these trends, seeking shelter in the PRC Constitution which guaranteed national minority rights.

Shadian was not just any place, for it had played an important part in the history of Chinese Islam, insofar as the area is located on the trade route of Southeast Asia and has maintained a thriving center of Muslim learning

---

13. Ma Shaomei, *Shadian Huizou Shiliao*.

which produced, inter alia, the first Chinese translation of the Qur'an. Shadian had also played a major role in the Du mid-19th Century Rebellion, which had created a Muslim state based on Dali, hence it had experience as a vanguard of Muslim ethnic self assertion, but also as a confrontational locus for Muslims of various political persuasions[14]. During the Cultural Revolution, when all religious activities were forbidden, and all mosques were shuttered across China Proper, many Yunnan Muslims, like Marrano Jews under the Spanish Inquisition, prayed in secret at home. Their children pursued their studies of the Qur'an with their akhongs, in the evenings, and even the fast of Ramadan was observed, while during the day Muslims engaged in their full-time occupations. The conflict escalated however, when the Mao-addicted Muslims criticized their conservative coreligionists and compelled them to commit the horror of horrors—eating pork—as a manifestation of total iconoclasm towards their own tradition and fealty to the demands of the Mao regime. Other abominable acts of anti-religious coercion were perpetrated when pork bones were thrown into water wells in order to irretrievably pollute the drinking water.[15]

This string of frictions and provocations culminated in a massacre perpetrated by the Chinese troops against the Muslims in July, 1975, resulting in the razing of entire Hui villages with spreading confrontations to other neighboring villages. After seven days of sustained fighting the entire picture of devastation and death became evident: around 1,000 Hui were massacred (half of them from Shadian) and 4,400 houses were destroyed. In the process, the PLA used not only guns and cannon, but also air bombardments, lending to the operation the nature of a full-scale war. This is how Ma described the final steps of the Hui rout in the Shadian District:

> Within the first and second days of August, the fight for the control of the strongholds of Jizhi and Quanfang villages continued. One side [the Government] had the advantage of modern weapons and equipment. The other [the Muslims] was only sustained by its religious spirit. The one possessed well-trained troops, the other only ordinary citizens. What sort of combat was it between these two [uneven] sides? The Shadian and Quanfang villages had almost no strength to resist following the intense cannon fire, howitzer shells, and indiscriminate killing. . . On August 3, the troops controlled about half of Jizhi village. Hand to hand fighting, shooting and gunfire were ubiquitous. In areas controlled by the troops, brutal mop-up operations were pursued. Injured and maimed Hui were captured, their

14. Wang Jianping, "Islam in Yunnan," 364–74.
15. See Israeli, *Islam in China*, 264–65.

> feet and hands were tied, and like slaughtered sheep they were thrown on the dirt track for for so-called "medical treatment." Some of them were summarily executed. . . On August 4, 157 Hui, including the elderly, women and children, surrendered to the troops, raising their heads and reciting verses from the Qur'an. When they approached the troops at the edge of the rice paddies, automatic fire was opened on them, and within one minute, corpses littered the ground, and the paddy waters were colored in red. After that, the troops checked the corpses one by one and delivered the *coup de grace* shot to whoever survived. Of the 157 surrendering Hui, only 5 were still alive at the end of the operation. Three of them were later shot at during the second mop-up, but they escaped unhurt. . . At six o'clock in the afternoon, high explosive detonations blew up the few remaining houses. Ma Baohua and the rest of the comrades heroically gave their lives. By the evening, the last work of annihilation was achieved and the massacre reached its end.[16]

This harrowing depiction of these events, reminiscent of the Nazi extermination operations in the killing fields of Eastern Europe and the Warsaw Ghetto, is matched by the heroic conduct of the Hui victims despite their being outnumbered and outgunned by the PLA troops and Air Force. Their recitation of Qur'anic verses while they were facing death was not only poignant as an act of extreme devotion to their faith, but serves today to augment the story of those eventful days, when the powerful PRC came out openly against its helpless citizens in an act of open, though undeclared warfare. This is the stuff that makes for the flowery narratives one can still hear today in Yunnan. Four years later, when the Deng Xiaoping regime began to mend the horrors of the Cultural Revolution and the abuses of the Gang of Four, the Yunnan Provincial Party Committee and the Kunming Military Region jointly issued Document No 7, entitled "Circular on the Rehabilitation Regarding the Shadian Incident." It stated :

> The Shadian Incident ought not to have been dealt with as a counter-revolutionary rebellion. It was wrong to solve the incident by military means. . . and the military leaders and the people of the Hui nationality who were involved in this incident should be rehabilitated.[17]

In another circular issued by the Provincial Minority Nationality Board of the Party, orders were given to rebuild the destroyed villages,

16. Translation by Wang Jianping.
17. Ibid.

including seven mosques, and relief funds and pensions were disbursed to the widows and widowers of the tragedy, as well as to survivors and orphans of the murdered. Some of them were provided state jobs, and the Shadian area was designated for preferential economic treatment However, it was not until 1987 that a final concluding document of the Yunnan Provincial Party Committee rectified the previous records, which had indicted some of the Hui leaders, including Ma Shaomei, and exonerated them from being accused of counter-revolutionary zeal, when Revolution was no longer hailed as the engine of the Chinese Communist Party in the new era of reform and free economic enterprise. It introduced several novel ideas, never seen or heard before:

1. What had been previously termed as an "illegal secret organization," was now spelled out as "*hizbullah*" (the Party of God), acknowledged as a "religious group founded under the abnormal circumstances of the Cultural Revolution," and therefore was now de-criminalized.

2. The previous accusation that those formerly indicted Hui had plotted to "betray their fatherland," was now removed since "it was never substantiated";

3. The accusation of beating, looting and smashing property, which was attributed to those indicted Hui, while substantiated, was now forgiven, in view of the general circumstances of the Shadian Incident.

In 1974, when a notice was circulated in the Shadian area ordering mosques to close down, more than one thousand outraged local Hui boarded a train to Beijing to present their complaint. But when thousands of Yunnan Muslims took control of the PLA barracks and arsenals in several counties of the province, and began manufacturing home-made weapons for themselves, the central government had to conclude that a military rebellion was brewing that needed full-scale intervention, necessitating the deployment of ten thousand troops against the seven Hui villages which seemed to have raised the banner of revolt, if not of disobedience. Just as in the Tiananmen tragedy two years later, the government, faced with massive disruption of daily life and defiance by small enthusiastic groups who had lost any sense of fear, had no choice but to confront the rebellious crowds before the country sank into chaos, and therefore acted with force. In any event, rehabilitation notwithstanding, the scope and mercilessness of the massacre left deep scars in the Hui landscape, exactly as had the slaughters in the 1870s which had quelled the Dali rebellion and drowned it in blood. In both cases, the obvious lessons were and remain that.

a. The greatest unforgivable sin in China was to rebel against the authorities of that immense unitarian state, namely the notion of fatherland that the Communist regime has been working hard to promote, no matter what the justifications or rationalizations of the unrest were;

b. When Muslim religious zeal, to the point of founding a Hizbullah on Chinese turf, is apparent, always on the verge of exploding when circumstances warrant, the state has to be wary of this sort of religious extremism, as it has been towards the Uyghurs of Chinese East Turkestan.

c. As the entire world has been watching the rise of radical Muslims around the globe, and every act of violence on their part immediately gains the status of "breaking news" internationally, China must control the foreign media's eagerness to penetrate the real crux of such events and diffuse them in the world.

Forty years after the Shadian Incident, which is still vividly remembered by the elderly of the Hui community, this time as its victims, unlike the 19th Century rebellions which had been initiated and led by Hui religious leaders, Yunnan Muslims are still not certain how they should recollect and commemorate the tragedy. Alice Su visited the spot in June 2016 and reported on her experience:[18]

> The Martyr's Memorial in Shadian, China, is a gray pillar topped with a crescent moon, set on a stone block engraved with names. It commemorates the so-called Shadian Incident, a massacre that took place in July of 1975, when the People's Liberation Army came to this small southwestern town to quell what the central authorities were calling an Islamist revolt. Then, as now, Shadian was inhabited almost entirely by Hui, members of one of the country's two main Muslim minority groups. In the years leading up to the incident, the Red Guards had attacked the Hui, destroying their mosques and forcing them to wear pigs' heads around their necks. When the P.L.A. soldiers arrived, they razed more than four thousand houses and killed some sixteen hundred villagers in one week. The Chinese government later apologized for the raid, blaming it on the Gang of Four—the ousted architects of the—and helping fund Shadian's reconstruction. But locals do not pay homage to the state at the memorial. The pillar is emblazoned with the *Fatiha*, the first chapter of the Qur'an, in green Arabic calligraphy, and, above it, in Chinese characters, the word *she-xi-de*. "That's the Arabic word *shahid*,

---

18. Su, "Harmony and Martyrdom."

instead of *lieshi*, the Chinese word for 'martyr,' " a man named Huang told me. (As with the other Chinese Muslims I spoke with, I will protect his identity by referring to him only by his surname.) "You know why? *Lieshi* would include the P.L.A. soldiers, wouldn't it?"[19]

The use of *Shahid* in this context is not only an assertion of self-identity and unique cultural tradition, but it also spells out the Muslim tradition worldwide, pursued by the Muslim Brothers, Hamas, Islamic Jihad , Hizbullah in Lebanon and in Syria and even by ISIS terrorists. The goals of its recurrent use is to announce that no Muslim dying for an Islamic Jihadi cause is in vain, because the Martyr is to dwell in the bliss of Paradise directly under the Throne of Allah; furthermore, it encourages others to seek to forego the ungratifying life on this earth in order to pass swiftly into the hereafter, accompanied by the 72 virgins that are promised by the Qur'an, and exonerated from the this-worldly sins of alcohol and sex, since in Heaven shari'a law is not applied. Only a fully dis-integrated minority in vast unforgiving China could possibly embrace this sort of ideology on which to raise their children and sustain their community. This indicates, more than anything else, that the full assimilation which had been the pride of the Hui and strengthened their sense of partnership and even partial ownership of the province, has melted away under the duress of the Cultural Revolution, especially following the Shadian Incident.

Shadian, now a 12,000 soul community (compared to the 7,000 during the Incident), almost all Hui, is still known among the Muslims of Yunnan for its Grand Mosque and its *Halal* barbecue. The immense mosque was built thanks to private donations, its gilded green domes patterned after those of the *Nabawi* (Prophet's) mosque in Medina, complete with imported date palms lining the entrance. The call for prayer, which overrides the sound of thunder during the frequent storms in Yunnan, is followed by fifteen minutes of Qur'anic teaching which unabashedly blares over the mosque's loudspeakers, though in Mandarin, in order to reach the largest audience possible. The history of the Hui in Yunnan, which is still recounted by the Shadian Muslims harks back to the period when Yunnan was not part of China, prior to Sayyid Edjell Shams al-Din Omar al-Bukhari, the Central Asian Muslim who served the imperial court, who brought Yunnan into its fold. According to Imam Ahmed at one of Kunming's mosques, many Hui still revere Sayyid Edjell, because he demonstrated that Islam could coexist with Chinese philosophy. "Chinese tradition teaches the *dao* of man, and Islam teaches the *dao* of heaven—the two are complementary," Ahmed said,

19. Ibid.

still desperately attempting to mend the cracks of the Incident. He said that Sayyid Edjell built Confucian academies alongside mosques and Buddhist temples, infusing foreign religion and culture with domestic ideals of harmony and hierarchy. "This is why Hui can mix with Han, but Uyghurs can't," Ahmed continued, referring to China's other significant Muslim minority. "We have Islam with Chinese characteristics." Nevertheless, relations between the Hui and the Han have not always been peaceful. In the nineteenth Century, during the Qing dynasty, tensions between the two groups erupted over how Yunnan's mineral resources were being apportioned. Qing officials ordered a *xi Hui*—a washing away of the Hui—slaughtering at least four thousand people in the course of three days in 1856. That massacre sparked a sixteen-year rebellion, which ended with another massacre, this time of at least ten thousand Hui. And that was the head count of Hui corpses only in that locality, while the extent of the slaughter of the Hui and the exile of others will be accounted for in the next chapters

After the Shadian Incident, as China's economy opened up, the Hui flourished again. They operated private copper, lead, and zinc mines, some of which outcompeted state-owned enterprises. Wealth, and the new liberal measures of the Deng period, brought them relative religious freedom, and with a steady flow of *zakat*, the Muslim equivalent of a tithe, Shadian's citizens built mosques and *madrassas* ( Muslim religious schools), giving scholarships to religious students and sending hundreds of Hui on the *hajj* each year to Mecca and Medina. Seeing the potential for Shadian to attract religious tourists from Southeast Asia, due to its particular history, provincial authorities began marketing the town as the "little Mecca of the East."( a long established title they have been struggling in vain to grab from Linxia in Gansu). Bracing for such a borrowed title and reputation, they decorated street signs in Arabic and as in Linxia and Lanzhou which use this symbolic Muslim color for the domes of some of their mosques, they built a green dome on the local administration building's roof. But things changed again in 2014, with yet another swing of the pendulum, when on March 1st of that year, a group of knife-wielding attackers began stabbing passengers at random in the Kunming train station, killing more than thirty and injuring more than a hundred and forty. Police shot four of the attackers at the scene, and three others were later executed; one woman was sentenced to life in prison. They were Uyghurs from the far-western province of Xinjiang, known for its restive separatism and ethnic strife.

When news emerged that the Kunming attackers had spent time in Shadian, droves of Han Chinese began criticizing the town's religious appearance, calling it "China's Islamic State," not necessarily a negative appellation for the Hui. The little Hui town became vilified as an enclave for religious extremism, where too many Muslims were allowed too much freedom. Popular online forums such as Tianya Club and Baidu became filled with Islamophobic vitriol. "Can these yellow-skinned Arabs stop disgusting us Chinese people?" one commentator wrote. "We know that *huaxia*" [the Han ethnicity's ancestral tribe and culture] "is a pile of shit in your hearts. Why are you still here?" As Han chauvinism swept the Chinese Internet, authorities instituted a series of "counter-extremism" policies, tightening at least the image of control over Yunnan's Muslims by planting flags in front of every mosque, painting green roofs white, and requiring all religious students and teachers from outside provinces to go home. Hundreds of Uyghurs were deported to Xinjiang.[20] Thus, government attempts to sooth the skeptical Hui following the Shadian abuses, were now drowned again in a sea of Han hatred towards the Muslims, much as had happened in Xinjiang after the violent events of 2009.[21]

While all of this was happening, Huang, a Muslim convert with a background in geological engineering, a native of Yangzhou prefecture, who had just moved to Shadian with his wife and daughter, explained: "We came for her education." Twenty years ago, he converted to Islam and started an unlicensed magazine devoted to philosophy, culture, and politics. After five years of private publishing and distribution via mosques, *halal* stores, and cultural centers, the magazine became well-known in Muslim circles, including in Xinjiang, which resulted in its being banned. "So I changed the name and stopped distributing there," Huang said with a shrug. His new publication has been circulating for fifteen years. Huang and his wife came to Islam from atheist Han Chinese families. They both had Hui friends who roused their curiosity, prompting them to learn about the religion for themselves. For Huang, spiritual hunger was directly linked to intellectual control, and filling one meant breaking out of the other. The purpose of his magazine, he said, was to awaken his compatriots in spirit and mind. "There is an emptiness in Chinese society," Huang told me over a dinner of spicy fish hotpot. Authoritarianism made people tools of the system, he said, without god or purpose in life, yet probably he was unaware that authoritarianism, and worse, was the norm in nearly all lands of Islam. "Chinese people have been taught slavishness for thousands of years: follow tradition and don't question authority," he said. "Then the Cultural Revolution destroyed tradition. What we have now is authority but no questions, because people don't remember how to ask them." Just as asking questions had led him to faith, he wanted faith to make people start asking questions. "Han

---

20. Ibid.
21. See Israeli, "China's Uyghur Problem," 89–101.

are an ethnicity with no real belief system, just superstitions and worshipping with no idea what or why," he said. "But most Hui have no idea what Islam means, either."[22]

Alice Su recounts the day she visited the Shadian Martyrs' Memorial with Huang, when he proudly took her on a tour of Yufeng Academy, an elementary school founded in the early twentieth century formerly run by the Hui scholar Bai Liangcheng, known for having reformed Hui curricula to include Confucian classics alongside lessons in Arabic and the Qur'ran. "Shadian is a cradle of Chinese Islamic civilization," Huang told her, as they strolled through exhibits honoring the town's prominent Hui people of the recent past: Ma Jian, who had studied at Cairo's Al-Azhar University in the nineteen-thirties, translated the Qur'an into Mandarin, and founded the Arabic department at Peking University; Lin Xingzhi, who performed the *hajj* thirty-eight times and became a diplomatic representative of the Republic of China in Saudi Arabia; and Lin Song, who was once photographed presenting a Chinese Qur'an to Yassir Arafat, Chairman of the PLO. Thus, the Shadian Hui people, while perhaps reminiscent of the Xidaotang in their eagerness to merge Islam with Han culture, not only jealously preserve their distinct Islamic civilization, by fostering Arabic and Qur'anic studies, evidence of which I observed during my field trip to Kunming and Dali in March 2015, but also maintain spiritual links with, and an innate sympathy for other Muslims across the world. Moreover, Chinese Islam was still able to attract Han and minority nationals in China to the faith due to its structured, task-filled religious tenets and sense of a closely knit community found lacking in the mass of new adepts of purposeless Chinese materialism.

Yet Shadian's scars, representing the split personality of the new prosperous and educated Hui, between material well being and spiritual search, were visible as well. A few streets away from the Academy, another respectable Hui bearing the title of Hajji Wang, who was thirty-one when the Shadian Incident unfolded, still reminisced about the trauma of those events. He and his six-year-old son had hidden outside the village, listening to the explosions and screams for seven days straight. "Every house had piles of dead people, some with babies still on their backs,." Now he and his family live in an airy villa with a bubbling fountain in its front garden, the archway over its entrance inscribed with the Arabic phrase *Bismillah ar-Rahman ar-Rahim*—"In the name of God, the most gracious, the most merciful," the coveted opening prayer for any saying or deed by Muslims everywhere. The family's wealth comes from a metals factory they own, and

---

22. Su, "Harmony and Martyrdom."

over the years they've given more than fifteen million dollars to Shadian's mosques and *madrassas*. "The old days were dark as hell," Wang said. "You couldn't think about faith. Class enemies were everywhere. Everyone was lying. Everything was fake. It's different now."[23]

Class enemies? Marxist rhetoric in the midst of opulent capitalism?. But that has been the standard discourse in new China, adopted by political, business and intellectual elites who have quickly adapted to talking unitarian communism, to maintain the one-party system which accepts no challenges, while practicing capitalism to satisfy the unquenched Chinese thirst for material wealth to compensate for both the past economic deprivations and for the present political limitations. In her last night in Shadian, Alice Su spent time with Huang and his neighbor Fu, drinking cup after cup of fermented *pu'er* tea as the Grand Mosque glowed outside Huang's living-room window. When she asked what the recurrent phrase "Islam with Chinese characteristics" meant, Huang pointed to the plaza facing the mosque and retorted: "There's a set of plaques there that says *ai guo ai jiao*—"love your country, love your religion/teaching." All the Hui will dutifully repeat this slogan, he added, but the question is what *ai guo* means. Does loving one's country mean loving its government? Holding it accountable? Asking for justice? If authorities destroyed the Grand Mosque today, would *ai guo* mean resistance? Fu snorted from across the table "Old Huang, you delusional intellectual, if the state wanted to destroy that mosque, they would. You couldn't do anything about it." Fu's father was one of ten Hui representatives who petitioned Beijing for help before the 1975 massacre. He now holds a high position in a local mining company, but has vowed never to go into politics. The Hui of Shadian want exactly what average people all over China want, Fu said—life without interference. That is why Yunnan's Hui didn't resist when the Uyghurs were deported. It didn't affect them, nor did the State's security measures before or after the Kunming station attack. "Politicians made up the idea that Shadian is a terrorist place so they could then say, 'We're so good at counterterrorism,'" Fu said. "Our lives here are exactly the same. The only change is that every politician has given himself a promotion." The single most Chinese characteristic of the Hui is probably that they are realistic, Fu added. "Let's be clear and objective about who we are. We're less than one per cent of the population. We're weaklings. There's a political game going on, and we are not part of it." Huang's response was no less fascinating and conclusive regarding the unresolved question of the Hui in Yunnan and the rest of China "If you want to put it that way, everyone in China is a weakling." Wasn't the difference between Muslims

---

23. Ibid.

and atheists that they had a standard of righteousness? Wouldn't Shadian's people stand up if their holy places were torn down? "Sure, blood would be shed, but so what?" Fu said. "We're a minority. We're drops. We're not going to dye the ocean."[24]

---

24.. Ibid.

Chapter Six

# The Du Wenxiu Heritage, The Burden of the Past

During my field visit to Yunnan in March 2015, in almost every conversation, encounter, interview and occasional exchange with local Hui people, the question of the Du Wenxiu rebellion inevitably arose. For, in spite of the more recently caustic memory of Shadian, the Islamic Kingdom of Du has been of much heavier weight in the consciousness of Yunnanese Muslims, judging by the embarrassment one causes when one raises the issue. Embarrassing because no one can deny that it was calculated to establish a separate Muslim entity in Confucian China, precisely at a time when the Qing Dynasty was harassed by internal dissent and rebellion of the Taiping, the Nien, secret societies in the south, sectarian movements in the north, and other Muslim uprisings in the northwest. To burst into yet another uprising at that time seemed rather a "treacherous" act on the part of the Muslims, who instead of rallying in loyalty and gratitude around their Chinese-Manchu host culture, ganged up against it in order to bring it down.

For the Muslims, those years of the Rebellion (1856–73), though they had offered a temporary glimmer of hope and euphoria, had ended up in a terrible defeat and a massacre of untold proportions, which turned the large Muslim minority, which was self-confident in its future and proud of its roots, into a docile, depressed and down to earth repository of sad realism about its present stature and lack of any prospects for the future, as the Shadian Incident has demonstrated. During my visit to Du's tomb, which I had expected would shine as the mausoleum of an unforgotten past hero, whose site would be the center of pilgrimage and worship, or at least of a somber reverence, I was shocked to find a neglected and dilapidated structure,

# The Du Wenxiu Heritage, The Burden of the Past 143

which had known better days. It was difficult to find the place amidst the wild and unattended growth of weeds, and the local Hui were reluctant to discuss that sad episode which had ended so tragically resulting in reducing the erstwhile prestigious Muslims of Yunnan both in size and stature. Only innocent Hui children who played in the courtyard of the building, when asked who was Du Wenxiu, parroted the answer he "was a Muslim leader who attended and did good to his people." They of course knew nothing of the great saga of the Dali Sultanate which had nearly succeeded in restoring Muslim independence, but also nearly produced the perdition of the Hui people of the province.

Muslim rebellions in China were not uncommon, especially under the rule of the last imperial dynasty, the Qing (1644–1911). However, in China Proper there was only one case recorded of a serious attempt by Muslims to secede from the Middle Kingdom and establish a separate Islamic entity, and that was the *Ping-nan Guo* (Pacifying the south State), founded and headed by Du Wenxiu during the abortive Muslim rebellion of 1856–73. It is true that a roughly contemporaneous attempt was made in Xinjiang, by Yakub Beg, to attain Muslim independence. But the Muslim Uyghurs who raised the banner of rebellion there were not part of the Hui minority, but Turkic speaking Muslims of East Turkestan. It is noteworthy, however, that although the Dali Muslim state attempted to secede and declare its detachment from chaotic China, it still used the traditional *Ping* appellation in its name, with the designation of a specific area of operation within China—*nan* (the south), which usually connoted the control of an area and bringing it to peace and tranquility, namely to subjugate a rebellious zone, or simply to achieve a regulated regime of peace and order. The grounds had been laid in a previous work by this author[1] of the modalities governing the Chinese-Muslim relationships in China which gave rise to the Muslim rebellions in general and to the Muslim desire to secede, when feasible, from the Chinese polity in particular. That work had set the stage for two analytical stages in these relationships, which apply paradigmatically to the Yunnan rebellion:

## Phase I: Uneasy Co-existence

Provides a description of Chinese ill-feelings towards the Muslims, and of the restraining policies of the imperial authorities which soft-pedaled these attitudes and made life under them barely bearable. Chinese Muslim leaders, who were essentially religious figures,

1. Israeli, *Muslims in China*.

namely *Ahungs (imams)*, were strictly parochial headmen catering to the needs of their communities in the religio-culture sphere.

## Phase II: Confrontation and Rebellion

Set in during the late Qing, when official pressures on the Muslim communities generated the escalation of the frictions between Chinese and Muslim, and marked the transition from a confrontation between world views into a head-on violent collision. The Chinese social, political, and economic *milieu* grew more hostile to the Muslims than ever before; in turn, Muslim attitudes and aspirations, both on the communal and individual levels underwent a deep process of change insofar as they became more attuned to an acute sense of the imperative of religio-cultural survival of the group, shooting sky-high in expectations and delusion. As a consequence, the characteristics of the Muslim population shifted from a low profile self-effacing style, into a «community in-arms." Since the purpose of mere individual socio-economic living became insufficient to fill those new needs, the collective will of the community now assumed an assertive clearly distinct self-identity in its environment which necessitated rebellion, and if possible also secession and independence. The ideological underpinnings for this rising unrest were provided by the Islamic revivalism of the nineteenth century in China.[2] Concurrently, charismatic leaders, sometimes seen as a *Mahdi* (the Divinely-Guided One in the Islamic context), appeared on the scene to lead the Muslim Jihad against Chinese oppression. One of these figures was Ma Hualong, whom we have distinguished above as one of the most formidable Muslim leaders in the Northwest during the chaotic mid-nineteenth century unrest that area. Another was Du Wenxiu, the driving engine behind the Yunnan Rebellion, who ephemerally succeeded in establishing and heading a Muslim Sultanate based on Dali.

## Phase III: Statehood and Demise

This phase tells the story of the Islamic polity created by Du within the confines of one province of imperial China, which had itself been wavering under the weight of domestic rebellion and foreign encroachment. Ping-nan Guo was a Muslim state, led by a Muslim who took on the Arabic-Muslim title of "Sultan Suleyman." He was a strange hybrid creature, perhaps unique

---

2. Ma Shouqian, "The Hui People's New Awakening"; See also Israeli, "The Muslim Revival," 119–38.

# The Du Wenxiu Heritage, The Burden of the Past 145

in the annals of both Confucian and Islamic civilizations. The next chapter will attempt to describe the Islamic ideology of that state and the way the Muslim rebels, who attained temporary independence, proposed to put their program into practice. We shall also try to explain how such a state functioned in the real world, and came to grips with the incongruencies inherent in the differences between Confucian institutions, from which it sought to disengage, and the Islamic ones that it aspired to cultivate. How did such a state sustain the allegiance of the traditional Chinese elite of literati, without which it could not govern, and at the same time that it engaged in iconoclastic efforts to depart from the traditional Chinese statecraft to espouse its Islamic counterpart? How did Islamic laws and fiats displace, supplement or supplant Chinese living customs and traditions? What was the nature of the newly-imposed Muslim state administration with its Muslim religious symbols? And finally, why did this 16 year experiment, as did its contemporaneous Chinese counterparts—the Taiping and Nian Uprisings—collapse before it could attain maturity?

The history of the rebellion, as well as the story of the Muslims in Yunnan, have been conclusively described, with an emphasis on the Chinese aspects thereof, in several major works, two of them by Chinese scholars, one in Chinese[3] the other in English[4], and two by American scholars of Chinese extraction: Alice Wei[5] and R. Chu[6]. A few articles on this matter were also published by Japanese scholars[7] and others. These scholars have all usually treated the rebellion as yet another manifestation of the unrest that tore China apart during the latter half of the nineteenth century, threatening to bring the ruling dynasty to an end. For, during those years, the Taiping, the Nien and the Muslim rebellions were rife, but their ultimate elimination by the end of the 1970s signaled what Mary Wright has called the "Indian Summer" of the Manchu dynasty, thus lending salience to the view that regarded all those uprisings as passing episodes in modern Chinese history. However, unlike other Chinese domestic rebellions, which had sought to modify the regime or overturn it, while at the same time growing within a Chinese historical context and manifesting no desire to abandon it or to escape from it, the Muslim uprisings were usually bent, by definition, on parting ways with the traditional system, and in the case of Du's uprising, even clearly seceding from it. Ma Hualong, the messianic leader of the Gansu-Shaanxi

3. Wang Xuhuai, *Xiantong, Yunnan Huimin Shiluan.*
4. Wang Jianping, *Concord and Conflict.*
5. Wan Wei, *The Muslim Rebellion in Yunnan.*
6. Chu, *The Reasons of the Yunnan Rebellion.*
7. E.g. Shiro, "Unnam Kaikyo to no Hamram" 31.

area, made such an attempt but failed, under the overwhelming pressure of Zuo Zongtang's relentless strategy of oppression and merciless military onslaughts which nearly annihilated the rebels. Du Wenxiu, the charismatic head of the Yunnan Rebellion, went even further and established his independent Muslim Sultanate which withstood Chinese pressures and internal dissent for sixteen years before it finally gave in and collapsed, again at a very high price of devastation and human lives.

Viewed from the Muslim vantage point then, the ephemeral *Ping-nan Guo* experience was by no means a passing episode but a link in a long chain within its own logic and dynamics. The Taiping, the Nian and other rebels came and went, but Muslims have been in China for over a millennium and have consistently, albeit not always actively and effectively, and certainly not successfully at all times, sought to disengage from the Chinese polity whenever the occasion arose and socio-economic conditions seemed opportune. Thus, there is merit in illuminating the Yunnan Rebellion in its Muslim context, not as just another heterodox uprising which was ultimately crushed, like all others, by the temporarily revitalized Confucian Empire, but as a Muslim awakening, struggling for secession, which succeeded over a limited period of time; not just another outbreak of Chinese domestic strife generated by socio-economic grievances of a particular ideological faction (like the Taiping) ethnic group (like the Hakka of the south), secret society (like the Triads in the south), sectarian movement (like the White Lotus in the North), or a deprived stratum of society (like the Nian), but as a separatist religio-cultural endeavor, by a group who found no accommodation within the Confucian order[8]; not as a temporary unrest characteristic of dynastic decline, but as a chronic problem which constantly brewed under the surface and at times erupted into violence.

Before we delve into the nature of the Islamic state in question, and into the character of the men who generated and were its leaders, a brief outline of the rebellion will be in order. What is called the "Yunnan Uprising" consisted in fact of two separate, though inter-related uprisings: one in the eastern part of the province, centered around the provincial Capital of Kunming (then Yunnan-fu), the other having its focus in the prefectural city of Dali in the Western part. What lent to these revolts the appearance of being part of a wider Islamic movement inexorably aiming at Islamizing all of China, as some western observers suspected at the time[9], was not only the simultaneous outbreak of the two uprisings in the same province of Yunnan, but also the contemporaneous unrest of Muslims in Gansu-Shaanxi

---

8. See Israeli, "The Incompatibility," 296–323.
9. See Vasilev, "Mohammedanism in China," 4.

and then Xinjiang. There is no denying that those scattered Muslim rebellions fed upon one another and may have been encouraged by the vision of a unified Muslim empire extending from Turkestan to the heartland of the Middle Kingdom. However, judging from the early surrender of the eastern part of the Yunnan rebellion on the one hand, and the adamant stand adopted by Du's revolt in the west on the other, there is no escaping the conclusion that the latter, who installed himself as the Sultan in Dali, must have been motivated by different impulses and visions, than Ma Rulong, the turncoat leader of the east, who soon turned to the Imperial authorities and even assisted them in repressing co religionists of the Dali Sultanate.

The Muslims of the eastern part of the province, more particularly those of Lin-an (south of Kunming) and Chu-xiong (half way between Kunming and Dali, were involved in the first anti-Chinese riots in the silver mines of Shi-yang. Ma Rulong, their leader laid siege to Yunnanfu, the provincial capital and was involved in mass killings of Han Chinese in early 1857. At the same time, Du Wenxiu declared his independent kingdom in Dali, but Muslims of northern and eastern Yunnan, including Ma Rulong and his troops, did not accept his claim to overall leadership and authority over Yunnanese Muslims. Ma Rulong soon crossed over to the imperial side in 1862, after his grievances, which were more material than ideological, were apparently satisfied. But it took another decade of bloodshed before the ravaged province of Yunnan could be brought back into the fold of the Empire. Du Wenxiu, while struggling to establish peace and order ( ping)- "pacification") in his Sultanate, had in addition to cultivate and project a Muslim image to his coreligionists in the province and in China at large in order to expand his potential constituency. In other words, while Ma's message was parochial, Du's was universal. Moreover, he attempted to lend legitimacy to his polity by seeking international recognition of the great powers of those days, Great Britain and the Ottoman Empire, something his rival Ma did not even envisage.

Arabic script documents are scarce, but Chinese sources written by Chinese Muslims or about them are abundant, some of them we have already reviewed above:

1. *The Hui Min Qiyi* (The Righteous Uprisings of the Hui People) is by far the most comprehensive collection of Chinese documents and other materials relating to the Muslim rebellions in China. Even though the collection covers only four uprisings which unfolded within a period of 25 years (1854–78), it provides a large variety of records, bound in four volumes, amounting to 2,000 pages of Chinese characters. The first two volumes pertain to the Yunnan Rebellion (1856–73), an indication

of its importance to the Chinese authorities due to its secessionist ambitions, except for one item containing materials on the Guizhou uprising (1854–73). The other two volumes cover the Guizhou, Gansu, and Xinjiang uprisings (1854–78). Besides reprints of well-known materials, such as excerpts from local gazetteers providing accounts of local campaigns, and selections from published papers and articles of imperial officials, the collection abounds in other less known materials, such as records engraved on stones, and a few documents from Muslim sources. The latter are of particular interest because they state the Muslim viewpoint, in contrast to the Chinese as reflected in official edicts and memoranda, and other imperial documents. The Muslim documents also contain very important information on the Muslim state organization of the Dali sultanate, in the course of the rebellion. These documents include lists of officials, laws and regulations, public statements, political decrees etc. Other important Muslim materials are reports written subsequent to the events either by eye witnesses, occasional travelers in the region, or by biographers of important figures in the rebellions.

2. This collection, though edited under the Communist regime by an eminent Chinese Muslim historian, Bai Shouyi, has many shortcomings stemming mainly from the editor's Marxist bias. In fact, Communist historiography has consistently considered rebellions under the imperial regime (Taiping, Muslims and the Boxers) as "class struggles" between peasants and the landlord ruling class. The editor had, accordingly, interpreted Muslim rebellions as a form of class struggle among the Chinese people. Moreover, being committed to taking the rebels' side, he may have excluded from his selective collection significant materials bearing evidence contrary to his viewpoint, or added apologetic introductory notes to documents that seemed to prove the imperial government's case. Therefore, the editor, despite his reputation as an historian and expert on Muslim affairs, cannot claim objectivity either in his choice of materials or in his judgments when he chose to include certain materials. The very title *The Rightful Muslim Uprisings* implies an obvious bias in this regard. As a whole, however, the HMQI (as they will be cited hereafter), if read with care, provide much valuable information not only about the Muslim rebellions in 19th Century China, but also about the Muslim community in China at large.

3. *Pingding Yunnan Huifei Fanglueh* (a Strategy for the Pacification of Muslim Bandits in Yunnan), is a five-volume collection of government

documents on the suppression of the Muslim rebellions in Yunnan. One fifth of this collection was included in HMQI (vol I) whose editor admits that omissions of some government documents from his collection were based on his subjective judgment. The lacunae in this collection, which were inevitable due to its official nature, are in part filled by another collection:

4. *Records of Yunnan Muslims*, compiled by Ma Shengfeng, a Hui native of Yunnan (1874–1935) who, through the Yunnan Muslim Advancement Association, collected materials, and especially from elders who told the compiler that they knew, saw and recorded information of the Yunnan Rebellion. Many of those stories were reprinted in HMQI; some of them are of great importance, such as a memoir written by a Muslim who was a close associate of Ma Rulong, one of the rebel leaders.

Many Chinese Muslim materials are known by their titles only, through different compilations by westerners. The most comprehensive bibliography of this sort was compiled by Claude Pickens, a missionary who spent a lifetime working among Chinese Muslims. Other compilations and field reports include Captain d'Ollone's mission to China, notably Yunnan, missionary studies over the 1920s, 1930s and 1940s by the legendary figures such as Rev. Ogilvie, who listed some 94 books, magazines and publications in Chinese, and Rev. Mason who listed more than 300 titles, many of them tracts and journals during the Republican era (1912–49).

Other than those Chinese-Muslim sources, and Chinese official accounts of the rebellion that are extensively cited by the first two collections mentioned above, there is a wealth of documentation generated by Muslim sources. Western powers, especially the British and the French, who took special interest in Yunnan due to its proximity to their colonies in Burma and Vietnam respectively, also contributed to our knowledge of that province through surveys, travelogues, missionary, geographic and geological reports. Although most of these reports were for the most part compiled after the uprising, the memories were still fresh for the elderly who could reminisce and have their statements collected and published, in spite of the inevitable occasional failure of memory in such horrific circumstances. Other western documents include the abortive attempts made by Du's temporary government to elicit recognition and support from the outside.

Chapter Seven

# A Muslim Sultanate in Confucian China

The Muslim Sultanate of Du Wenxiu in Dali, although a far cry from the more ancient Nanchao Kingdom, nonetheless rested on the same foundations of an independent political entity in that very same area. The Muslims in Yunnan of the 19th Century were so numerous and their standing in the province so reputable that they seemingly were secure and had nothing to fear. Nonetheless, there was a series of clashes between them and the predominant Han which can help explain the events that led to Du's rebellion, when all his and his compatriot-religionists' complaints to Beijing were to no avail. Therefore, his fateful decision to rebel was not only the result of his evaluation of the chaotic state of eclipse of the Dynasty during his visits to the Capital, but also due to what he may have viewed as the unbearable harassment of the Hui in his province, which left them no choice but to rise and secede. In a series of monographic reports from various parts of Yunnan about these clashes, very plausible illustrations were recounted that led to the great rebellion:

1. In 1839, almost two decades before the outbreak of the rebellion, a dispute over land between Han and Hui escalated into violence and mutual killing. It was reported that Zhang Jingyi, a local corrupt official who took bribes, decided in favor of the Han, who launched an onslaught on the Hui in Mengmianting, killing hundreds of them (disputed estimates ran between 700 and 1700). Furthermore, as many Han officials in office bore resentment against the Hui, they did nothing to rescue them from the massacre. Ultimately, the Qing Dynasty

acted against Qu Tingyuan, who led the massacre, and executed him, but tempers remained inflamed.[1]

2. Since 1840 in the Yongchang area of the Baoshan County, Shen Ying, an "evil gentry" as reported by the Muslims, used to bully the Hui with his underlings. In April 1845, at Banqiao, east of the city, another clash broke out between Han and Hui, because the latter used to sing while transplanting rice seedlings in their rice paddies. Shen Ying took the opportunity to expel the Hui, and in May, when a Shaanxi Muslim, Ma Da, was teaching 31 people martial arts at the Banqiao mosque, he was arrested while other Muslims escaped. Qing officials destroyed the mosque and burned more than ten Hui villages just outside the city. So the Hui went to other cities, like Shunning, Menghua and Yunzhou, gathered hundreds of Hui people and launched an uprising. On May 25th, they attacked the Jinji village, the home of Shen Ying, but failed. They retreated to Mengtingzhai village where they built forts and recruited 1,000 Hui for its defense. The Hui troops attacked the Lianhuasi Temple at Dongshan, then killed a Qing general in the prefecture. On September 2, Qing troops searched and killed 8,000 Hui people inside and outside the city and burned all the mosques and the Hui villages in the prefecture. After the Hui failed to conquer Jinji, they retreated suffering some 3-4 hundred casualties, but they pursued their struggle under the leadership of Huang Baba. Then, Du Wenxiu, Liu Yi, Ding Canting and Mu Wenke successively travelled to Beijing to state their grievances. Thereupon, in 1847, Lin Zexu, the famous Qing hero who battled the British during the Opium War in 1839-40 but was later banned due to his failure, who was now the Governor General of Yunnan and Guizhou, was dispatched to deal with the Han-Hui conflict. He ordered the arrest of 430 people, apparently most of them Han, and meted out varying degrees of punishment, including execution, mandatory military service, and banishment, much to the pleasant surprise of the Hui defendants.[2]

3. In connection with the persecution of the Hui in Yongchang in 1845 as cited above, where many Hui people were attacked without provocation, Du Wenxiu went with others to Beijing to complain, resulting in the Emperor Dao Guang dispatching Lin Zexu in 1847 to investigate the issue about which it was reported that in 1848, 178 Hui notables complained on behalf of the Hui victims in Baoshan. Lin Zexu had already made his way to Yixi, to control Qishao and his group, which

1. Wenzhiao entry, *Zhongguo Huidzu, Dazidian*, 158.
2. *Zhongguo Hui-zu da zidian*, 158-59.

had bullied the Hui. But then, when the Hui complaint arrived at the Governor's office in Dali, one of his officials decided to outdo the document by forging another "complaint," written in blood on a sheet of white silk, with all the names of the signatories of the original one, but in terms critical of the Qing Dynasty. Without questioning its veracity, Lin immediately ordered the arrest of the Hui notables who had allegedly signed it, resulting in the banishment of 100 and the execution of another 76 of them. This blatant act of injustice was cited as the direct cause of Du Wenxiu's rebellion.[3]

4. Again in connection with the Yongchang massacre, and the complaint by Du and his Hui colleagues, accompanied by some members of the families of the victims, the entourage arrived at the Emperor Dao Guang in Beijing, approached the Court in two successive groups, and succeeded in having the Emperor order Lin Zexu to conduct a thorough investigation, however the Hui of Yunnan were understandably disappointed by the final outcome which resulted against them. Thereafter, when Du was in Dali on a business trip and in the neighborhood, he contacted some Hui notables of integrity, organized them into secret groups and started to ponder the possibility of an uprising against the Dynasty in view of the terrible Han-Hui conflicts that he witnessed and was unable to redress in spite of his vigorous attempts.[4]

5. Another outrageous incident against the Hui exploded in 1850, still under the Dao Guang Emperor, when the "gold rush" near Talang (Mojiang today) yielded lucrative remuneration to its exploiters, accompanied by some villainous trouble makers who instituted gambling, robbing and other criminal activities, as is customary in lawless areas where making quick profits became more important than human lives and human relations. Thus, during gambling between two Hui businessmen and others, when the loser refused to pay the winner 100 gold taels, fighting ensued, and a local gentry took over the mine to restore order. Hui businessmen presented a petition to the local government in Talang asking for the permanent official presence in the mine to deter trouble makers, and the petition was forwarded to higher authorities. On September 10th, the bullies murdered 100 people, including the Hui businessmen involved. The higher authorities ordered the local government to quell the disturbances, but the latter dragged their feet, arguing that they lacked enough troops to crush the trouble-makers. The Hui who were victims of the disturbances kept

3. Ibid., 159.
4. Ibid., 159.

complaining, but beyond dismissing the local officials and prosecuting them, the authorities failed to seize the mine from the criminal element.[5]

6. Following the "Gold rush" came the "Silver rush" in the mines of Shiyangchang (Shuangbai today) in 1853. Both Hui and Han businessmen were flocking there to mine silver. In March, when two Hui Ma brothers were attempting to purchase a mine from the Jiangxi Han owner, blows were exchanged, and the two brothers were asked to pay for medical treatment of the injured Han, but they refused. They also rejected a plea by a local gentry to compensate another Han mine owner for equipment they had taken. The two injured Han then plotted their revenge, organizing with the bandits who had butchered the Hui in 1850 at the Talang gold mine. Hundreds were organized who converged on the silver mine yelling : "Kill the Hui people!" Fighting ensued between the parties on March 28th, when 180 Hui people were massacred, mosques and Hui villages were burned, and tens of thousands of silver taels of public and private silver were looted from the mine. The authorities of the province gathered a militia and tried suppressing the culprit brigands. Thus Ma Xueyu, from the Hui village Huilong, gathered more than 150 Hui and led them to attack Shiyangchang via two different routes, killing 300 Han from Linan. On July 20th, official Pan gathered 1,000 men and set out to take revenge on the Hui, which caused both Hui and Han civilians to run for their lives, resulting in the loss of Shiyangchang by the Hui. Then Cui Shaozhong, a Hui, went to Huilong village and asked help from Ma Rulong, a practitioner of martial arts, who was to become a major actor in the Yunnan rebellion. Thereupon Ma Ruling gathered 800 Hui and Han people, who conquered Shiyangchang in December, defeated Pan De and his gang, inflicting 3–4 hundred casualties. It would be Pan De who in 1855 would lead the bandits to kill the Hui people in Ejia, and in 1856 in Chuxiong. Thus, the silver mines were repeatedly targeted by both sides, escalating tensions between Han and Hui.[6]

7. The Ma Long Incident of 1855 happened after the sliver mine dispute had occasioned the death of 1,000 Hui from 300 different families. In April of that year, the silver mine was again attacked at Malong, resulting in the death of 100 Hui, led my Ma Yunzhen and Ma Ming.[7]

5. Ibid., 159–60.
6. Ibid., 160.
7. Ibid.

8. Another major incident unfolded a year later in April 1856, when Ma Lingshan, a provincial level notable entered Kunming, at the head of 1,000 Hui and took a position in the Shunchengjie Mosque in order to protect the Hui of the city from the threats of the Han in Linan. But the Governor, Shu Xingge, took that measure as a rebellion, therefore ordering all the local governments in the province to recruit enough troops to kill Hui people in a circumference of 400 kms around the city. Thus, between April 16-18,th Han people, including soldiers and officers, militiamen and civilians, butchered some 20,000 Hui in Kunming, with only a few succeeding in escaping the violence.. The constant escalation in the killing of Hui led to Du Wenxiu's uprising in West Yunnan.[8]

This string of serious incidents in itself attests to the fact it was not only the constant Muslim unrest in China, nor the condition of chaos throughout the Empire which triggered the major Muslim rebellion in Yunnan. Add to that the efforts made by Du Wenxiu and others to calm the mood by first petitioning the Court in Beijing, before he rose against it, shows that the pre-revolutionary ambience in the province had been a response to the mounting unbearably high numbers of butchered Muslims on each occasion, as officials of the Kingdom evinced neither the capacity nor willingness to put their realm in order, while gangs of bandits and disorganized militia enjoyed free reign to do as they wished, leaving the victims without protection from the authorities. Thus, realizing that in the present chaos every group had to fend for itself if it wished to survive, Du and his colleagues must have arrived at the conclusion there was no other option but rebellion and secession from the Empire. In short, it was not only a matter of "quarrels over the mines," or the historical residues of the long Han-Hui confrontation in the province which mattered, but for the Hui minority it came to the primary essentials of securing life and survival for themselves. In view of the long series of confrontations in which the Hui were usually the main victims, it stands to reason that Du and other Hui leaders had realized that while avoiding direct clashes with the overwhelming Han would be a more promising avenue of co-habitation, with the constant disorder, the rule of criminal gangs, and the helplessness of the official government to control events converging together, the Hui saw no other avenue to safeguard their existence and launched the rebellion. Therefore, rather than seeing the Muslim uprising, like its Gansu contemporaneous counterpart, as an attempt to claim their separate identity, exploiting the chaotic circumstances in the Empire to their benefit, maybe we should regard that entire venture as a

8. Ibid.

desperate measure of self-defense, the only one that was considered feasible, and bearing some chances of success, at least until order was re-established and an effective central government was re-installed.

A description of the outburst of the open Hui uprising in Yunnan may corroborate these preliminary impressions. We are talking about the reign of the Dao Guang (1820–50) and the Xian Feng (1850–61) Emperors, in whose time the West had interfered militarily in the Opium War, and thereafter (from 1839 on), local uprisings (Taiping, Hui, Nian and others) tore the Empire apart. It was not until the Tongzhi Restoration (1861–75) that a similitude of order and of renewed imperial authority was re installed, as all rebellions were crushed («pacified» in euphemized terms), including the Yunnan one. It is remarkable that together with the Muslim symbols Du tried to uphold in order to attract his constituency, he himself dubbed his Dali Sultanate "Ping-nan Guo" = Pacify the Southern State, exactly as to fit within the imperial design of pacifying its rebellious south. For Du Wenxiu, his Muslim Sultanate was not the "south" of anything except the Chinese Empire which the Emperor also, and his officialdom, wished to pacify. His appeal, then, was more Chinese than Muslim, and his entire endeavor as the charismatic leader of his rebelling fief was to juggle between his ostensibly Muslim rebellion (otherwise he had no reason to rebel) and the Chinese ties that linked him to the central rule and to the Han part of the population of his Sultanate.

This source[9] acknowledged that the rebellion was influenced by the Taiping, probably not in the sense of overturning the regime in all of China and replacing it by the new egalitarian Heavenly Kingdom with proto-Christian coloring, nor in the sense of the utopian society that Hong Xiuquan had in mind if he had succeeded in his social revolution. Du Wenxiu's urgent need, as we have seen, was to survive and to secede from the Empire, in order to enable him to erect an alternative Muslim society, the sole idea that could appeal to his Muslim constituents. He probably calculated that if the Taiping were successful, it would be easier for him, as for others, to abandon the Imperial Unitarian strict centralism and to engage on a new path. He could not know, of course, that in the Indian Summer the Empire would experience under the Tongzhi Restoration, the reinvigoration of the Emperor and the officialdom, headed by such great men as Zuo Zongtang and Ceng Guofan, and that the central power would rally and crush all rebellions, beginning with the Taiping, one after the other, including the Muslim uprisings in the Northwest and Southwest.

9. Ibid., 161.

At the outset, rather than a major effort by the rebels in a certain part of the province, several local Muslim uprisings broke out in several locations simultaneously:

1. Between the Spring and the Summer of 1856, Ma Jinbao and Lan Pinggui staged an uprising in Yaozhou (Yaoan today);
2. Du Wenxiu led another rebellion in Menghua (Weishan today);
3. Ma Linghan mounted another in Kunyang;
4. Ma Rulong in Jianshui;
5. Ma Fuchu in Xingxing (Yuxi today); and
6. Xu Yuanji in Chengjiang.

These were the main outbursts of Muslim violence in the province, accompanied by attempts to take advantage of the chaotic situation and gain some degree of defensive self-rule, only one of which, headed by Du, would gain prominence and get close to realizing some concrete goal. The others, which were less successful and ended less dramatically than Du's saga, where he was seized and beheaded, and therefore could be counted as a martyr by his followers, and has an established patrimony and a tomb to bear witness to its veracity, were doomed to oblivion. This is much like the battles in China between the many contenders for rule in the *inter-regnum* between dynasties, and only the successful among them became founders of new dynasties, while the others are relegated to the status of rebel- bandits, like a Li Zicheng in the transition between Ming and Qing (1644).

Most of the insurrectionary armies were composed of Hui people, but other ethnic groups were also recruited, some Han, Yi, Bai, Dai, Naxi Hani, Lisu and others, all members of disaffected groups who felt abandoned to their fate in the midst of the overwhelming chaotic situation at the center, and the corrupt and ineffective bureaucracy around the periphery. By the nature of things, the recruits were artisans, peasants, miners and small traders who had nothing to lose in view of the takeover of trade, and economic life in the province by the gangs of bandits with no government in control. Due to the unity of purpose of the rebels on the one hand, and the inherent benefit of joining forces into a more formidable army corps on the other, those six different throngs gradually merged into two main forces, which would henceforth constitute the main actors in the uprising: the West Yunnan group was led by Du Wenxiu, and the southeastern Yunnan headed by Ma Rulong and Ma Fuchu, who were based in Xingxing and Guanyi. Ma Rulong, who thought of himself as a great general and aspired to the conquest of the Capital Kunming (at the time Yunnan-fu), and laid siege to it on three occasions in 1857, 1860 and 1861. Apparently, however, when he realized the futility of his endeavor, in view of the imperial armies that were converging against him, he changed direction, rallying to help suppress the uprisings in his area, thus earning the derogatory title of a "turncoat" in the eyes of many Hui people, who had at first been hopeful about Muslim autonomy.

Conversely, Du Wenxiu in 1856 conquered Xiaguan in August and Dali in September, where he established a government manned by his military and civilian officials, also encompassing representatives from other ethnic groups. Du was then aware of the Taiping successes and was intent in joining forces with them in their revolt against the Qing Dynasty. Therefore, he announced a series of new policies:

a. His kingdom considered all the ethnic groups equal and it was strictly forbidden for one group to abuse the others. That was probably his reaction to the years of suppression and persecution by the Han against the Hui and other ethnic groups; but it was also a kind of rebellion against the hierarchical bureaucratic system that was dominated by the Han. He wanted his administration to be a coalition of minorities, given that none of them was numerous enough to dominate the scene demographically;

b. He decreed that people wear their natural long hair, and ignore the Manchu mandatory fashion of wearing a pigtail by the Han Chinese, which was seen as a sign of suppression;

c. Nonetheless, not to cut himself totally from the Han-Chinese patrimony, he also put Han Chinese in important positions in his administration;

d. He also pledged to develop the economy in order to make amends for the years of destitution and impoverishment caused by chaos and banditry, and to rehabilitate people's livelihoods;

e. He promised to resettle the many refugees who were flocking to him from other parts of Yunnan, some from other adjoining provinces which were torn by war, insecurity, deprivation and banditry;

f. He revived the old water conservation projects which had fallen into disrepair during the war and chaos, harking back to Seyyid Edjell, the first Muslim governor under the Mongol Yuan, who was also credited with the construction of the large irrigation plants of the province. These plans were, naturally connected with the rehabilitation of the devastated agriculture, which had always been the main source of wealth of that rich and fertile province.

g. To encourage trade and cottage industries, which had thrived there before the destructive 19th Century, much of which had been in the hands of the enterprising Hui . By contributing to economic activity and boosting the people's livelihood, he wished to alleviate the burden of the people enabling them to become a more prosperous and loyal citizenry;

h. One of the reforms he promised was to abrogate certain exorbitant taxes and levies which had been imposed during the waning years of the dynasty, which due to the need for more income to ensure security, given the abandoned and ravaged lands, the peasants were unable to pay.

Exactly like the Taiping who did not have the chance to put to the test their ambitious program within the decade and some years of their rule, so did Du's promising plans go unfulfilled after the decade-long existence of his Sultanate came to its end. But while he was struggling to build his kingdom, he accomplished some quite remarkable achievements:

1. Du's troops defeated repeatedly the Qing army onslaughts;
2. His administration came to encompass in its heyday some 53 counties;
3. In 1867 he sent 200,000 troops led by Cai Tingdong and other 18 senior officers to also attack Kunming from the East. They conquered several villages and forts along the way and laid siege to Kunming in October from the South, the West and the North.

Du Wenxiu was a native of Jinji Village in the Baoshan county, in a family of businessmen. In his youth he studied poetry and at the young age of 14 he was allocated the scholarly title of *Xiucai* under the Qing examination system at the county level. At 16 he became a recognized scholar who earned some government grants, but he concurrently also studied Islamic texts, hence his mastery and emotional attachment to both cultures, something that he would demonstrate in his adulthood in his attempts to avoid revolting against his Chinese gentry status, or bringing his Muslim creed to collide with his Chinese upbringing. In 1845, some local Han leaders in Baoshang incited killing the Hui. In September more than 8,000 Hui people from 1,300 families were slaughtered around Yongchang, and Du had to escape for his life to Zhaozhou, southeast of Dali. In 1847 Du went to Beijing, together with Liu Yi, to complain, as a result of which Governor General Lin Zexu ordered an investigation as mentioned above. Apparently, in order to maintain the appearance of a balanced view, the General duly prosecuted hundreds of trouble-making bandits, but also suppressed the Hui's attempts at self-defense. So much so that in 1851-5, when both the gold mine of Talang and the silver mine of Shiyangchang, which had been exploited by Hui, were taken over by Han bandits, who also set fire to Hui villages, Du Wenxiu staged his uprising in August 1856 in Menghua (Weishan today).[10]

Interestingly enough, this source claims that Du's intention was to combine Han and Hui together so as to remake China, erasing all evil, where common people would be relieved from the misery of their daily lives. He was also reported to have responded to the Taiping call to join in launching a revolution against the Qing, reject the imposed Manchu hair style which symbolized the submission of the Han to the foreign dynasty, and adopt the Chinese calendar of the Heavenly Stems and Earthly branches, instead of the current dynastic calendar which counted time according to the year the incumbent Emperor came to power. After he defeated the Imperial armies and conquered his kingdom, he collaborated with Ma Rulong in August 1860 to wipe out the Qing troops in the province, and occupy Chuxiong. In June 1861 they also conquered Yongchang and more than 20 towns in western Yunnan. In 1862 their troops conquered more territory, including Weiyuan. In 1865 the Qing forces counter-attacked but were defeated in November. In 1866, Du's forces also defeated Ma Rulong's troops who had surrendered to the Qing in Dayao. In November, 1867, when Du ordered his soldiers to redeploy, he dispatched his grand expedition of 200,000 against Kunming, the provincial capital, but when they failed, they retreated to Yixi. In October, 1872, with Qing forces at the gates of Dali, Du ordered a last stand against them, but succumbed to their overwhelming superiority. He convened his people and declared his readiness to sacrifice himself in order to save the lives of his followers. He took his poisoned potion and delivered himself to the Qing camp in Wuliqiao, where his head was cut off.

On the next day, Qing troops occupied Dali and Du's saga ended with his execution as a rebel-bandit, who dared to rise against a ruling dynasty. Therefore, he was condemned in Chinese history as an evil trouble maker, in spite of his genuine efforts to rescue his Hui people from suppression and elimination. His patrimony remains mixed to this day among the Muslim population of Yunnan: a hero for some, due to his courage and sacrifice in trying to obtain for his persecuted people a path to an honourable existence; a fool-hardy for some, due to his arrogance and presumption in trying to rise against the mighty Chinese dynasty which has never forgiven anyone who challenged its traditional order, at the price of a massacre that has cut in half the Muslim population in the province of several million, and occasioned a humiliation and loss of dignity and pride which used to characterize the

---

10. Dictionary of the Hui People, 285-86.

Hui population in the entire Chinese Midwest. Du's uprising lasted, some 16 years and succeeded in uniting various ethnic minority groups, while rehabilitating water conservation projects, opening up virgin soil for cultivation, introducing the cultivation of cotton and improving farming techniques, abrogating exorbitant levies and taxes, and making people's lives more easily bearable. All of which was expressed in the determination of the populace to resist the Qing forces against all odds. Therefore, among various ethnic groups of Yunnan, he is remembered with respect and awe, regardless of how the authorities consider him.[11]

Conversely, the other major figure of the Yunnan Hui Rebellion, Ma Rulong, also known as Maxian, was the mirror image of Du Wenxiu, is much more controversial and difficult to evaluate in any conclusive fashion[12]. For, he began like Du as a conscientious Hui leader who cared for his people, but then reversed course as a turncoat General in the service of the dynasty which massacred his people. It is easy today to accuse him of a cynical approach in which his personal benefit and status mattered to him, as a coward who facing the overwhelming power of the Dynasty elected to choose the winning side, or as a wise leader who preferred to submit to the mighty Qing than to condemn his helpless Hui people to total elimination had he chosen to fight to the finish. He was also said to have addressed the troops under his command and argued with them in favor of pacification, on the merit of the "long history of good relations between Muslims and Chinese, thanks to which the Hui had achieved Muslim integration socially and politically," and tried to convince Du to follow suit.[13] But it is difficult not to look at his career with awe and respect. He was born at Huilong Village in the province, to a poor family, but nevertheless passed the examination and won the *Xiucai* title. In 1853, when the Hui silver mine in Shiyangchang was taken over by bandits, he led a contingent of 800 Hui people to defeat the gangsters from Linan, and also staged an uprising in Jianshui. Later, in collaboration with others, Ma Ruling organized a large army corps in 13 different camps and took the bombastic title of "generalissimo," leading the Hui uprising in Yinan. In April, 1856 he occupied most of the towns in the LInan and Chengjiang prefectures, and in 1857 he launched his aborted attack on Kunming. In February, 1862 he led his army to Xinxing and Guangtong, and in August, in cooperation with the Hui insurrectionary army in Dali, he defeated the Qing troops once again.

11. Ibid., 161.

12. HMQI, II, 358–66, there are details of Ma Rulong's and of his subordinate Ma Futu, who remained loyal to him to the end.

13. Ibid.

The shift in Ma's fortunes began in October, 1861 when he attacked Kunming for the second time, but failed and retreated again. In November he tried for the third time, but in February 1862, when he was summoned by the Qing Inspector General in the province, Xu Zhiming, to surrender, he returned to the rule of the Dynasty all the territory he had occupied, and was appointed in return as the Commanding General of Linyuanzhen and given charge of "pacification affairs," namely the ferocious wolf was made a docile lamb, hardly an explainable turn about for such a warrior with such a warring record. Thereupon, he dispatched his deputy, Yang Zhenpeng, to Dali, to urge Du Wenxiu to follow his example and surrender, but Du was resolute rejecting any such deal. In February, 1863 Ma Rong, one of Ma Rulong's subordinates, secretly contacted the Dali insurrectionary army, broke into the city and killed a local governor, without his master's permission or knowledge. Ma Rulong, who was in the meantime promoted to Provincial Commander-in-Chief, rushed to quell that manifestation of indiscipline, and ultimately executed the culprit in Kunming in 1864. After Du's troops laid their abortive siege to Kunming in 1868, Ma Rulong's forces held fast in its defense until March 1869 when the siege collapsed. In January 1874 Ma was appointed Provincial Commander-in Chief in Hunan, and traveled to Beijing by order of the Emperor. He died later in Sichuan from his old wounds.

But in February 1868, the pendulum swung the other way, as Commissionner Cen who fought for the Qing, in conjunction with Ma Rulong who had switched to the government side, thwarted Du's offensive. Cen counter-attacked, while Du's two illustrious commanders, Li Yuanfang and Ma Xingtang were killed, generating the withdrawal of Du's forces, and the quick advance of the Qing soldiers occupying much of the territory previously included in the Sultanate. In 1872 the Imperial troops laid siege to Dali the capital, thus crushing all the insurrections in the Southeast. Besieged Dali soon ran out of ammunition and supplies, and without any hope for help from the outside, Du's rebellion was doomed. In November Dali fell. Li Guolun, a senior leader in Du's government led the rest of the loyal troops in defense of Tengyue (today Tenchong), but the overwhelming superiority of the Qing troops left him no chance.[14] When Ma Rulong rejected the plea by one of Du Wenxiu's subordinates to surrender, as Du laid siege on Kunming, he then declared his loyalty to the Manchu troops, and warned that their intention to protect the Muslims would turn against them, and that the Muslim rebellion in Yunnan would bring suffering on the Muslims in all 18 provinces of China. He also expressed his disappointment with

14. Ibid., 285.

the Muslim leaders of East and South Yunnan, who appealed for help from West Yunnan when the area was strong, but turned eastwards when the West weakened. Thus, he presented himself as the real fighter and savior of the Muslims, their reputation and their descendants. Unlike others who regarded him as a turncoat at the time, he praised himself for his loyalty to the Dynasty, to his ancestors and to the commitment to avoid calamity to the entire community by remaining the «pillar of the golden path." Thus he encouraged the rebellious West to surrender as long as the proffered conditions were favorable, for his religion was identical to that of West Yunnan.[15]

According to Wang Xuhuai, the complicated relationship between Du (the hero of the time) and Ma (the turncoat of the time), should be divided into three separate periods:

1856-60—In that early period, the two had a close relationship, which began when they both studied the Muslim classics under Ma Dexin. In 1856, when separate Muslim unrest broke out at many locations, it was widespread and uncoordinated due to the bad communications between various areas. But in 1860 the Provincial Tartar General attacked Du's armies and threw the area of Dali into turmoil. Then Du appointed Ma to attack Zhu Xiong in order to cut the Manchu route to its inland area, and defeated him. That was the first occasion the two collaborated in battle, and Ma proved of great help to Du.

1860-2—Despite that earlier period of military collaboration, the relationship between the two failed to go deeper, and their respective forces seemed to stand separately from each other. In 1860 Ma left Zhuxiong and headed eastward, alternately fighting and negotiating with the Qing army. Moreover, he included Dali under his governance and took on the title of "generalissimo" which clashed with, and challenged the authority of Du himself. But, when in 1861 Ma besieged the capital of Kunming, he asked for Du's help, Du declined, much to his old ally's dismay. That signaled their final break and the open competition for leadership between them, which led to Ma's surrender to the Qing in 1862. That seemed to him his best option since Du would not contemplate a submission to the Dynasty and Ma himself was reluctant to subordinate himself to his opponents if he should join forces with him. So, the high rank and remuneration he gained from the Qing satisfied him and satiated his aspirations.

1862-73—From Ma's appeal to surrender, their relationship was in crisis. So, though his capitulation to the Qing was managed behind the scene by Ma Dexin, it ended up to be beneficial for Ma Rulong, due to the support he enjoyed from the highly reputed Ma Dexin. Then, due to the high rank

---

15. HMQI, Vol III, 148.

bestowed on him by the Dynasty, he would have been able to subjugate Du, had the latter also survived via negotiation and surrender, and not perished due to his stubborn rebelliousness.[16]

In the aftermath of the uprising, for four entire days, a massive, unrestricted massacre of the Hui in Kunming and its environment exploded as a wave of anger and vengeance on the part of the Han, for all the years of rebellion, unrest, tension, friction, hatred and compressed restraint that Muslim subversion had generated in the province, came into the open, leaving a scene of cruel butchering that considerably thinned the Muslim presence in the province on the one hand, and left an unforgettable sobering reminder among the Muslim community, as to where a rejection of the present order in China, or the revolt against their minority status in the midst of the overwhelming Han majority, can lead. No event or talk with Chinese Muslims anywhere in China can avoid mentioning or hinting at that mammoth tragedy and its lingering effect. The Hui, who by all accounts used to be dubbed as "arrogant," and "self-confident," sensing that they were the masters of that "Muslim country" in which they were in essence a minority, have definitely lowered their heads, in resignation if not in submission, and withdrew into their little enclaves of Islam where they continue to voice their bitterness silently and also to find solace there. Their occasional outbursts of resentment, when they talk among themselves, or when they feel safe confiding to foreigners their concerns, are but a meek echo of the turbulence and humiliation that is still brewing within, and for good reason.

It is however necessary to underline that the butchering of the Hui in Yunnan following the aborted rebellion, which led to a massive exodus of some of the survivors to neighboring Thailand, where a vibrant Chinese Muslim community still exists in the northern city of Chiang Mai, did not unfold everywhere in the same fashion. For example, during the fighting, the Hui of Dongxiang and Naguxiang villages did stand up to defend themselves, in view of the deep distrust and bitter impact of the Muslim rebellion. But notables from both sides, the Han and the Hui, tried to dialogue to ensure some sort of continued coexistence as of old, despite the unrest. In 1857, the Hui of Naguxiang gathered at their mosque and chose Na Taishou and Na Hai to go to other neighboring villages to dialogue with some Chinese gentry, with whom they came to an agreement for a mutual Han-Hui protection deal. Thus, on July 8, 1858, when the Hui were laying siege to Hexicheng', also threatening Dongxiang, the two parties again met to confirm their pact. The result was that even though the Hui gained the upper hand in this confrontation, no single Han person was killed, and vice-versa,

---

16. Wang Xuhuai, *Xiantong, Yunnan,* 158–62.

when the Han were about to win. There was even an exchange of presents between the parties to solidify that understanding.[17]

A repeated corroboration of Ma Rulong's claim that the Hui in Yunnan had enjoyed a good enough relationship with the Han majority to deter them from rebellion, was not only confirmed in the amicable deals concluded between the two parties in the aftermath of the disastrous rebellion which had diminished the status of the Hui and rendered them more tractable, but also prior and during the uprising, with such moderate and peaceful Hui leaders, as Ma Dexin, who sought accommodation rather than confrontation with the overwhelming Han majority. Some of those leaders, who were spread all over the province, came to represent parochial interests and therefore had a stake in maintaining the peace. Topographically, the uprising was directed from three different sections: the West, the South and the East. While the West was under the aegis of Du Wenxiu, and the East under Ma Liansheng and Ma Rong, the dissident South was under the domination of Ma Dexin and Ma Rulong. In the East, both Ma Liansheng and Ma Rong who were neither strong nor charismatic, and therefore when they were caught and executed in 1864, their influence and effect completely disintegrated and they left no noticeable impact in their wake.[18]

Initially, Ma Dexin's influence on the uprising and its leaders was quite intimate, because he had a very magnetic impact on both Du Wenxiu and Ma Rulong, to the point that many said that he was the *eminence grise* behind the rebellion and that it was his brainchild. He was accused of alternately rebelling and then surrendering in order to trigger the pacification of his area of Yunnan, viewing peace and quiet as the most predominant principle of his political activity. He was born in Xiaguan in the Dali prefecture and was thought to have come to the world some time between 1794 and 1797. In his youth he studied the Muslim classics in his home and later traveled extensively to Shaanxi and Sichuan, after which he took a liking to Confucianism which he explored in depth. In 1841 he travelled via Burma and the Indian Ocean to Arabia and Istanbul where he studied astronomy, geography and the Muslim classics. On his way back via various provinces, he reached Yunnan from the West River, and devoted himself to scholarship and religion, after he had studied at various schools in Arabia, their rites, political systems, local customs and the like. He also acquired many rare books and introduced them to China for the first time. In 1848, he taught in the village of Huilong in Yunnan and assembled many disciples around him, among them both Du Wenxiu and Ma Rulong. He wrote and translated so

---

17. Ibid.. 161–62.
18. Wang Xuhuai, *The Muslim Uprising in Yunnan*, 109.

many books (some 30) that he became a counselor for many civil and military officials. He had become so proficient in Arabic, that his knowledge of Chinese started to lag behind that of his disciples, but he won the reputation of his erudition, scholarship and religious authority. He was murdered by Zen Dexin, but before that he had achieved the status of the foremost Yunnanese Hui leader, who died before his pacific ideals were accomplished.[19]

A contemporary report on the rebellion by a Western source not directly committed to either side in the uprising, summed up the events thus:

> The Panthays in Yunnan had multiplied and become a flourishing and distinct community. They preserved their separate nationality and customs, but were nevertheless obedient to Chinese laws. The Chinese and Tartar officials are said to have been oppressive, and the foreign population was specially marked out for the exercise of more than ordinary severity. Their industrious habit and general aptitude, made the Mahommedans profitable subjects; whilst it rendered them at the same time victims to unjust and extortionate masters. Then, a feeling of enmity and hatred was engendered, with the usual results. The Loosonphoo silver mines of Yunnan were worked by Panthays, under the superintendence of Chinese officials. On a certain day a dispute arose at the mines, and the miners, exasperated by unjust treatment, had recourse to force, and murdered every Chinese officer they could find. The revolt of the miners was followed by a general armed rising of the Panthays through Yunnan. Being far inferior in numbers to the Chinese, they at first took to the woods and mountain fastnesses, from thence they carried on a fierce guerilla warfare. Meeting everywhere with success, they were joined by large numbers of neighboring semi-independent hill tribes of Shans. . . and others, and they soon extended their operations to the plains and to the siege of large towns. And the local government, receiving no assistance from Beijing, finally succumbed, the insurgents became supreme, and a separate Panthay government was established in Dali, which was then a city of secondary importance, but where the Mahommedan element had always been very strong. Feeble attempts have been since made from time to time to recover the lost province, by the dispatch of imperial troops from the capital. But the Chinese have never been able to make head against the Panthays, and the troops sent have generally been repulsed, before they could even penetrate within the Yunnan frontier.[20]

19. Ibid., 126–27.
20. Fytche, "Memorandom on the Panthays," 296–303.

> The present Mahommedan government of Yunnan is presided over by a military chief named Suleiman by the Muslims and Du Wenxiu by the Chinese. He has assumed the insignia of royalty . . . by the exclusive and prerogative use of yellow clothing and appurtenances. The Chief is assisted by four military and four civil ministers, the principle one of whom is established at Momein, a large town close to the Shan border, west of Yunnan. There is little departure in the matter of administration from the old form of Chinese government, except being more military in its character. Taxation is extremely light, being restricted as far as can be understood to a moderate assessment of land. The Mahommedans pride themselves of their Arab descent, many of them are able to converse in Arabic and their prayers are all in this language. . . After twelve years of absolute government in Yunnan, it is not improbable to suppose that their future independence is secure. . . Panthays say that last year an Embassy was received from the Emperor of China in which the Imperial government sued for cessation of hostilities and volunteered to cede Yunnan to the Panthays, provided they would come to terms and commit no further acts of aggression on neighboring provinces, but the offer was indignantly refused . . .

This obviously over-optimistic assessment of the rebellion while it was still raging and at the height of its apparent success, was probably leaning more on the failure of the ruling Dynasty, whose end was correctly predicted, than on the intrinsic strength of the Du Sultanate. Another major visitor[21] to the Sultanate, even earlier than the previous one, and probably equally disinterested to support either side of the conflict, added some crucial details on the Sultanate unknown from other sources:

a. Provincial governors of Dali bore the unmistakably Islamic title of Qadi (judge, magistrate) and wore a perfectly orthodox beard and clothing.[22]

b. The Sultanate enlisted Chinese officials who switched loyalty to it,[23] and they kept their haughtiness and privileges under it;

c. Parallel to the exclusive yellow dress of the Sultan, in imitation of the Chinese Emperor, the Governors' palaces under Du Wenxiu were built, furnished and decorated in the Chinese style, and the governors themselves wore a blue satin embroidered robe reaching to their feet,

---

21. Sladen, *China via Bhamo*, 138–59.
22. Ibid., 138.
23. Ibid.

which corresponded to the dress of the Chinese governors under the former [i.e. Ming] Dynasty[24]. Thus, while Du and his court were rebellious towards the Manchu Qing, their loyalty to the Chinese order never failed. This tends to demonstrate that the Hui rebels, while seceding from Imperial China for a while, did not renege on their Chinese roots altogether; they stood for a change of dynasty, not of the Chinese order.

d. The Sladen Mission to Burma and Yunnan was intended to establish commercial relations between Du's Sultanate and the British government and to make the customs arrangements on the border of the Shan states. Probably due to Dali's sense of siege around it, it felt the acute necessity of reviving trade with Burma via Bhamo. This vital necessity of the Dali government was expressed by the assistance the Dali government was ready to give to the British mission, as well as by the dispatch of a government mission from Dali to Rangoon. However the Burmese government was lukewarm and did not take any further steps to accommodate direct trade communications. Thus, the Yunnanese population was forced into the arduous and expensive alternative of reaching Mandalay with a limited caravan once a year rather than be completely excluded from the most valuable of their trade resources. However, the Mission, having met Du's Governor and been assisted by him, could not proceed into Yunnan itself due to «inopportune circumstances," as there were insubordinate forces blocking the route to Dali.

e. The Panthays of Yunnan were greatly elated for the recognition they received from their Muslim coreligionists in India and Burma, and attached great importance to it.

f. The Dali government had the wisdom to allow the Shan states of Yunnan to govern themselves in peace and prosperity, rather than impose on them alien chiefs and governors, unlike the Shan states further to the south that depended on the Burmese government, where the hereditary chiefs had been deposed or placed under the governance of Burmese officials, with the consequence that they were subject to chronic disturbance, and industry had yielded to indolence and poverty.[25]

---

24. Ibid., 139 and 148.
25.. Ibid. pp. 151-9.

Conclusions

# Two Arenas, Two Patrimonies and One Uniting Islam

The rationale for encompassing such two different provinces in China under the appellation Midwest is not only their geographical location within the large Chinese landmass, but also the traits that unite them:

1. Both are border areas of China, with a mix of local Chinese and incoming ethnic groups, usually from the West, and they bear ethnic characteristics not typical of the almost purely Han areas of the eastern regions;

2. Maybe due to their ethnic makeup, or to the fact that Muslims settled there at an early time, under various circumstances, those two provinces became "Muslim country," although at their peak they never constituted the majority of the population, perhaps local majorities at most, especially in Ningxia, where Han settlement and Han natural growth soon overwhelmed them numerically and confined them to their small minority status.

3. Due to the distance from the Capital on the one hand and their proximity to the vast expanses of the Tibet-Qinhai-Xinjiang-Mongolia wilderness, the Hui in the Midwest could acquire their high visibility in the face of the lack of cultural challenge from others, except for the dominating Han.

4. It is a fact that the Midwest, either due to the above-mentioned factors or for other reasons, was the place where Muslim rebellions brewed, exploded into the open and attempted secession;

# Two Arenas, Two Patrimonies and One Uniting Islam 169

5. Though those two areas are only nominally "Hui"-dominated in their Muslim population, in fact they consist only in their minority of Muslims and other Islamized minorities, like the Uyghurs, the Dongans and the Salars who all have Turkic connections and links to Central Asia.

6. From the evidence collected in the literature[1] and in the field trips, it is clear that while during the heyday of the Muslims in the Midwest, prior to the Rebellion era, when they were numerous, self-confident and more literate in Islamic culture, their knowledge of Arabic, and their use of it, were much more widespread. Today, not only ignorance of Arabic and Islam, especially among the younger generation, is more prevalent, but the eagerness to use them and to proclaim and advertise them in public has grown more reticent for fear of unnecessarily "waking the sleeping dogs" of the rebellions which have left an unmistakable stigma on the Muslim reputation.

The Chinese sources on the Hui in those border regions, all tend to impute the frequent frictions between Han and Hui, which all too often escalated into local unrest or into major rebellions, such as that of Du Wenxiu and Ma Hualong, to socio-economic competition, jealousies and permanent suspicions which pitted the majority Han against the Hui minority or vice versa. But the reality was much more complicated than a simple story of a rift over a gold or a silver mine. For, every time a quarrel burst into the open, it was the violent expression of deep and long term bitterness which had brewed under the surface for generations. Initially, it was perhaps the fruit of a built in Hui resentment and refusal to accept the steep descent from the privileged status the Hui had under the Yuan and, especially under Seyyid Edjell in Yunnan, into the abyss of an underprivileged and outnumbered minority in later centuries, which in the 19th Century necessitated a Hui coalition with other minorities before they could dare to launch their major and almost suicidal rebellion. This all leads to the conclusion that pragmatic leaders like Du, and Ma Hualong, made their fateful decision to launch their respective rebellions only after they made efforts at reconciliation in view of their hopeless demographic inferiority, when they were backed into a corner, and finally launched their fateful initiative given the lack of choice and as a matter of last resort and instinct of survival.

Although it remains questionable whether and to what extent the Muslim rebellions in the Midwest were triggered and or/dominated by the New Sect (*Xinjiao*) sentiment, it was clear to the Hui then, and still obvious

---

1. See e.g. the Fytche Report of 1878, page 300.

to the Hui today that the Sect, traces of which are hard to detect today, has become the scapegoat of anti-Muslim sentiment and the legitimate object of persecution, despite the self-righteous Chinese pronouncements of distinction between good (*liang*) Hui and Hui bandits (*fei*), namely between good-innocent Muslims and bad-rebellious Muslims, thus pretending that it was not the anti-Muslim sentiments that guided the Han, but merely the positive and negative behavior among the Muslims. From all the testimonies about the rifts and quarrels that were enumerated above between Han and Hui, it is hard to conclude that only "bad Hui" participated in unrest, nor is it evident that the Han fell victims to the Hui greed and aggression, but exactly the reverse, it was systematically occasioned by the general atmosphere of chaos in the country, and the frequent collaboration of the greedy bureaucratic gentry with the criminal gangs.

For in effect, after more than a millennium in China, they have become totally Chinese as much as they have remained totally Muslim. In the Northwest, in the midst of the obsessive sectarianism that had taken hold of the Hui in the 19th Century, that large majority may have seemed to outsiders as a confusing mixture of mystic sectarianism and millenarianism, lumped together under the designation of the New Sect, which sought seemingly to distinguish itself from the Chinese environment by adopting militant ways, while it retained its silence and reluctance to discuss their identity, or deny any knowledge of it. This was due not necessarily to total ignorance of the matter, but probably from the embarrassment entailed in admitting dissension in their midst. In fact, to this day, as we have seen, the Hui tend to minimize the role of the New Sect in the rebellion and to deny any affiliation with it. Conversely, Muslims in China to this day tend to emphasize Qing oppression and general Han discrimination as the main motives for unrest. It is certainly true that the New Sectarians were the main carriers of the Muslim resentment which was due to both the Qing repression, but added to that was a certain amount of ideological thrust, and both matter, ideology and discontent can be related as mutually reinforcing aspects of the same social phenomenon: discontent boosting the search for an ideology as a base for rebellion, and ideology thriving on discontent.

Ideology helps to perform two main social functions: one, directly societal, of binding society together, and the other—fulfills the individual's need for satisfying one's identity. Politically, it becomes significant by its relation to authority inasmuch as the latter is legitimized on the basis of those ideologies and provides a moral basis for social manipulation, or lays claim to superior planning and rationality[2]. This does not mean, however, that

---

2. Apter, *Ideology and Discontent*, 18–21.

# Two Arenas, Two Patrimonies and One Uniting Islam

traditional Chinese Islam (what is usually called the Old Sect) did not provide enough ideology to thrive upon. For, the revivalist movements among Chinese Islam in the Northwest have swayed enough Muslim audiences to their side that even those not affiliated with the New Sect have found themselves supporting the rebels who carried the mood of the day. But on the whole that Muslim resurgence remained pragmatic and conservative and sought no more than an accommodation with the Chinese system and a return to the "live and let live" formula which had prevailed prior to the Qing. Not that coexistence with the Chinese system was ideal, but it was deemed to be the only practical way of surviving as long as the pressures were kept at a tolerable level, and the environment could be said to exist within tolerable parameters. This may explain the various Muslim leaders of the old Hui establishment, including Ma Dexin and Ma Rulong, who laid down their arms once they judged their main demands fulfilled.

Ma Dexin himself, in his mission to convince the recalcitrant Du Wenxiu to follow suit, elaborated on the material advantages which the Muslim population would enjoy if peace should be restored, as contrasted with the disaster that the community would incur were the rebellion to be pursued:[3] Ma was not only a reputed scholar, but also a leader of the community, who had to come to grips with the "ideal vs actuality" dilemma and resolve it. As Malcom Kerr has pointed out:

> Underlying the Islamic tradition of social thought, is a pessimistic consciousness of the tension between ideal and actuality, the spiritual and the temporal, virtue and power, Allah's command and man's conduct. In past centuries, Muslim scholars did not customarily think it their business to reconcile between these two sets of contrasting elements. Instead, they elaborated their conceptions of the ideal and left Islamic societies to deal with actualities, by evolving its own practical but largely unacknowledged psychology and social mechanisms. But the spread of secular culture in the modern Muslim world has changed this. Instead of rendering the sense of tension obsolete, it has sharpened the tension and made its resolution a vital problem[4].

So much so that Zuo Zongtang, who was in charge of crushing the rebellion in the Northwest, wrote in a memorial to the Throne:

> Previously, in 1781, two Hui people, Ma Mingxin and Su Sushi Erh[5] returned from Western countries and Arabia, where they

---

3. Rocher, *La Province Chinoise du Yunnan*, 80.
4. Kerr, *Islamic Reform*, 1.
5. There is no agreement in the sources as to when Ma Mingxin returned from

claimed they had become aware of the secret way to attain salvation... They founded the New Sect and raised rebellions... Since Ma Hualong, the Sect has become widespread. Under the cloak of tradesmen, they sent out missionaries to spread this evil faith everywhere.... The reason why the New Sect must be prohibited is that it claims its origin in God and indulges in preposterous prophesizing. The Sect's conduct is strange and often lures unthinking Hui into slavery. The followers of the Sect are often unwittingly pushed into plotting uprisings, and they would be prepared, without hesitation, to face execution ... which makes it a real danger to the Empire.... Some captured Muslims have testified to the effect that Ma Hualong knows the future, can predict the numbers of visitors who would come to visit him from afar.... Others testified that Ma often manifested his divine abilities, healed diseases, accorded child-bearing to barren women... Those who joined the Sect confessed their sins before Ma Hualong, who whipped them and then granted them redemption after he interfered with God on their behalf.... Even though the Hui are usually skeptical, they change once they accept the New Sect Teaching, and seem possessed with madness... Under siege, when the Hui suffered famine and had to eat human flesh, none came out to criticize Ma Hualong and his family, who had availed themselves of large quantities food supplies. Even when they were in a hopeless situation, the idea that the Great Ahung would in some way save them, was a comfort to them.. .Even after Ma gave himself up, many Muslim leaders continued to flock to him, prostrated themselves before him, and would not redress themselves unless an order came from Ma himself[6].

In other memorials of 1868, Zuo wrote:

If anyone hesitated to join them, they all attacked him and threatened him with their weapons until he yielded. There are even cases where sons who are believers would kill their fathers if they rejected them[7]

Numerous Hui people from Yunnan and Gansu, having left their homes and being full of enthusiasm over their rebellion,

---

his trips to Arabia and Central Asia. Two dates are mentioned: 1761 and 1781.

6. For translations of this Memorial, see also Chu Wen-djang, *The Muslim Rebellions*, 156–58; and also Parker, *Studies in Chinese Religion*, 258–59.

7. *Huimin Qiyi* (HMQI), 9–10.

are there [in Shaanxi]. Chinese who have been forced to convert to Islam are also there[8].

The earliest Chinese documents referring to the New Sect, did not even mention the Old Sect, namely the common Chinese Muslims, because official Chinese attention was focused on the troublesome new intruder, while "regular" Islam had been taken for granted for centuries. In a memorial of 1781 by Bi Yuan, the Governor of Shanxi, who helped crush the Muslim rebellion in Gansu in 1781, and again in 1784, and was promoted in consequence to the Governorship General of Hu-Kwang (Hubei and Hunan) in 1788[9], made the first distinction between the two:

> There are no less than thousands of Muslim families in Xian, and they have seven mosques, the biggest dating from the Tang. Each of these houses of prayer has one or more religious leaders called Ahung. Each congregation of Hui goes to its own particular mosque to pray, and they are independent of each other. . . . There are none who belong to the New Sect. . . . The Hui have lived in China since ancient times, and they are no different from ordinary inhabitants. . . . When the Salar[10] tribe rebelled the Hui of Shaanxi were alarmed at the prospect that they might be involved, but this having nothing to do with the Hui people of the interior, I ordered them to go about their affairs in peace. . . . I shall keep a vigilant eye, and in case any of the New Sect or other vicious faiths attempts to create trouble, they will be arrested . . . so that they may be totally extirpated. . . .[11]

Thus, the contrast was between the Common Hui and the New Sect, not between two rival sects, both of which would have been persecuted as heterodox evils. One year later, in an edict of the Qianlong Emperor, the term Old Sect was used to designate the good (*liang*) Hui, as opposed to the New sectarians, who were dubbed the *Hui Fei* (the Hui Bandits):

> Su Sushi San of Gansu belongs to a seditious sect in the Muslim faith called the New Sect (*Xinjiao*), which has now been wiped out[12]. The Hui of the Old Sect are numerous in all provinces and particularly in Shaanxi. . . . Their prayers are traditional and

8. Djang, *Muslim Rebellions*, 129.

9. Yuan (1730–1797) a scholar and official, who was appointed Governor of Shanxi in 1773, in *Eminent Chinese of the Qing Period*, 622–24.

10. The Salars are Muslims of Central Asia who were identified with the New Sect Movement under the leadership of Su Sushi-san.

11. Ford Documents.

12. The Emperor refers to the Salar Rebellion of 1781 which had been suppressed.

have nothing seditious in them. . . . The outbreak of rebellion in Gansu last year resulted from a controversy between the New Sect and the Old Sect. . . .[13]

In another case the Qianlong Emperor decreed that:

> When Su Sushih San rebelled last year, the Hui of the Old Sect led the people in helping the government troops to defeat and catch the rebels, for which I commended and rewarded them[14].

Are we then to infer that in Yunnan, as in Gansu, the pro-government Hui, who helped quell the Dali rebels, were in fact common Muslims of the Old Sect, who were pitted against New Sect rebels? In fact, in both the Gansu and Yunnan rebellions, there were several cases of this strange alignment of Hui forces against their brethren, a weakness that has dramatically contributed to the failure of the uprising, once the Empire succeeded in its traditional policy of *divide et impera* which activated one faction of the rebels against another. This suggests that the Old Sect must have regarded the New Teaching as a deviation of the traditional faith of Islam. D'Ollone in effect reported:

> The Yunnan Muslims spoke to us on Ma Hualong and his sect with such marked disgust that they left no doubt that some of those heretics were present in the neighborhood. I repeatedly got the impression of being prevented from encountering some Muslims in the Huilong homestead near Lingnan-fu.

Interestingly, during my trip of September 2016 to Linxia, I too was prevented by Chinese Muslims from visiting the neighboring city of Lintan, the seat of the Xidaotang and the burial place of Ma Qixi its founder, which some Muslims today are still interested in hiding, as they were then, due to the embarrassment the Cult of Saints that is involved with it, which they dub as *Kombejiao*, poses to them. This term was still in use, though discreetly, in Lintan in 2016. Again, according to d'Ollone's eye witness testimony:

> The Xinjiao cult, also known as Kombechiao, i.e. the cult of tombs, professes prayers on the graves of saints, who are believed to be preoccupied with earthly affairs and to dispense their benedictions after their departure. Ma Hualong, who taught this very doctrine, and is credited by his followers to be endowed with supernatural gifts that he inherited from his father. The adherents of the Old Sect (Jiujiao or Laojiao) vigorously reject

---

13. Ford Documents.
14. Ford Documents.

> these creeds and these practices. In old times there were confrontations between the two sects, which today pretend not to recognize each other. My regular informers who belong to the Old Sect have refused to serve as our intermediaries to the people they abhor. It is perhaps because they were aware of our good relationship with the adherents of the Old Sect that the head of the New Sect has refused to see us.

A contemporary Chinese Muslim described the Old-Sect-New Sect differences in similar terms:

> The New Sect is limited to a few large cities, while the Old Sect was dominant throughout the rest of China... The Old Sect followed the Chinese tradition of wearing white mourning garments, while the New Sect forbade wearing special clothes of mourning... The Muslim community was divided with one side favoring reform—the |New Sect, and the other opposing changes, and known as the Old Sect. Each side suspected the other and accused it of heresy. It was a shame to have such a hiatus develop...[15]

One conclusion which can be drawn from all this, whatever the historical motivations of the unrest in the Chinese Muslim Midwest, and however dramatic and virulent the ideological and personal divisions between the various branches of Islam, namely the enormous massacres and their impact on the Hui population during and as a result of the 19th Century unrest, causing its diminution, the crushing of its aspirations and the smashing of its self-confidence and pride, they have all converged to create a new sobriety that is tinged with sadness and a sense of resignation among the Midwest Hui population. From being the main actors in the Muslim revival of the 18th and the 19th Centuries in the Northwest, and the main engines of reform and renewal, which may have triggered and sustained some of the rebellions, the Hui of this border area of China have reconciled to the idea of their marginal status in that enormous land, as a diluted insignificant minority. To the extent that anyone among them still entertains any pretensions of grandeur or autonomy, his eyes are set on the Muslim Uyghurs of Xinjiang, further to the West, who, like their Tibetan compatriots, have been watching their national and cultural turf irretrievably invaded, colonized and Sinicized under the cloak of rapid economic "development."

---

15. Dawood, *Islamic Culture in China*.

# Bibliography

Alles, Elisabeth. *Musulmans en Chine:Une Anthropologie des Hui du Henan*, Editions de l''Ecole des Hautes Etudes, Paris, 2000.
Anderson, John, *Mandaly to Momien*, Mc Millan, London, 1876, p. 228.
Apter, David (ed.) *Ideology and Discontent*, Free Press, London, 1964, pp. 18–21
Bai Shouyi, *Huimin Qiyi* (The Rightful uprisings of Muslims), Shanghai, 1953, 4 Volumes.
Bales, W., *Zuo Zongtang*, Shanghai, 1937. R. Israeli, *Muslims in China*, p. 169
Bennigsten, A. and S. W imbush, *Mystics and Commissars: Sufism in the Soviet Union*, Berkeley, 1985.
Bosworth, Edmond (ed), *New Encyclopaedia of Islam*, Leiden, Vol XX, pp. 300–301.
Broomhall, Marshall, *Islam in China: a Neglected Problem* London, 1910
Bruinessen, Martin van, "The Origins and Development of the Naqshbandi Order in Indonesia", in *Der Islam*, Band 67, Heft 1, 1990, pp. 150–179
*Chen Jiexian (ed) Proceedings of the 4th East Asian Altaistic Conference*, Taipeh, 1971,
Chu, R., *The Reasons of the Yunnan Rebellion*, an MA Thesis at the University of Toronto, 1967.
Chu Wendjang, *The Muslin Rebellions in Northwest China*, 1862–78, Mouton, The Hague, 1966,
Davies, H.R., *Yunnan: the Link Between India and the Yangtze*, Cambridge, 1909, pp. 334–6
Ding Hong, "The Pattern of the Xidaotang," Zhong Yang Ming zu Daxue Xuebao ( Journal of the Central National Minorities University), No 5, 1996, p. 50.
Drake, F."Muhammedanism in the Tang Dynasty", *Monumenta Serica*, VIII (1943), pp. 23, 34.
Feng Jinyuan, *Zhongguo de Yisilan Jiao* (Chinese Islam, (1994)
Fields, Lanny, *Zuo Zongtang and the Muslims: Statecraft in Northwest China*, 1868–80, Brown and Martin, Kingston, 1978
Fletcher, .J., "the Sufi Paths(Turuq) in China," in *Etudes Orientales*, No 13–14, Liban 1994
Fletcher, Joseph, "Central Asian Sufism and Ma Mingxin's New Teaching," *in Chen Jiexian (ed) Proceedings of the 4th East Asian Altaistic Conference*, Taipeh, 1971, pp. 88–90.
Fytche, Colonel Albert, (Chief Commissioner to British Burma), "Memorandom on the Panthays or Mahommedan Population of Yunnan," in General A. Fytche, *Burma, Past and Present*, Kegan Paul, London, 1878, pp. 296–303.

Fytche, General A. *Burma, Past and Present*, Kegan Paul, London, 1878, pp. 296–303.
Ford Documents. Joseph Ford has prepared but never published "Excerpts From Chinese Documents drawn from Wang Taiyu's *Chenjiao Zhenquan* and Liu Zhi's *Tianfang zhi-sheng Shihlu*
Gao Zhangfu, *Xibei Musilin Shehui Wenti Yanjiu* ( Studies into the Societal Issues of the Muslims of the Northwest), Gansu Minzu Chubanshe, 1991
Gao Zhanfu, *Xibei Musilin Shehui Wenti Yanjiu* (Research into the Question of Muslim Society in the Northwest, (1991)
Ghosh, Stanley *Embers in Cathay*, New York, 1961
Gibbs, H. (translated from Arabic, *The Travels of Ibn Battuta*, The Haklyut Society, London, 1994, pp. 847–902.
Gill, Captain William, *The River of Gold Sand*, London, 1880, Vol II, Chap 8: "In the Footsteps of Marco Polo and of Augustus Margary," pp. 303–5.
Gladney, Dru, *Muslim Chinese: Ethnic Nationalism in the People's Republic*, Harvard, 1991
Hartmann, Martin, *China, The Encyclopaedia of Islam*, Leiden, 1913.
Hille, Marie-Paule, *Le Xidaotang, une Existence Collective a l"Epreuve du Politique: Ethnographie historique et Anthrolopologique d'une Communaute Musulmane Chinoise (Gansu, 1857–2014)*
*Huimin Qiyi* (HMQI), Edited by Bai Shouyi (Righteous Uprising of Muslims), three Vol
*Imanaga Seiji, Chugoku Kaikyoshi Josetsu* (An Introduction to Chinese Islam), Tokyo 1965
Israeli, Raphael, "Ahung and Literatus: a Muslim Elite in Confucian China," *Die Welt des Islams*, XIX, 1–4, 1979, pp. 212–22.
Israeli, Raphael, "The Muslim Revival in 19th Century China, *Studia Islamica*, XLIII, pp. 119–138.
Israeli, Raphael, "The incompatibility between Islam and the Chinese Order," *T'ong Pao*, LXIII, 1978, pp. 296–323.
Israeli, Raphael, "Myth as Memory: Myth and History in Chinese Islam," in *Muslim World*, Spring 2001.
Israeli, Raphael, "Islam in the Chinese Environment," in R. Israeli, *Islam in China :Religion, Ethnicity, Culture and Politics*, Lexington Books, Lanham, 2002, pp.295–312.
Israeli, Raphael and Adam Gardner-Rush, "Sectarian Islam and Sino-Muslim Identity in China," *The Muslim World*, Vol 90, No 3–4, Fall 2000, pp. 439–452
Israeli, Raphael, "Translation as Exegesis: Translations of the Qur'an into Chinese," in P. Riddell and T. Street (eds) Islam: Essays in Scripture, Thought and Society, Brill, Leiden and NY, 1997, pp. 81–103
Israeli, Raphael . "China's Uyghur Problem", *The Israel Journal of Foreign Affairs*, Vol Four, 2010/5770, No 1, pp. 89–101.
Israeli, Raphael, "Medieval Muslim Travellers to China", *Maritime Silk Road Studies*, no. 1, 1997, pp. 94–104.
Israeli, Raphael, "Is there Shi'a in Chinese Islam?", *Journal of Muslim Minority Affairs*, IX, No 1, January, 1988, pp. 49–66.
Israeli, Raphael, "Muslims in the People's Republic of China," Asian Survey August, 1981, Vol XXI, No 8, pp. 901–919.
Israeli, Raphael, *Islam in China : a Study of Cultural Confrontation*, Curzon Press, London, 1978, especially Chap II

# Bibliography

Israeli, Raphael, *Islam in China :Religion, Ethnicity, Culture and Politics*, Lexington Books, Lanham, 2002.
Jashock, Maria, and Shui Jingjun, *The History of Women's Mosques in Chinese Islam: a Mosque of their Own*, Curzon, Press, London, Richmond, Surrey, 2000.
Kerr, Malcolm,*Islamic Reform: the Political and Legal Theories of Muhammad 'Abduh and Rashid Rida*, UC Berkeley, 1966, p. 1.
Lewis, Bernard, *The Assassins* : A Radical Sect in Islam, Basic Books, NY, 1968
Li Shujiang and Karl Luckert, *Mythology and Folklore of the Hui*, Albany, 1994
Lipman, Jonathan, Familiar Strangers: a History of Muslims in the Northwest, Univ. of Washington Press, Seattle, 1997
Lipman, Jonathan, *Hyphenated Chinese : Sino-Muslim Identity in Modern China*,1996
Liu Zhi, *Tianfang zhi-sheng Shihlu*
Ma Kesun, "Zhongguo Yisilanjiao Yikhewanpai de Changyi", in *YIsilanjiao zai Zhongguo*, Yinchuan, Ningxia, 1982, pp. 439-58
Ma Zishi, delivering a lecture in Cairo in 1934, cited Hu Fangquan's "Zhongguo Huijiao Gaikuang," published in *Zhongguo Yisilanjiao Cankao Ziliao Xuanbian*, Yincguan, Ningxia, 1985.
Ma Shaomei, *Shadian Huizou Shiliao* ( Historical Materials of the Hui People in Shadian, Kaiyuan, Yunnan, 1989. This source was translated by Wang Jianping
Ma Haiyun, "The Mythology of the Prophet's Ambassadors in China: Histories of Sa'ad Waqqas and Guess in Chinese Sources," in *The Journal of Muslim Minorities*, XXVI, December 2006
Ma Shaomei, *Shadian Huizou Shiliao* ( Historical Materials of the Hui People in Shadian, Kaiyuan, Yunnan, 1989. This source was translated by Wang Jianping
Ma Shouqian, "The Hui People's New Awakening from the end of the 19th Century to the Beginning of the 20th Century," read at the *International Conference on the Legacy of Islam in China*, Harvard University, 1992
Ma Tong, "Chinois ou Musulmans?," Translation into French by C. Halfon from an interview with Abu Yussef Ma Tong?," in *Etudes Orientales*, No 13-14, 1994, 1948-9.
Ma Tong, *Zhongguo Yisilanjiao Jiaopai yu Menhuan zhidu shihlue* (a Survey of the factions and menhuan in Chinese Islam), Lanzhou, 1981
Ma Tong, *The Origins of the Islamic Sects and Menhuan in China*, Ningxia, 2000.
Ma Tong, "Xidaotang," in Wan Yibing ed., *Zhongguo Yisilanjiao Baike Quanshu*, Sichuan Sheshu Chubanshe, Chengdu, 1994
Ma Tong, *Zongguo Yisilan Jiaopai yu menhuan zhidu shilue* ( A History of the Islamic Sects and Menhuan in China) (1981)
Ma Tong, *Zhongguo Yisilanjiao Jiaopai yu Menhuan zhidu shihlue* (a Survey of the factions and menhuan in Chinese Islam), Lanzhou, 1981
Ma Tong, *Zhongguo Yisilan Jiaopai menhuan Suyuan* (The Origin of Chinese Islamic Sects and Menhuan, (1986)
Morgan, Kenneth (ed), *Islam: the Straight Path*, Ronald, NY, 1958.
Nohara, Shiro, "Unnam Kaikyo to no Hamram" (Rebellions of the Yunnan Muslims),*Kaikyoken* (Islamic World), I, 1938, pp. 31ff.
d'Ollone, HMV, *Recherches sur les Musulmans Chinois*, Leroux, Paris, 1905, p. 105
Parker, E.H. Studies in Chinese Religion, London, 1919
*Pingding Yunnan Huifei Fanglueh (*a Strategy for the Pacification of Muslim Bandits in Yunnan), is a five-volume compilation

*Records of Yunnan Muslims*, compiled by Ma Shengfeng

*Qing jen geng yuan*

Reichauer, E. and J. Fairbank, *East Asia : the Great Tradition*, Houghton Mifflin, Boston, 1958

Riddell, P. and T. Street (eds) *Islam: Essays in Scripture, Thought and Society*, Brill, Leiden and NY, 1997, pp. 81–103

Rocher, Emile, *La Province Chinoise du Yunnan*, 2 vol.Leroux, Paris, 1879, p. 80

Shih, Vincent, *The Taiping Ideology*, Seattle, 1967

Saunders, W., "Chinese Muslims," in *Friends of Muslims*, VIII, 1934

Sladen, Colonel, Apendix II to Anderson's book, pp. 456–7, purports to be the translation of Chinese a official document accounting for the coming and establishment of Islam in China

Sladen, E. B., *China via Bhamo*, Rangoon, 1869, pp. 138–159

Sladen, in Apendix II to Anderson's book, pp. 456–7, purports to be the translation of a Chinese official document accounting for the coming and establishment of Islam in China

Su, Alice, "Harmony and Martyrdom Among China's Hui Muslims", The *New Yorker*, June 6, 2016.

Ting Dawood, *Islamic Culture in China*, in Morgan, in Kenneth (ed),*Islam: the Straight Path*, Ronald, NY, 1958.

Vasilev, V., *Mohammedanism in China*,( translated by R. Loewenthal), *Central Asia Collectania*, No 3, Washington DC, 1960, pp. 4ff

Vissiere, A. *Etudes Sino-Mahometanes*, I, Leroux, Paris, 120–1

*Xibei Minzu Yanjiu* (Studies into the Hui people of the Northwest).

Wan Lei, *The Hui Minority in Modern China :Identity and Struggles*, Fatih University, Istanbul, 2012, . Jonathan Lipman, *Familiar Strangers: a History of Muslims in the Northwest*, Univ. of Washington Press, Seattle, 1997.

Wan Yibing (ed)., *Zhongguo Yisilanjiao Baike Quanshu*, Sichuan Sheshu

Wang Jianping, *Concord and Conflict: the HUi Communities of Yunnan Society in a Historical Perspective*, Lund, 1996 Chubanshe, Chengdu, 1994, pp 600–601

Wang Jianping, "Islam in Yunnan", *Journal of the Institute of Muslim Minority Affairs*, London 13, No 2, pp. 364–74

Wang Jianping, "Islam in Yunnan," *Journal of the Institute of Muslim Minority Affairs*, London 13, No 2, pp. 364–74

Wang Taiyu, *Chenjiao Zhenquan.*

Wang Xuhuai, *Xiantong, Yunnan Huimin Shiluan* (the Muslim Uprising in Yunnan Under the Xianfeng and Tongzhi Emperors, Academia Sinica, Taipei, 1968.

Wei, Alice, *The Muslim Rebellion in Yunnan*, a PhD dissertation at the University of Chicago, 1974.

Wright, Mary, *The Last Stand of Chinese Conservatism : the Tongzhi Restoration*, 1862–74, Introduction, Atheneum, NY, 1967.

Yang Huaizhong, "Gan Ning Qing Huizou zhong de Sufeipai" (the Sufi factions among the Muslims of Gansu and Ningxia), *Ningxia Shehui Kesue*, 1986, No 4, p. 10.

Zhao Zhangwu, "Shanshinian lai zhi Zhongguo Huijiao Wenhua Gaikuang," in Bai Souyi (ed), *Zhonguo Yisilanjiaoshi Cungao*, Ningxia 1982, pp. 385–405

*Zhong Guo Huitzu Da Ci-dian* (The Great Dictionary of Chinese Islam), Jiangsu Guji Chuban Shi, 1992

## Bibliography

*Zhong Yang Ming zu Daxue Xuebao ( Journal for the study of the Centralnational Minorities)*

Zwemer, Samuel, "Islam in Gansu, *The Moslem World*, Hartford,, Vol 10, p. 381, 1919.

# Analytical Index
## Names, Places, Terms and Events

**A**

Abbasids, 116
Al-Azhar, 127
Al-Qa'ida, 40
Arab/Arabic/Arabia, viii, 4–5, 15, 18,
    21, 38, 48–52, 54, 58, 115, 153
Arafat, Yassir, 127
Asia,
    Central, 48, 50, 54, 83–84, 116–18
    Muslim Republics in, 50, 55
    West, 118

**B**

Banna Hassan, 42
Beijing (See also Oven Street), 58, 113
Britain, 8
Buddhism, 7, 22, 48, 67, 72
Burma/Myanmar, 152, 155
    Sladen Mission, 155

**C**

Canton/Guangzhou, 27, 46, 91
Chiank Kaishek, 57
Christians, vii, 35, 54, 72, 115
    Catholics, 72, 86
    Jesuits, 71
    Missionaries, 62
Confucianism, 7, 21, 33, 35, 61–62,
    67, 72, 130, 134, 152
Cultural Revolution, 7–8, 15, 38, 55,
    58, 118–19, 120, 123

**D**

Dali, vii, 9, 11ff, 117, 120, 123, 134,
    145, 147, 153
    Sultanate, vii, 12, 115, 117, 132,
        136, 138ff
    Erh-Hai Lake, 9, 11, 114, 116
Daoism, 74, 80–81, 100, 107–8
Deng Xiaoping, ix, 58, 63, 70, 121
Dongan, vii, 34
    Rerbellion, 4
Du Wenxiu, vii, 9, 11, 47, 113–14,
    118, 130ff, 138ff, 157
    Sultan Suleyman, 132, 154

**E**

Edjell/ Adjell, Seyyid, 10, 117,
    123–25, 145, 157

**F**

Falungong, vii, viii, 53
France, 9
Fujian
    Academy of Science, 37

**G**

Gansu, vii, viii, ix, 1ff, 15ff, 113–14,
    132
    Daxia River, 2
    Panhandle, 1
    Qilian Mountains, 2
    Uprising, 136

Gobi Desert, 1
Gombei, 6-7, 71, 77
　jiao, 162
Great Leap Forward, 58, 63
Guangxi, 8
Guangzhou, ix
Guizhou, 8
　Uprising, 136
Guomindang, 57

## H

Han Dynasty, 22
Hanzhou, 46, 55
Hizbullah, 121-22
Honk Kong, ix
Huang Ho / Yellow River, 2, 4

## I

Ibn Battuta, 46-47, 115
Ibn Taymiyya, 51
Iran/ Persia, 35, 48, 54
ISIS, 40, 68
Islam
　Gedimu, 19, 30, 32, 39, 41-43, 45, 64, 71, 74, 76, 85-86
　Hanafite, 5, 45, 71, 91
　Ikhwan, 32, 39, 42-43, 50, 51, 61
　Muslim Brothers, 33, 35, 41, 63, 123
　Qurban Festival, 29
　Salafis, 32, 42, 51
　—'s Schools of Law, 35-36
　Shi'ite, 5, 35, 40-41, 1000
　Sunnite, 17, 40
　Umma, 28, 34, 39-40
　Wahhabis, 36, 38, 42, 44, 50-52, 55, 68
Israel/Palestine, ix, 28, 64

## J

Jihad, 40, 123, 132

## K

Kaifeng, 54
　Jewish Community of, 54
Kang Yuwei, 65

Kazakh, vii
Kunming, vii, 9-11, 116, 125, 134, 145-47, 150, 151
　Yunnan-fu, 134, 145
Kuwait, 4, 7, 37

## L

Lanzhou, vii, ix, 1-2, 31, 43, 47, 56, 58, 125
Li Keqiang, viii, ix, 18
Lintan, vii, viii, ix, 5ff, 43, 62ff, 162
　River Tao, 63
Linxia, vii, viii, ix, 1, 5ff, 30-31, 43, 47, 52, 55-56, 64, 125
　Autonomous Region, 1, 31
　Mecca of China, vii, 5, 19, 27, 49

## M

Ma Anliang, 59, 62, 108
Ma Dexin, 150, 152-53, 159
Ma Hualong, 47, 56ff, 132-33, 157, 160
Ma Mingren, 64-65, 70
Mao Zidong, 2, 35, 37-38, 57-58, 63, 113, 120
Ma Qixi, viii, 6, 11, 61ff, 94ff
Ma Rulong, 57, 135, 144-45, 147-48, 149-50, 152, 159
Ma Wanfu, 50
　Ahl al-Sunna, 50
Ma Zhongyin,
　Rebeliion, 64
Mecca, vii, 5, 19-21, 23, 38, 48, 52, 62, 77, 94, 125
　Ka'ba, 77
Mekong River, 9
Menhuan, 5, 30, 34ff, 41, 44, 46-47, 49, 64-65, 71, 77
Middle East, viii, 5, 38, 50, 52-3
Ming Dynasty, 4, 38, 63, 100, 117
Ming Xuecheng, 70ff
Mongolia, 2, 10-11, 30-31, 114, 156-57
　Inner, 2
　Kublai Khan, 115, 117
　Yuan Dynasty, 38, 41, 47, 115, 145, 157

## Analytical Index

### N

Naqshbandiya, 30, 48–49, 61, 76, 83
  Jahriyya, 31–32, 42, 44, 48, 61–62, 71, 74, 76, 82–83, 93
  Khufya, 30, 41–42, 44, 48, 61–62, 64, 76, 83, 93–94
New Sect, 34ff, 39, 42, 160–64
Ningxia, 2, 17, 19, 23, 24–27, 29, 34, 45, 49, 55, 156
  Na Homestead, 15, 29

### O

Old Sect, 43–44, 64, 161, 164
Opium War, 139
Ottomans (see also Turkey), 28, 52, 135
Oxen Street (see also Beijing) Mosque, 52–53

### P

Panthay, 114, 153
  Rebellion (see also Yunnan), 9–10, 113, 154
People's Congress, viii, ix
Polo, Marco, 12, 115
Prophet Muhammad, 20–23, 28, 51, 72, 77–78, 82, 87, 89–90, 93, 102, 106
  Birthday of, 29–30, 77

### Q

Qatar, 4
Qing Dynasty, vii, 5, 24, 26, 46, 47, 53, 56, 63, 102, 117–18, 130, 138, 140, 145–46, 159
  Daoguang Emperor, 58, 139
  Documents, ix
  Kangxi Emperor, 71, 96
  Qianlong Emperor, 162
  Shunzhi Emperor, 94
  Tongzhi Restoration, 57, 83, 143
Qinghai, 2, 30, 45, 49, 58, 63, 78
Quanzhou, 46
Qur'an, viii, 5, 7, 15, 17, 21–22, 38, 42, 49, 51, 67, 72–74, 76, 86, 119, 121, 123, 127

### R

Red River, 9
Rushdie, Salman, 58–59, 113

### S

Salar, vii, 31, 34, 64
Salween River, 9
Saudi Arabia, 4, 7, 35, 37, 52, 55, 127
Shaanxi, 2, 31, 114, 118, 132
Shadian (see also Yunnan), Martyrs Memorial, 125–27
Shan State, 155
Shanghai, ux
Shenzhen, ix
Sichuan, 8, 36, 63, 70, 98, 118
Silk Road, 4, 37
Song Dynasty, 47, 72, 116
Sufis, 30, 35, 44–48, 50, 62, 71, 76, 84, 92ff, 106–7
  Khaltawiyya, 48
  Kubrawiyya, 41, 47–48, 61, 93
  Qaderiyya, 41, 48–49, 61, 80, 84–85, 93–94, 97–98, 100ff, 106–7
  Yasawiyya, 48
  Zawiyya, 40

### T

Thailand, 151
  Chiang Mai, 151
Taiping, 47, 57–58, 62, 64, 69, 130, 134, 137, 143, 145–47
Tang Dynasty, 21–23, 29–30, 114, 116
  Tai Zong Emperor, 20, 24
  Xuanzong Emperor, 23, 26
Tibet, 8–11, 30, 58, 64, 70, 108, 156, 163
Turkey/ Turkestan (see also Ottomans), 4, 7, 31, 38, 55, 117, 123, 130, 135

### U

UN
  UNESCO, 9
Uyghurs, vii, 11, 58, 114, 118, 123, 125, 128, 163

## V

Vietnam/Indochina, 8, 114

## W

Wang Haoran, 52–53
War-
　World War II, 4, 55
Women's mosques, 32

## X

Xian, 4
Xi Jinping, viii
Xinjiang (see also Uyghurs)—2, 23, 30, 54, 57–58, 63, 126, 156, 163
　Rebellion, 57, 136
　Yakub Beg, 131

## Y

Yangtse River, 116
Yi (minority), 10
Yunnan, vii, ix, 1ff, 8ff, 44–45, 113ff
　Expedition, 118
　Nanchao Kingdom, 115–16
　Party Committee, 121–22
　Ping-nan Guo, 130, 134, 142

## Z

Zhang (minority), viii, 11
Zhejiang, 55
Zuo Zongtang, 40, 47, 57, 59, 133, 143, 159

www.ingramcontent.com/pod-product-compliance
Lightning Source LLC
Chambersburg PA
CBHW071446150426
43191CB00008B/1252